British Design

British Design:
Tradition and
Modernity after 1948

Edited by
Christopher Breward,
Fiona Fisher and Ghislaine Wood

Bloomsbury Academic
An imprint of Bloomsbury Publishing Plc

B L O O M S B U R Y
LONDON · NEW DELHI · NEW YORK · SYDNEY

Bloomsbury Academic
An imprint of Bloomsbury Publishing Plc

50 Bedford Square	1385 Broadway
London	New York
WC1B 3DP	NY 10018
UK	USA

www.bloomsbury.com

BLOOMSBURY and the Diana logo are trademarks of Bloomsbury Publishing Plc

First published 2015

British Library Cataloguing-in-Publication Data
A catalogue record for this book is available from the British Library.

ISBN: HB: 978-0-8578-5712-5
PB: 978-1-4725-0537-8
ePDF: 978-1-4742-5621-6
ePub: 978-1-4742-5622-3

Library of Congress Cataloging-in-Publication Data
British design : tradition and modernity after 1948 / edited by
Christopher Breward, Fiona Fisher and Ghislaine Wood.
pages cm
"This book originates in a conference entitled Spaces and Places: British Design 1948–2012."
Includes bibliographical references and index.
ISBN 978-0-85785-712-5 (hardback) – ISBN 978-1-4725-0537-8 (paperback)
1. Space (Architecture)–Great Britain–History–20th century. 2. Space (Architecture)–
Great Britain–History–21st century. 3. Design–Social aspects–Great Britain–History–20th century.
4. Design–Social aspects–Great Britain–History–21st century. I. Breward, Christopher, 1965- editor.
II. Fisher, Fiona, editor. III. Wood, Ghislaine, editor. IV. Spaces and Places: British Design 1948–2012
(Conference) (2012 : Victoria and Albert Museum) V. Title.
NA2765.B75 2015
745.0941'0904–dc23
2015010277

Typeset by Integra Software Services Pvt. Ltd.
Printed and bound in India

CONTENTS

NOTES ON CONTRIBUTORS

Fiona Anderson is Senior Curator of Fashion and Textiles at National Museums Scotland. She previously worked as Lecturer in Design and Visual Culture at Edinburgh College of Art. Fiona has also worked at the Design Museum, the Victoria & Albert Museum, London, and as Curator of the Conran Foundation Collection. She has lectured in the history and theory of fashion, textiles and design at a range of institutions, including Central Saint Martins, Brighton University and the Royal College of Art. Her recently published research includes a major book, *Tweed*, for Bloomsbury Publishers, which explores the cultural history of all types of tweed from the 1820s to the present.

Janine Barker is a PhD candidate in the Faculty of Arts, Design and Social Sciences at Northumbria University, Newcastle-upon-Tyne. Funded through the AHRC Collaborative Doctoral Award in partnership with the Shipley Art Gallery in Gateshead, Janine's research focuses on the German émigré Henry Rothschild and his craft shop Primavera, which operated in London and Cambridge, 1946–1980. Prior to this she worked as a Collections and Archives Assistant at Alnwick Castle in Northumberland and completed an MRes which explored notions of identity, history, heritage, tourism and authenticity.

Christopher Breward is Professor of Cultural History at the University of Edinburgh, where he also holds the positions of Principal of Edinburgh College of Art and Vice Principal of the University (Creative Arts). He was trained at the Courtauld Institute of Art (BA) and the Royal College of Art (MA, PhD), London, and has subsequently taught at Manchester Metropolitan University, the Royal College of Art and London College of Fashion. Before taking up his post at Edinburgh, he was Head of Research at the Victoria & Albert Museum, London. Christopher has published widely on the history and theory of fashion and its relationship to masculinities and urban cultures. Key publications include *The Culture of Fashion* (MUP 1995), *The Hidden Consumer* (MUP 1999), *Fashion* (OUP 2003), and *Fashioning London* (Berg 2004).

Cheryl Buckley joined the University of Brighton as Professor of Fashion and Design History in 2013. Before taking up this appointment, Cheryl was Professor of Design History and Associate Dean for Research at the University of Northumbria in Newcastle-upon-Tyne. She was a founder member of the journal *Visual Culture in Britain* in 2000, Chair of the Design History Society from 2006 to 2009, and has been Editor-in-Chief of the *Journal of Design History* since 2011. Her research concentrates on twentieth-century design, particularly fashion, ceramics and interiors. Her publications include *Designing Modern Britain* (2007), *Fashioning the Feminine* (2002), and *Potters and Paintresses* (1991). She is currently co-writing (with Hazel Clark) *Fashion and Everyday Life in Britain and America, 1890–2010* (Bloomsbury, 2015).

Catherine Burke is Reader in the History of Childhood and Education at the Faculty of Education, University of Cambridge. Her current research examines the relationship between innovation in teaching and the design and decoration of formal and informal teaching and learning spaces; the participation of children and young people in the design of education; and the history of twentieth-century school architecture and its pioneers. She has published books and articles on the history of school architecture and the participation of children in the design of schools, as well as on contemporary school architecture. She is currently President of the History of Education Society, UK, and editor of the Sources and Interpretations section of *History of Education* journal. Catherine's books include *A Life in Education and Architecture*: *Mary Beaumont Medd 1907–2005* (Ashgate, 2013) and *The Decorated School*: *Essays in the Visual Culture of Schooling* edited with Jeremy Howard and Peter Cunningham (Black Dog, 2013).

Fiona Fisher is a researcher in Design History and a member of the Modern Interiors Research Centre at Kingston University, London. Her research interests include the visual, material and spatial culture of late nineteenth- and early twentieth-century urban leisure environments and of domestic modernity in the post-war period. She is co-author of *The Picker House and Collection*: *A Late 1960s Home for Art and Design* (Philip Wilson, 2013) and co-editor of *Performance, Fashion and the Modern Interior*: *From the Victorians to Today* (Berg, 2011). Her study of British architectural practice *Kenneth Wood Associates* will be published by Routledge in 2015.

Paul Gorman writes about visual culture. His journalism has been featured in many of the world's most prominent publications and his books include *Mr Freedom: Tommy Roberts – British Design Hero*, *The Look: Adventures in Rock & Pop Fashion*, *Reasons to Be Cheerful* and *Legacy: The Story of the Face* (to be published by Thames & Hudson in 2016). His current activities include *Rethink/Re-Entry*, a monograph of the British artist Derek Boshier (Thames and Hudson, autumn 2015) and a series of projects relating to the life and work of the late artist and cultural iconoclast Malcolm McLaren. Gorman also lectures, curates exhibitions and consults on archives, sourcing material and addressing authentication issues for such institutions as the Victoria and Albert Museum, London and New York's Metropolitan Museum of Art.

Owen Hatherley is a freelance writer based in London and the author of six books, *Militant Modernism*, *A Guide to the New Ruins of Great Britain*, *Uncommon - an essay on Pulp*, *A New Kind of Bleak*, *Across the Plaza* and *Landscapes of Communism*.

Maurice Howard is Professor of Art History at the University of Sussex, was President of the Society of Antiquaries of London (2010-14) and is currently President of the Society of Architectural Historians of Great Britain. He has written books on early modern architecture, most recently *The Building of Elizabethan and Jacobean England*, published in 2007. He has had a long association with the Victoria and Albert Museum, where he co-curated the Gallery of European Ornament (1992), was Senior Specialist Advisor for the Tudor and Stuart sections of the British Galleries (2001) and contributed essays to the books *British Design 1948-2012: Innovation in the Modern Age* (on 'Nation, Land and Heritage') (2012) and to *Treasures of the Royal Courts: Tudors, Stuarts and the Russian Tsars* (2013), which accompanied exhibitions of the same titles. He curated the exhibition 'Sir Basil Spence at the University of Sussex' to celebrate the 50th anniversary of the foundation of the university in 2012.

Christine Lalumia lectures and writes on the design and garden histories of the late nineteenth and twentieth centuries. After twenty-one years as Deputy Director of The Geffrye Museum of the Home, London, she left in 2011 to pursue a freelance career. She is a consultant lecturer and tutor on the MA in Contemporary Design at Sotheby's Institute of Art, London, where she co-edited *Creative Britain: Perspectives on Twentieth Century and Contemporary Design*, a journal of occasional papers (2012). She recently co-edited a second volume, *Materials, Methods and Makers* (2014). Christine lectures regularly at the Victoria & Albert Museum, London, and is a co-convenor of the History of Garden and Landscapes Seminar at the Institute of Historical Research.

Jules Lubbock is Emeritus Professor of Art History at the University of Essex. In October 2014 he mounted an exhibition, 'Something Fierce: University of Essex, Vision and Reality' about the architecture and history of the university to celebrate its 50th anniversary (http://issuu.com/uniofessex/docs/gallery_guide_22163/1?e=7878038/9258926, retrieved 19.3.2015). His essay "'To Do a Leavis on Visual Art' The Place of F.R. Leavis in Michael Baxandall's Intellectual Formation", is in *Michael Baxandall, Vision and the Work of Words*, edited by Peter Mack & Robert Williams, Ashgate, 2015. *Storytelling in Christian Art from Giotto to Donatello* was published by Yale University Press in 2006. He is currently writing a revisionist account of Ambrogio Lorenzetti's Sala della Pace in the Palazzo Pubblico in Siena.

Harriet McKay is a curator and academic with a specialism in interior design history. She has worked at the Geffrye Museum of the Home, London, the Sainsbury Centre for Visual Arts, Norwich, and ran the National Trust's first Modern Movement property to be open to the general public. She has taught Museology and Heritage Studies in the School of World Art and Museology at the University of East Anglia. Her current research interests include twentieth-century South African design and material culture and the impact of apartheid on the region's visual culture. She teaches at the Royal College of Art and at Suffolk New College and with two colleagues has recently set up a craft-design project which works to ameliorate conditions for people living with HIV/AIDS in Khayelitsha township, Cape Town.

Alan Powers writes and curates on twentieth-century British art, architecture and design. His books include *Britain* in the series *Modern Architectures in History*, and *Eric Ravilious, Artist and Designer*, and he is an editor of the series *Twentieth Century Architects* (Twentieth Century Society with English Heritage and RIBA Publishing).

He has been guest curator for exhibitions at the Design Museum, Kettle's Yard, the Royal Academy and the De La Warr Pavilion. A former Chairman of the Twentieth Century Society, he taught for many years at the University of Greenwich and was Professor of Architecture and Cultural History to 2012.

Penny Sparke is Professor of Design History and the Director of the Modern Interiors Research Centre at Kingston University, London. She graduated from Sussex University in 1971 and was awarded her doctorate in 1975. She taught History of Design from 1972 to 1982 at Brighton Polytechnic and at the Royal College of Art in London from 1982 to 1999. Since the mid-1990s, her work has focused on the relationship between design, gender and the interior. Her books include *As Long as It's Pink: The Sexual Politics of Taste* (Pandora, 1995), *An Introduction to Design and Culture: 1900 to the Present* (Routledge, 2004), *Elsie de Wolfe: The Birth of Modern Interior Decoration* (Acanthus 2005) and *The Modern Interior* (Reaktion, 2008).

Abraham Thomas is the Director of Sir John Soane's Museum in London. Prior to this, from 2005 to 2013, he was Curator of Design and Lead Architecture Curator at the Victoria & Albert Museum, London, where he curated exhibitions including 'Heatherwick Studio: Designing The Extraordinary' (2012), '1:1—Architects Build Small Spaces' (2010), and the V&A's bicentenary retrospective exhibition on the nineteenth-century designer Owen Jones (2009), and subsequent international tour. His publications include research on key nineteenth-century British designers working in the Middle East, such as Owen Jones and James Wild, as well as published work on twentieth-century fashion drawings, graphic design and photography.

Richard J. Williams is Professor of Contemporary Visual Cultures at the University of Edinburgh, UK. His most recent book is *Sex and Buildings: Modern Architecture and the Sexual Revolution* (London: Reaktion Books, 2013). You can read his blog at http://richardjwilliams.net.

Ghislaine Wood is Deputy Director of the Sainsbury Centre for Visual Arts, University of East Anglia. She is a curator specializing in twentieth-century art and design and has worked in the Research Department at the Victoria & Albert Museum for many years. She has curated several major international exhibitions including 'British Design 1948–2012' (2012), 'Surreal Things: Surrealism and Design' (2007), 'Art Deco 1910–1939' (2003) and 'Art Nouveau 1890–1914' (2000). Her publications include British Design from 1948 (2012), Surreal Things: Surrealism and Design (2007), The Surreal Body: Fetish and Fashion (2007) and Art Deco 1910–1939 (2003). Her current projects include a major exhibition on the design of Ocean Liners to be shown at the V&A in Spring 2018.

Martin Wood is a Textile Designer, Decorator, and Garden Designer. He has written extensively on twentieth-century decorative history, including studies of John Fowler, Sister Parish, Nancy Lancaster and Laura Ashley. He has lectured on these subjects in the UK and the United States.

EDITORS' FOREWORD

This book originates in a conference entitled 'Spaces and Places: British Design 1948–2012', which was co-convened by the Victoria and Albert Museum's Research and Learning Departments and the Modern Interiors Research Centre at Kingston University, London. The conference took place in May 2012 in conjunction with the V&A's Olympic year exhibition 'British Design 1948–2012: Innovation in the Modern Age' and brought together academics, curators, independent researchers and authors with a shared interest in spatial manifestations of post-war British design. The case studies that follow explore a cross-section of British spaces of the post-1948 period and suggest some of the ways in which they were transformed by design and in turn played a role in the transformations within British culture and society. They are prefaced by two introductory chapters. The first, by the exhibition's curators, looks back at the exhibition and the spatial framework within which British design and British design identities were explored. The second contextualizes the case studies through a discussion of spatial transformations in British society after 1948.

ACKNOWLEDGEMENTS

We would like to thank Matilda Pye for her organization of that conference. Our thanks go to the keynote speakers, David Kynaston and Owen Hatherley, and to the speakers, Fiona Anderson, Janine Barker, Cheryl Buckley, Catherine Burke, Alison Clarke, Paul Gorman, Piers Gough, Maurice Howard, Joe Kerr, Christine Lalumia, Jules Lubbock, Harriet McKay, Joe Moran, Julian Powell Tuck and Alan Powers, several of whom have written chapters for this volume. We would also like to thank Martin Wood, Abraham Thomas and Thomas Heatherwick for their contributions. We are grateful to Rebecca Barden and Abbie Sharman at Bloomsbury and Mark Eastment at the V&A for their support in the development of this anthology.

British Design 1948–2012: Innovation in the Modern Age: A Retrospective View

Christopher Breward and Ghislaine Wood

In the stifling summer of 1948, London, a city poleaxed by the physical, economic and emotional effects of seven years of conflict, hosted the first post-war Olympic Games with a sense of trepidation. And yet, the Organising Committee's official report optimistically remarked that the Opening Ceremony in Wembley Stadium 'was packed with 85,000 people. The scarlet of the Guards Band, the white of the choirs, the many coloured dresses of the ladies and the shirts of the coatless male spectators blended with the orange red of the track, the vivid green of the grass in the centre and the gaily coloured flags, to form a never-to-be-forgotten spectacle.'[1] With great haste, no little ingenuity and at minimal cost, British sporting and governmental bodies had mustered once again the famous 'spirit of the blitz' to ensure that the promotion, administration and accommodation of what would become known as the 'Austerity Games' were fit for purpose. Even the Victoria and Albert Museum (V&A) played its part, presenting the last ever Olympiad 'Sport in Art' Competition Exhibition through eight galleries at a total cost of £3,000.[2] By the time of the closing ceremony, the committee could report that 'with this sad farewell, there was also combined a spirit of peaceful contentment, and indeed exaltation, that in spite of the trials and tribulations of a troubled world, and in spite of all the dismal prophecies as to the likely failure of the Games, they had risen, and triumphantly risen, to greater heights than they had ever reached before, and had stirred a real hope in the hearts of millions of men and women throughout the earth in the possibility of mankind living together in happiness and peace'.[3]

Sixty-four years later, in the summer of 2012, London hosted the Olympic Games once more. Whilst the scale, sophistication and cost of the design of the Olympic Park in East London bore little comparison with 1948, there were some superficial similarities in terms of the broader context, not least of a world facing significant long-term challenges in relation to natural and financial resources and political and social stability. The 'look' of the Games may have changed, but its 'spirit' remained remarkably unchanged; and this contradiction was captured perfectly in the twenty-first-century logo designed by Wolff Olins (although the bold design attracted some controversy on its initial release to a British press traditionally sceptical of the value of corporate and public branding). As Olins' Press Release explained:

> London's Organising Committee needed a powerful brand, one that could inspire and engage with a global audience of four billion people. A brand that could make the Olympic and Paralympic Games more relevant, accessible and inspiring than ever … These Games were to be everyone's. They would call for people to challenge themselves—to try new things, to go further, to discover new abilities … The emblem is 2012, an instantly recognizable symbol and a universal form … It is unconventionally bold, deliberately spirited and unexpectedly dissonant, echoing London's qualities of a modern, edgy city. Containing neither sporting images nor pictures of London landmarks, the emblem shows that the Games is more than London, more than sport. It is for everyone, regardless of age, culture and language.[4]

As in 1948, the V&A also staged a major exhibition, co-curated by the authors of this chapter, to coincide with the hosting of the London Olympics, though this time the focus was not sport. Instead, 'British Design 1948–2012: Innovation in the Modern Age' traced the changes that have informed the design, appearance and use of buildings, objects, images and ideas produced by designers born, trained or based in Britain since the 'make-do and mend' ethos of the Austerity Games [Fig. 1]. The range and scope of the project was huge, and its content echoed the connections and contrasts that linked 1948 and 2012. The earlier examples from the 1940s and 1950s supported an interpretation of design in Britain that was in some ways paternalistic, parochial and fiercely patriotic and yet at the same time optimistic, democratic, and highly principled, bent on creating a new and better world for its citizens. By the 1960s and through the 1970s and 1980s, our selection of case studies demonstrated an increasing curiosity amongst artists and designers for the progressive character of design cultures in Europe and North America but also a tendency towards individualism and creative anarchy informed by the economic, political and social crises of the era. And from the 1990s to the present, the focus was on a slicker, more self-conscious, and globally aware form of presentation, attuned to the ever-diversifying tastes of multiple audiences and consumers and wryly critical of the models that succeeding modernists, postmodernists and neo-liberals have bequeathed to the youngest generation of British design talent.

Britishness and identity

Inevitably an exhibition and publication on British design raised questions of definition, particularly around the whole issue of what might constitute the boundaries and characteristics of its subject. We were then indebted to the work of a number of scholars from several disciplines whose insights informed our approach. Surprisingly, the theme has not been a central concern to art and design historians (with some notable recent exceptions to be discussed later), but 'Britishness' is an idea that has continued to interest social and cultural historians since at least the late

FIGURE 1 *British Design 1948–2012: Innovation in the Modern Age, Victoria and Albert Museum, London, 31 March to 12 August 2012. Exhibition Design: Ben Kelly Design. Photography: Philip Vile.*

FIGURE 2 *British Design 1948–2012: Innovation in the Modern Age, Victoria and Albert Museum, London, 31 March to 12 August 2012. Exhibition Design: Ben Kelly Design. Photography: Philip Vile.*

1950s, when 'structuralist' and 'culturalist' professors of English Literature, History and Sociology in British universities argued over the place of theory in the arts and humanities and provided fuel for the emergence of the uniquely British Cultural Studies project.[5] This line of academic enquiry, which connects Richard Hoggart to E. P. Thompson to Dick Hebdige to Raphael Samuel to Stuart Hall to Angela

McRobbie, was one entirely focused on the issue of British identity and its relation especially to questions of social class, race and gender in a period of post-industrial and post-colonial decline.[6] The resulting literature—expansive, passionate and generally infused with Marxist good intentions—will naturally form a bedrock for any project engaging with the material, visual and stylistic implications of post-war British design. However, its agendas and focus often work against the interpretation of representations and objects usually associated with the V&A and with the culture industry more generally.

The concept of Britishness has also provided a fruitful terrain for academic debate amongst political and social historians. Linda Colley famously tracked the invention of the spatial, governmental and economic entity defined as the United Kingdom of Great Britain and Northern Ireland, from its initiation in the Act of Union of 1707 to the accession of Victoria in 1837.[7] Colley demonstrated how relations with mainland Europe and North America and the effects of the British Empire encouraged the superimposition of an overarching British identity on much older regional and national identities. Crucial to her argument are the contributions of a 'pantheon' of British writers and artists to this patriotic project (interestingly, the work of architects, scientists and engineers is rather underplayed), who are mobilized to suggest that the forging of Britishness has always been an essentially imaginative and creative process (an approach initiated by Nikolaus Pevsner in his examination of the characteristics of English Art).[8] Even more usefully for our purposes, Colley's research suggests that some of the underlying identities that a homogenizing British identity supposedly replaced (Scottishness, Welshness, Englishness, Northernness, etc.) have re-emerged and become far more important in the recent past and present, demonstrating the contingent nature of nationalistic and ethnic categories.

The 'imaginative' construct of Britishness evoked by Colley is one that has also concerned recent authors, whose interest has focused on rather romantic (but nonetheless contested) conceptions of national belonging, rooted in the narratives of landscape, community and biography.[9] Benedict Anderson's influential work on 'imagined communities' first posited an understanding of modern nations as fluid cultural phenomena rather than material entities fixed on the map.[10] In the post-colonial, globalized, connected world of the twenty-first century, the old imperialist desire to demarcate has been somewhat superceded by a consumerist tendency towards what the geographer Steve Daniels has termed a 'symbolic activation' of nationhood, managed through an ongoing articulation of 'legends and landscapes, by stories of golden ages, enduring traditions, heroic deeds and dramatic destinies, located in ancient or promised homelands with hallowed sites and sceneries'.[11] The history of twentieth-century Europe is, of course, scarred by the adaptation of similar representations by the fascist ideologies of 1930s Germany and Italy or more recent nationalist parties in Spain, Ireland, France, Poland and Russia. But British institutions, politicians and activists from the Crown through William Morris to the National Trust and English Heritage have, according to some, also tended to borrow from its nostalgic repertoire, albeit in gentler terms, inadvertently stifling technological and social innovation along the way.[12] The return to more radical concepts of Albion by anti-establishment writers including Patrick Wright, Jon Savage, Ian Sinclair and Peter Ackroyd in the 1980s and the 1990s and the resurgence of independence movements and forms of local governance in Scotland,

Northern Ireland and Wales more recently suggest that the debate on nationhood and culture is not yet exhausted (and was particularly intense at the time of writing in the run-up to the 2014 referendum on independence in Scotland).[13]

Writing and exhibiting British design

Given the rich seam of literature generated by questions of British national identity, it was then unsettling to discover how rarely histories of design engage directly with these complex issues. Fiona MacCarthy and Cheryl Buckley have been the only design historians to face up to the challenge in a sustained manner.[14] With the exception of publications on fashion, film, craft and a recently developing scholarship on visual culture, the historiography of post-war British design and architecture has instead tended to concentrate (albeit very thoroughly) on institutionally focused case studies couched in the constraining language of modernism rather than embracing the vibrant social, aesthetic and material narratives which imbue the terrain with colour and critical relevance.[15] Questions of identity and cultural value are more comprehensively addressed in recent literatures on late twentieth-century popular cultures and subcultures, particularly histories of music and entertainment but also of exhibitions, consumer cultures, the built environment and urban life. The more perceptive cultural and social histories of Britain produced in the past decade have turned to these themes of a peculiarly British sense of stylization and creativity for inspiration.[16]

Beyond the academic disciplines, an accessible, almost touristic anthropology of 'British' character-traits, typified by the journalism of Bill Bryson and Ian Jack, has enjoyed regular success in the non-fiction best-seller lists in recent years.[17] Whilst there is a danger inherent in these sorts of texts of retreating into the comfort of stereotypes, they did offer us another model for thinking through the ways in which the wider concept of Britishness in design culture might be applied in an accessible and stimulating manner, for an imaginative, object-centred survey of the make-up of modern Britain drawing on these various lines of enquiry seemed to us to be long overdue. It has become almost a truism to suggest that Britain's creative role in the world can be described through often-opposing qualities that range from the eccentric and transgressive through the romantic and sentimental to the pragmatic and ingenious, but few have attempted to document the ways in which these characteristics have been consciously developed or inscribed in the nation's material landscape over time.

The exhibition 'British Design 1948–2012: Innovation in the Modern Age' attempted then, by displaying over 300 objects and images drawn from the fields of architecture, urban planning, fine art and sculpture, product, furniture, graphic, textile, ceramic, fashion and digital design, glass and metal-working, jewellery and illustration, design for performance, film and advertising, to construct just such a story. In so doing, it followed a number of survey shows that also presented the 'best of British' and invited visitors to deconstruct the unique and shared qualities that define British manufacturing output: The Council of Industrial Design (COID) sponsored 'Britain Can Make It' hosted by the V&A in 1946 and the less well-known 'Enterprise Scotland' at the Royal Scottish Museum Edinburgh in 1947, 'Sheffield on Its Mettle' in 1948 and 'The Story of Wool' at Bradford in 1949. All of these showcased contemporary British products and promoted the COID line 'that exports were paramount, good design crucial and thoughtful consumption essential' in facing the challenges of post-war reconstruction.[18] The Arts Council and the British Council have also played an important part in promoting British design both at home and abroad.

Alongside these organizations and events, the V&A had a crucial role in the collecting and disseminating of contemporary British design in the post-war years largely through the work of the Museum's Circulation Department. Described as a 'museum within a museum' and 'one of the real splendours of the V&A', the Circulation Department organized exhibitions which toured schools, colleges, museums and galleries throughout the country until the mid-1970s while also developing an active contemporary acquisitions policy.[19] These acquisitions (whose distinctive object numbers started with 'Circ.') formed a significant proportion of the objects displayed in 'British Design 1948–2012'. The educational remit of Circulation was paramount and was clearly allied to the founding principles of the V&A. A broad exhibition programme helped to inform and educate audiences and change attitudes towards contemporary design ideas, and important shows included Carol Hogben's 'Modern Chairs' held at the Whitechapel Art Gallery in 1970, which subsequently toured Oxford, Aberdeen and Greenwich, and a number of single media shows focusing, for example, on British studio pottery and modern glass. A thoughtful series paired contemporary designers to explore the inter-relatedness of different media—the jewellery of Gerda Flöckinger with the glass of Sam Herman and the textiles of Peter Collingwood with ceramics by Hans Coper.[20] This more experimental approach to themes and material typified the work of Circulation, which actively explored the relationships between different disciplines. As Elizabeth Knowles, a curator in Circulation, recalled, 'contemporary fine art and design were dealt with together in a way that gave a specific current relevance through the sixties and early seventies. There was a rapid broadening of understanding of the interrelatedness of art and design, and of the recent history of art where design and photography, painting, graphic art, printmaking and so on had developed together. At one level, this was illuminated by the growth of "Sunday Supplement" culture at that time.'[21]

A particular strength of Circulation's collection and exhibition policy was in the area of textile design. Throughout the 1950s and 1960s, displays of contemporary textiles were sent around the country, predominantly to art schools, and the department built strong relationships with most of the leading manufacturers including Liberty's, Heals, Edinburgh Weavers, Hull Traders, Helios and Horrocks. Through acquisition and gift, thousands of examples entered the collection, making textiles one of the richest areas for the study of twentieth-century design in the V&A. A series of exhibitions also combined both historical and modern design and proved hugely influential. The English Chintz exhibition of 1960 brought the story of Chintz up to the present day and included work by Hans Tisdall, John Drummond and Lucienne Day. As the *Ambassador* magazine commented, 'the wealth of our design tradition becomes an inexhaustible point of departure for every kind of design from the most literal to the most abstract interpretation'.[22] Barbara Griggs writing in the

Evening Standard confidently predicted that the exhibition would 'exercise a major influence on fashion', reporting that 'Bernard Nevill, lecturer at the Royal College of Art, has persuaded the textile students there to produce a series of Morris-inspired designs'.[23] The V&A's historical collections throughout the period have continued to provide inspiration and a vast, and well-used resource, for contemporary designers and manufacturers.

The controversial announcement of the closure of the Circulation department in 1976 threw into stark relief the lack of cultural provision for the regions. The V&A was accused of 'metropolitan myopia' and a petition signed by more than seventy artists, art critics, college principals, and historians was handed to the Department of Education and Science by David Hockney.[24] It stated: 'We cannot see why a cut of this order need necessarily deprive the whole country of a standard-setting and cost-effective service which continues to fulfil the vision of the original founders of the V&A.'[25] Despite the closure of Circulation, the V&A continued to showcase British design during the 1970s and early 1980s through the activities of the materials departments (especially Prints, Drawings and Paintings—now renamed Word and Image). Exhibitions such as Margaret Timmers' 'The Way We Live Now: Designs for Interiors, 1950 to the present Day' of 1978 not only provided an invaluable comprehensive survey of the British design scene at that date but also acquired a large number of important works on paper for the collections. The collaboration with the Conran Foundation, which resulted in the opening of the Boilerhouse project within the V&A in 1981, finally provided a dedicated space for contemporary design shows and a number of important exhibitions helped establish design as a genre separate from the decorative arts.[26] Subsequent development of the Gallery of 'British Art and Design 1900–1960' in 1983 and the Twentieth Century Gallery in 1992 (partly re-displayed in the West Room of the National Art Library in 2008) together with a continuing series of thematic exhibitions have ensured a long-standing engagement with, and consideration of, the shifting nature of British design practice, informed over the same period by the burgeoning discipline of design history.[27]

Beyond the V&A, the exhibition 'British Design: Image & Identity' held by the Boijmans van Beuningen Museum, Rotterdam, in 1989 offered a very different 'outsider' perspective, informed (as the curators saw it) by the collapse of British manufacturing in recent decades and the rise of a distinctive postmodern British-style culture in the 1980s. In the curator Frederique Huygen's words:

> The identity of British design is no easy thing to pin down… Fashionable tendencies intermingle with tradition, visual styles from elsewhere are quickly absorbed, and most design areas testify to a great diversity. Influences come from the street, from tradition, from modernism and classicism… There is little question of a single British Identity, in visual terms, that holds true for all design sectors. Any such leitmotiv is elusive indeed.[28]

In the spirit of a prevailing postmodernism, Huygen favoured a pluralistic reading that emphasized diversity and the formation of multiple identities as a way of interpreting the 'character' of British creativity. More recently, curators have chosen to set British design achievements in a sharper, more pragmatic, and arguably modernist perspective, where questions of local identity and 'personality' are subsumed by the greater demands of globalization. In 2009, the Design Museum in London staged and published 'Design in Britain: Big Ideas (Small Island)' in this spirit, celebrating the achievements of generations of British designers but recognizing, once again, the challenges facing the sector in a world where 'there is no *British* design; there is only *design in Britain*'.[29] The context for this exhibition was a series of important monographic shows staged over the last twenty years, focusing on the work of major British designers including practices as diverse as those of Archigram, Alan Fletcher and Philip Treacy.

'British Design 1948–2012' incorporated elements of all these significant predecessors, but in its approach, which aimed to interrogate the constituents of an evolving design sensibility through an examination of the key places and spaces of the production and mediation of objects and ideas in Britain (the state, the city, the land, the home, the studio, the street, the factory, the laboratory and the architect's practice), it offered what we believed was a more situated and nuanced account of how we got to where we are and how that journey had impacted on the look and feel of the objects and images that are all around us. Importantly, the integration of the fine and decorative arts into broader cultural histories within the exhibition helped to disrupt traditional boundaries between disciplines. The three big themes of the exhibition: Tradition and Modernity, Subversion, and Innovation provided a spatial framework over three galleries for overlapping chronological divisions that were broadly the same (reconstruction in the 1950s and 1960s, a challenge to consensus from the 1960s to the 1990s and the shift from a manufacturing to a service and creative economy from the 1970s to the present). These were held in balance by the inventive exhibition design of Ben Kelly Design, with graphic interpretation by Graphic Thought Facility [Fig. 2].

Kelly's design was sensitive to both the long chronology of the exhibition and the huge range of material, but above all it embodied the playful, narrative qualities associated with so much British design over the last sixty years. As Hugh Pearman observed in his review of the exhibition, 'Kelly … imparted a studio aesthetic of stuff leaning against walls'[30] and indeed the informality of the design had its roots in the playful pop aesthetic and materials of the 1960s. Kelly acknowledges the influence of Max Clendinning, one of British pop design's major figures, whose privileging of bright colour, bold line and a disposable aesthetic made him a key interior designer of the period. Much of Kelly's graphic style, best exemplified in his iconic design for the Hacienda club in Manchester, clearly owes its lineage to Ralph Adron's visualizations of Clendinning's work.

However, Kelly's design aesthetic of easel-like leaning display structures (whether for carrying textual information or the display of objects) went beyond a benign pop vocabulary, evoking also the temporary nature of 'Festival' architecture and the very artificiality of the exhibition environment itself: an artifice made explicit through stripped down supports, bold palettes, and the use of unrefined materials such as raw Douglas fir. Kelly's self-conscious design underpinned the shifting narrative of the key spaces of design agency through the post-war period and into the millennial era—the Festival of Britain, the city, the home, art schools and artist's studios, reclaimed industrial spaces, the street, and finally the harsh factory environment with its stark open plan arrangement and brilliant cold light, beautifully evoked in the last gallery by lighting designers Studio ZNA. The look and feel of the exhibition was also, above all, resonant of a British design culture which is often ambiguous and dislocated but also playful and highly imaginative, and more often than not unremittingly populist.

Critical responses to 'British Design 1948–2012' in the popular press and design media acknowledged the curatorial challenge and internal tensions implicit in our attempts to disrupt the well-worn narratives of a manufacturing nation in decline or the triumphalist grand-standing of 'Cool Britannia' whilst also appealing to a wide, non-specialist audience highly likely to be travelling to London in the summer of 2012 for sport rather than culture—and in search of easily digested experiences and familiar stories. Nevertheless, the overlapping themes and chronology of the exhibition hoped to throw fresh light on the response of British designers and associated industries to a shrinking manufacturing sector, highlighting new industries that came to the fore during the 1980s and after, particularly in the service sectors. For instance, the narrative of the first gallery which focused on the reconstruction of Britain in the post-war period and the predominantly socialist impetus for building projects was contrasted with the architectural examples selected for the last gallery which focused on the changes wrought in the 1980s and 1990s, when the financial services sector took over from manufacturing to reshape city centres. Perhaps it was unsurprising then that architecture was a particular focus of critical discussion and disagreement in the reviews, as the selection was on high-profile projects executed in the years of the booming service economy, 'big bang', and the hegemony of global corporations.

It is also interesting to note that there was far more critical consensus about the content of the exhibition the further material was away from the present, redolent as this content was with nostalgic affection for a world of lost values and aspirations. Undoubtedly, the first gallery with its focus on design in the 1950s and 1960s was deemed the most successful, while the inclusion of the video games industry in the last gallery was less well received, its disruptive ambience an unsettling coda to the reassuring materiality of solid, useful things. A number of critics explored the shifts in style over the period—from the Welfare modernism that informed the rebuilding of cities' centres and the infrastructure of Britain in the post-war period to the dynamics of 1960s change explored in the second gallery, which consciously shifted the terrain away from European modernism to the increasing influence of American consumer culture on a new Art School generation and ultimately to the advent of postmodern sensibilities. As Edwin Heathcote writing in the *Financial Times* observed, 'the post war dream of a social contract and increasing equality collapsed in to the atomization and alienation that would lead to our aggressively individualist era'.[31]

In retrospect, it is also important to contextualize the V&A's British Design exhibition against the backdrop of the London Olympics and Paralympics. Although the exhibition did not attempt to document design for the Olympics (including only Wolff Olins' vindicated 2012 logo, a model of Zaha Hadid's remarkable Aquatics centre and images of the Michael Hopkins Velodrome), the success of the Olympics project itself was perhaps the greatest statement of the vibrancy and dynamism of Britain's contemporary design sector. The Olympics utilized a vast range of British design talent in the service of the leisure industries, including graphic, service and environment designers, planners, architects, engineers, landscape designers and digital, fashion and body augmentation designers. From the Team GB kit by Stella McCartney to the new Alias typeface or Someone's spare Olympic pictograms, design took centre stage in the spectacle and clearly signalled Britain's claims to creativity and inclusivity (or at least the claims of LOCOG, the London Organising Committee of the Olympic and Paralympic Games, to ownership of those values).

Although often stereotyped as being heritage-obsessed, the Olympics presented Britain as a vibrant contemporary culture that mines the past for fresh visions of the future and this was made particularly clear in Danny Boyle's opening ceremony, which again clearly privileged the dynamism and creative anarchy of British popular culture. In essence, the 2012 Olympics also stood as the ultimate framing device for the British Design exhibition, which in itself could not help but reflect the spirit in which the games were presented. Like Boyle's parallel pageant, and in echo of the rhetoric that accompanied the London Olympics in 1948, 'British Design' achieved its aim of encapsulating an ephemeral moment of hope and self-reflection. And as Tanya Harrod wrote of the exhibition in the *Times Literary Supplement*, it also 'succeed[ed] in telling a story of radical and irrevocable change in British Society'.[32] Writing two years later in a Spring that has seen unprecedented flooding, following an extended period of renewed and savage austerity in British public and private life, and before a referendum that may alter the make-up of the United Kingdom in a fundamental manner, that sense of radical change and an understanding that design cultures might capture its texture and feeling in the event of the exhibition seems more heightened than ever. '2012,' however, seems a long time ago.

Notes

1   The Official Report of the Organising Committee for the XIV Olympiad (The Organising Committee for the XIV Olympiad: London, 1948), 221.

2   Official Report, 1948, 196–7.

3   Ibid., 540.

4   http://www.wolffolins.com/pdf/2012_case_study.pdf

5   G. Turner, *British Cultural Studies* (London: Routledge, 1990).

6   R. Hoggart, *The Uses of Literacy* (Harmondsworth: Penguin, 1958); E. P. Thompson, *The Making of the English Working Class* (Harmondsworth: Penguin, 1963); S. Hall and T. Jefferson, *Resistance through Rituals: Youth Subcultures in Post-War Britain* (London: Hutchinson, 1975); D. Hebdige, *Subculture: The Meaning of Style* (London: Methuen, 1979); R. Samuel, *Patriotism: The Making and Unmaking of British National Identity* (London: Routledge, 1989); and S. Hall, 'Culture, Community, Nation', *Cultural Studies*, 7/3 (October 1993): 349–63.

7   L. Colley, *Britons: Forging the Nation 1707–1837* (London: Yale University Press, 1992).

8   N. Pevsner, *The Englishness of English Art* (Harmondsworth: Pelican, 1956).

9   D. Matless, *Landscape and Englishness* (London: Reaktion, 1998).

10 B. Anderson, *Imagined Communities: Reflections on the Origin and Spread of Nationalism* (London: Verso, 1983).

11   S. Daniels, *Fields of Vision: Landscape Imagery and National Identity in England and the United States* (Cambridge: Cambridge University Press, 1993), 5. See also E. Hobsbawm and T. Ranger, *The Invention of Tradition* (Cambridge: Cambridge University Press, 1983) and A. Goodrum, *The National Fabric: Fashion, Britishness, Globalization* (Oxford: Berg, 2005), 59–61.

12   M. Wiener, *English Culture & the Decline of the Industrial Spirit 1850–1980* (Harmondsworth: Penguin, 2004).

13   P. Wright, *On Living in an Old Country* (London: Verso, 1985); J. Savage, *England's Dreaming* (London: Faber & Faber, 1991); I. Sinclair, *Lights Out for the Territory* (Harmondsworth: Penguin, 1997); and P. Ackroyd, *Albion: The Origins of the English Imagination* (London: Chatto & Windus, 2002).

14   Fiona MacCarthy, *British Design since 1880: A Visual History* (London: Lund Humphries, 1982) and C. Buckley, *Designing Modern Britain* (London: Reaktion, 2007).

15   For surveys of British Fashion see A. De la Haye, ed. *The Cutting Edge* (London: V&A, 1996); C. Breward, B. Conekin & C. Cox, eds. *The Englishness of English Dress* (Oxford: Berg, 2002); C. McDermott, *Made in Britain: Tradition and Style in Contemporary British Fashion* (London: Mitchell Beazley, 2002); and A. Goodrum, *The National Fabric: Fashion, Britishness, Globalisation* (Oxford: Berg, 2005). For Film see P. Cook, *Fashioning the Nation: Costume and Identity in British Cinema* (London: BFI Publishing, 1996) and Sarah Street, *British National Cinema* (London: Routledge,, 1997). For Craft see T. Harrod, *The Crafts in Britain in the 20ᵗʰ Century* (New Haven: Yale University Press, 1999). *The Journal of Visual Culture in Britain* provides a number of useful essays on British art. David Jeremiah, *Architecture and Design for the Family* (Manchester: Manchester University Press, 2000) offers a reading of state and private planning in twentieth-century Britain, and A. Powers, *Britain: Modern Architectures in History* (London: Reaktion, 2008) constructs a polemical history of iconic projects and buildings.

16   G. McCay, *DIY Culture: Party & Protest in Nineties Britain* (London: Verso, 1998); L. Hunt, *British Low Culture: From Safari Suits to Sexploitation* (London: Routledge, 1998); M. Bracewell, *England Is Mine: Pop Life in Albion from Wilde to Goldie* (London: Flamingo, 1998); B. Conekin, F. Mort and C. Walters, eds. *Moments of Modernity: Reconstructing Britain* (London: Rivers Oram Press, 1999); and K. Davey, *English Imaginaries* (London: Lawrence & Wishart, 1999). J. A. Walker, *Left Shift: Radical Art in 1970s Britain* (London: Macmillan, 2002); M. Bracewell, *The Nineties: When Surface was Depth* (London: Flamingo, 2002); B. Conekin, *The Autobiography of a Nation* (Manchester: Manchester University Press, 2003); M. Hilton, *Consumerism in 20ᵗʰ Century Britain* (Cambridge: Cambridge University Press, 2003); J. Harris, *The Last Party: Britpop, Blair & the Demise of English Rock* (London: Fourth Estate, 2004); R. J. Williams, *The Anxious City: English Urbanism in the Late Twentieth Century* (London: Routledge, 2004); M. Donnelly, *Sixties Britain* (London: Pearson, 2005); S. Reynolds, *Rip It Up and Start Again: Post Punk 1978–1984* (London: Faber & Faber, 2006); D. Sandbrook, *Never Had It So Good: A History of Britain from Suez to the Beatles* (London: Little Brown, 2006); D. Sandbrook, *White Heat: A History of Britain in the Swinging Sixties* (London: Little Brown, 2007); A. Marr, *A History of Modern Britain* (London: Macmillan, 2007); D. Kynaston, *A World to Build: Austerity Britain 1945–48* (London: Bloomsbury, 2007); D. Kynaston, *Smoke in the Valley: Austerity Britain 1948–51* (London: Bloomsbury, 2007); D. Kynaston, *Family Britain 1951–57* (London: Bloomsbury, 2009); B. Harrison, *Seeking a Role: The United Kingdom 1951–1970* (Oxford: Oxford University Press, 2008); R. Hornsey, *The Spiv and the Architect: Unruly Life in Postwar London* (Minneapolis: University

of Minnesota Press, 2010); P. Addison, *No Turning Back: The Peacetime Revolutions of Post-War Britain* (Oxford: Oxford University Press, 2010); B. Harrison, *Finding a Role? The United Kingdom 1970–1990* (Oxford: Oxford University Press, 2010); and O. Hatherley, *A Guide to the New Ruins of Great Britain* (London: Verso, 2010).

17 B. Bryson, *Notes from a Small Island* (London: Black Swan, 1995); J. Paxman, *The English* (Harmondsworth: Penguin, 1998); C. Fox, *Watching the English* (London: Hodder & Stoughton, 2004); and I. Jack, *The Country Formerly Known as Great Britain* (Jonathan Cape, London, 2009).

18 Buckley, *Designing Modern Britain*, 118.

19 Norman Rosenthal, 'Circulation', in the *Spectator*, 12 February 1977. V&A Archive MA/19/13 Press Cuttings 1965–77.

20 Both exhibitions were shown in 1969. Collingwood and Coper toured until August 1969.

21 Note from Elizabeth Knowles (Underhill) to Joanna Weddell. 8 December 2010.

22 'The new chintz tradition', *Ambassador* (May 1960): 103.

23 Barbara Griggs, 'From a Museum – A Design for the Future', *Evening Standard* (4 January 1960) in the 'Fashion News-Focus' section.

24 Letter to the *Times*, 10 November 1976. From Professor George L. Huxley, Department of Greek, the Queen's University of Belfast, Belfast.

25 'Artists Oppose V&A Cut', *Times* (16 December 1976): 8.

26 Boilerhouse exhibitions included 'Images for Sale' (1983), 'Kenneth Grange at the Boilerhouse' (1983), 'The Good Design Guide: 100 Best Ever Products' (1985).

27 C. Wilk, 'Collecting the Twentieth Century', in *A Grand Design: The Art of the Victoria and Albert Museum*, eds. Malcolm Baker and Brenda Richardson (London: V&A Publications, 1997), 350–53. Margaret Timmers' (Dept of Prints, Drawings and Photographs and Paintings) exhibition 'The Way We Live Now: Designs for Interiors 1950 to the Present Day' was a groundbreaking survey of contemporary domestic design.

28 F. Huygen, *British Design: Image & Identity* (London: Thames & Hudson, 1989), 173.

29 D. Sudjic, *Design in Britain: Big Ideas (Small Island)* (London: Conran Octopus, 2009), 7.

30 Hugh Pearman, *Crafts* (May/June 2012): 66.

31 Edwin Heathcote, *Financial Times* (1 April 2012).

32 Tanya Harrod, 'Ziggurats and Gherkins', TLS (18 May 2012).

The Spaces and Places of British Modernity

Penny Sparke and Fiona Fisher

Many dramatic changes occurred in the social, cultural, economic, technological and political circumstances of Britain in the half century following the Second World War. These had multiple repercussions, notable among them a number of transformations to the nature of many of the country's physical spaces, both 'inside' environments contained within built structures and 'outside' ones situated beyond their boundaries.

In the years after 1948 many new forms and meanings were given to the visual, material and spatial culture of Britain's spaces. Those spaces included private domestic living rooms inhabited by people across the class spectrum; semi-public interiors—those in government buildings and educational establishments for example; and public spaces within commercial buildings, such as retail outlets, and other sites, both urban and non-urban, devoted to leisure and pleasure, including objects of transport. In the outside spaces much of the built environment and many of the cities of post-war Britain were altered beyond recognition.

Those spatial transformations took place within a historical context of, first, a renewal and, subsequently, a decline of manufacturing industry; a democratization of consumption, taste and the concept of lifestyle, firstly across classes and then across age groups; an expansion, from the mid-1950s onwards, of the middle classes; the creation, in the early decades, of extensive building programmes, both of private residences and of the urban fabric and the country's infrastructure; a huge expansion of technological know-how and its implementation; and of an unprecedented embrace, at least in the first half of the period, on the part of the British public, of the concept of modernity. As Bernhard Rieger and Martin Daunton explained in their book, *Meanings of Modernity: Britain from the Late-Victorian Era to World War II*, 'the tensions [between modernity and tradition] that had already strained various established narratives of British modernity in the interwar years erupted fully after 1945 and led to significant re-negotiations of the semantics of the modern in the United Kingdom'.[1]

In his keynote to the V&A's 'Spaces and Places' conference, the historian David Kynaston saw British modernity as having four phases in the period between 1948 and 2012:

> The first period clearly comes after that immediate post-war big freeze... I'm thinking of the period from roughly the mid-'50s, I guess, through to roughly the mid '60s when there is this very powerful top down modernity zeitgeist at work, particularly in the area of the built environment, and it's the era of course of the white heat of technology, Harold Wilson's famous phrase from 1963... The second phase I would mention are the 1970s—a very contested decade. One might perhaps think of the '70s as the long '70s, given that it's clear that by the late '60s some kind of reaction was in place against that rather sort of brutalist, top-down, male driven modernity that had dominated from the mid '50s to the mid '60s... Ronan Point, when high rise temporarily anyway really sort of hit the dust as it were... the women's movement obviously, the green movement... all those community papers... Laura Ashley, of course, famously a reaction... and then hovering over the whole decade that presence... David Bowie. I think he represents identity taking over from class... The two other phases I'll just touch on briefly, I guess the '80s and Thatcherism and obviously its origins were in many ways backward-looking. It was in some ways an attempt to reinvent Gladstonian liberalism.... And then the final phase... the noughties... it does seem to me that internet, emails, mobiles, much else has profoundly affected our day to day living and our working practices, so profoundly that now to read a novel set in the period just before all this happened and the characters haven't got access to all this stuff kind of seems weird actually.[2]

The concept of modernity has been widely debated, in particular its complex relationship with architectural and design modernism. Bernhard Rieger and Martin Daunton focused on its meanings in the earlier period in Britain, leading up to 1945, showing how it is a phenomenon that brings together the social, the political, the economic and the cultural and claiming it as a 'useful category for historical analysis'.[3] Their 2001 introduction to their edited text set itself against the analysts of British culture in the period who saw it as a picture of national decline, one in which tradition and aristocratic values held sway. They demonstrated that it was also an era, an 'interlude' perhaps, in which the idea of the 'modern' had significant currency. That sense of modernity, the authors claimed, manifested itself widely and in many forms, artistic modernism being just one of them.[4]

One way to see the period focused upon in this book is as one that witnessed the rise and fall of architectural and design modernism and the rise and rise of popular culture, the latter bringing with it a new definition of design that took consumption rather than production as its starting point. That relationship between production and consumption was not without its inner tensions, however. While the new technologies, an embrace of the future both by designers and by the population at large, and the new social and political agendas of the early post-war decades led to a desire to embrace the idea of the 'modern' and to represent it in the styles of many buildings and their interiors, other aspects of material culture continued to reflect a fear of change and a need to hold on to past values. In many cases, modernity and tradition were both represented in the same spaces. In the early post-war decades, the modern was especially evident in those spaces that were linked to new state initiatives—the seats of higher education to which the sons and daughters of non-university-educated citizens could now enter (see **Chapters 7 and 9**); the living rooms of the houses on the new estates created in the wake of slum clearance and the modern homes of the middle classes (see **Chapter 4**); and, especially in the 1960s, the interiors of new kinds of retail outlets selling new things to newly empowered consumers (see **Chapter 2**). In other spaces, above all, those still linked to the upper classes (see **Chapter 3**), to seats of power, to memories of earlier eras and agendas, and to objects that communicated a notion of 'Britishness' (see **Chapter 5**) tradition maintained a strong grasp.

While the relation of modernity with modernism has been widely discussed, their 'other'—the notion of tradition—had received less attention in this context. The term is widely used as a catch-all to denote an attachment to values that are rooted in the past and the aesthetic models that are assumed to flow from embracing them, most notably the use of historical styles. Work has been undertaken to show that this is a simplistic association and that embracing modernity may, in certain circumstances, result in the adoption of historical styles or at least a mixture of traditional with modern idioms. In the case of the early twentieth-century American interior decorator Elsie de Wolfe, for example, her adoption of French eighteenth-century decorative styles was a modernizing response that brought a new sense of lightness and openness into interior spaces that represented a rejection of the dark cluttered spaces of the earlier Victorian era.[5] The same could be said of the revival of the Georgian style in British furniture in the 1950s.

To understand the tensions (and sometimes the happy coexistence) between modernity and tradition in the era in question, and their complicated effects on post-war British architecture and design production, requires careful contextualization and an attempt to understand what it meant to the British public at the time. What looks historical to us now might have appeared modern at the time. A subtle negotiation between looking backwards and looking forwards was taking place throughout the period, albeit in different ways at different moments

Writing in 1957, the architectural historian Talbot Hamlin argued that 'One of the cardinal problems of modern life is its relation to the past'.[6] In the article, 'The Place of Tradition in Modern Design', he set out to define tradition and to distinguish 'real tradition' from 'false fashion' and proposed the following definition:

Tradition is that flow of energy from the past of the human race which still has motivating power. The tradition that exists at any time is the result of man's struggles and activities in the past—his successes and failures—but it is also a very real power in the present. It is that part of the past which the constant erosion of time has left undamaged, like a rock in a racing stream. It is very much alive, for it is inconceivable that any of us can act without that act being at least partly formed by our own past; and that past, in turn, has been itself conditioned because of what went before. Tradition is therefore immortal, going on from generation to generation. It comprises all the lessons mankind has learned, which are still of help to him or which still form and control many of his unconscious activities.[7]

Where interior and exterior spaces were concerned, each decade after 1945 experienced a different kind of negotiation between the modern and tradition. Many of the interior spaces of the 1950s sought their modernity partly in Britain's own past, especially that of the eighteenth century, when classical forms and proportions and a strong visual elegance reflected the taste and affluence of the upper classes. The neo-Georgian style of the 1950s was manifested in much modern architecture as well as in the splayed and tapered legs of slim sofas which rejected the heavily stuffed upholstery of the Victorian era. The modern domestic style of 1950s Britain favoured a light airy look that reflected an era in which opportunity for increased material affluence and social advancement was a reality and there was a widespread desire to shed the dark browns of an earlier age and embrace colour. Nowhere was this more in evidence than at the 1951 Festival of Britain held on London's South Bank. Traditional pageantry co-existed with the modern, for example, in the Lion and Unicorn Pavilion at that event, demonstrating that the revitalization of architecture and design did not necessitate a total rejection of the past.

'Contemporary' 1950s furniture and furnishings also looked beyond Britain to modern styles developed elsewhere. The Scandinavian modern movement was particularly attractive as it, like its British inter-war equivalent, had side-stepped the hard metal and black leather modernism of Germany and France and embraced a softer idiom that welcomed natural materials and light patterns. The craft-based modernism that emanated from Sweden and Denmark was joined in late 1950s Britain by another foreign influence, a technologically and fine art-defined version of modernism from Italy. While at the top-end of the market the modern Italian interior style, characterized by sculptural forms, was influential, its popular equivalent could be found in coffee bars, with their see-through glass coffee cups, and on the streets in the form of the 'Vespa', the little motor-scooter that provided a primary means of transportation for the 'Mods', one of the 1960s' most visible, newly emergent youth groups. Alongside the influences of Scandinavia and Italy, the United States played a key role in influencing the visual language of youth in the 1950s and of many of the products that accompanied them, from radios to blue jeans. At another level of the market, the pioneering designs of the Americans Charles Eames and Eero Saarinen influenced the materials and forms of much British-produced, modern-style furniture, such as pieces designed by Robin Day for Hille.

The importance of foreign influences on British cultural modernity had largely vanished by the 1960s when a home-grown body of designers emerged—many of them from the newly structured art schools—to create a new style of dress, textiles, furniture and life-style accompaniments for the new pop-oriented consumers. Rather than receiving foreign styles and cultures Britain set the pace internationally for a number of years and its pop musicians, fashion designers and graphic designers received international acclaim. That phenomenon was repeated in the 1980s, 1990s and 2000s, decades in which British designers (and British design education) remained highly influential across the globe.

By the late 1960s, the modern concept of lifestyle, which reinforced the notions of individualism and personal identity, products of the consumer boom that began in the late 1950s and which took over from the idea of an undifferentiated mass society, had been fully democratized. In the 1960s, individualism had been stoked by the home accessories retailer, Terence Conran, through his store 'Habitat' which offered a range of objects which, although eclectic and variously sourced, combined to create a unified environment that constituted the accompaniment to a modern lifestyle that appeared classless. At least in terms of the marketing of design and style, that decade had seen Britain become a significant force in the international marketplace. This did not mean that everyone had joined the pop bandwagon of course and traditional values were still embraced, most visibly at both extremes of the social spectrum in the private interior spaces of the home.

As Kynaston explains with such evocative examples, from the 1970s onwards a pendulum swing saw a significant loss of faith in the concept of the future. It was accompanied by a re-invention of tradition, a revival of the notion of 'Britishness' that had its roots in the past. The social mobility and growth of consumerism that began in the late 1950s took a dip in the 1970s, the decade in which Britain saw a high degree of social and political unrest and, like the rest of the industrialized world, experienced significant economic challenges. Sub-cultures—Punk in particular—and their accompanying styles, thrived in those years, however. The new climate favoured market-led design and the private spaces of the home became the focus for identity formation as well as a focus for the mass media which initiated an exploitation and spectacularization of it that has continued up to the present. The 1980s was the era, in Britain, of 'designer culture', a phenomenon that heroized and mythologized the designer, defined as the creator of 'added value' in the marketplace. From, in the 1950s, an ideological concept used by the establishment to attempt to raise the living standards, tastes and aspirations of society at large, 'design' had, by the 1980s, been transformed into a commercial strategy used to encourage people to enter into economic exchange.

A huge gulf separates 1950s Britain from 2000s Britain where the built environment and urban spaces are concerned. That change has been brought about by the continued privatization and commercialization of public space. In 1992 the French anthropologist Marc Augé famously coined the term 'non-place' to describe those modern urban spaces—airports, leisure halls and airports among them—that he believed did not have the capacity to give their users an identity or to contain any degrees of 'socialization or symbolization'.[8]

When Augé wrote his influential text it was possible for him to speak about an 'unprecedented expansion of spaces of circulation, consumption and communication'.[9] This was as true of Britain as elsewhere. The expansion had happened from the 1980s onwards and had eclipsed the state's early post-war commitment to creating social housing, schools and universities that were accessible to all. Back in the 1950s and 1960s several British cities had been transformed beyond all recognition in the hands of planners and late modernist architects. By the 1970s programmes of regeneration, begun in that decade, often involved destroying early post-war buildings and developing older parts of the cities, such as ports and warehouse areas. The shifts in urban thinking have been dramatic over the period and today's postindustrial urban Britain looks very different from the early post-war visions on architects' drawing boards.

Since the publication of Yi-Fu Tuan's *Space and Place: The Perspective of Experience* (1977), there has been much debate among geographers about the complex meanings of those terms.[10] In broad terms, in the context of their practice, architects and designers use the former as a basic component of their creative language, a kind of blank canvas to be manipulated and formed, while the latter term is often used in connection with spaces that have become inhabited, used and familiar. Most importantly 'places', seen from this perspective, have the capacity to give their inhabitants a sense of identity.

The relationship between privacy and publicity—another theme that emerged at the conference—was, and remains, a complex one in the period. The ambiguity, or permeability, between them was exacerbated by the expansion of the role of the media, especially by the arrival, first, of television and, more recently, the personal computer, which, to a considerable extent, have replaced, or at least redefined, the visit to the public exhibition or the cinema respectively and arguably increasingly 'domesticized' the experience of the 'outside'. The terms 'private' and 'public' are also used in the context of the state ownership, or otherwise, of industry and a country's infrastructure. The relationship between the public and private sectors, thus formed, in Britain in the period in question, and their authority or otherwise over the creation of spaces and places and what goes on within them, is a central theme in this book. Kynaston used the word 'activators' to describe a group of establishment figures, several of whom worked for the state, who exerted their authority over the masses in the 1950s and 1960s.

> it was being driven by a class of people whom I call, because I do not think there actually is a word in the dictionary as it were for this group of people, so I kind of invented a word, and I hope one day it may catch on, but have my doubts. And I call them activators. I think intelligentsia is too narrow, chattering classes is too flip. Coleridge used to talk about the clerisy, but who understands that. So—activators—and in the field we are talking about I guess the Council of Industrial Design, later Design Council, classic activators. But I'm thinking more generally yes, of politicians, of Whitehall mandarins, of newspaper editors, of newspaper columnists and critics, of architects, of planners of that whole elusive group, opinion-formers. I'll call them activators.[11]

The story of post-war Britain can also be seen as one of ever-increasing privatization and, with it, arguably, an erosion of a sense of society and of the concept of social class. As individualism and private identity came to the fore, Britain's spaces were increasingly designed and developed to cater for their requirements.

The chapters in this volume explore a range of British post-war environments from the perspectives of architectural and design history, social and cultural history, and are loosely grouped by theme, covering retail environments; the home; the semi-public spaces in a passenger liner and in government interiors; new spaces of education; and the wider urban context within which a number of them were situated. Their authors address the ways in which British designers employed the resources of the past within a context of modernity and in which tensions between tradition and modernity played out within a range of settings through the agency of consumers, 'activators', and other cultural intermediaries and in relation to other historical and contemporary creative practices, among them art and music.

The opening chapter in the volume 'The Primavera Story: 1946–67' by Janine Barker and Cheryl Buckley discusses the gallery and shop that Henry Rothschild established in London's Sloane Street in 1946 and the role that it played in the exhibition and sale of traditional and modern crafts from Britain and abroad.

Through his approach to the acquisition and display of 'an eclectic mixture of the old and new, the traditional and the avant-garde', the authors argue, Rothschild 'refused rigid divisions between modern/traditional and design/craft' and not only supported a range of British craftsmen and woman but also created an important space in which British crafts could be seen within an international context. Barker and Buckley point to the significance of the teaching of craft in Britain's post-war art schools and to the value of Basic Design in fostering experimentation with materials and form and liberating young designers from the constraints of the workshop tradition.

Paul Gorman's chapter 'Tommy Roberts: From Kleptomania to Two Columbia Road' is similarly focused on the work of an influential individual who made a major contribution to London's vibrant boutique culture from the 1960s. Roberts was another important patron of 'fresh talent emerging from London's art schools' and a supporter of the type of collaborative creative engagements that Britain's post-war art school training encouraged. In the various shops that he created he combined his private passion for 'weird bits of junk from the past' with an acute eye for emerging British and international cultural trends in 'street style, furniture, gastronomy, home-wares, interiors and collectibles'. From the immersive psychedelic and pop interiors of Kleptomania and Mr Freedom in the 1960s to the 'discreet' and 'gallery-like' Two Columbia Road, which opened in 2000, Gorman charts a series of negotiations with modernity and modernism that anticipated and informed broader shifts in retail design and popular taste.

Martin Wood's chapter 'John Fowler, Nancy Lancaster and the English Country House' discusses the country house interiors designed by John Fowler and Nancy Lancaster in the second half of the twentieth century and the way in which they fulfilled their clients' aspirations for modern comforts within an idealized traditional setting. Carefully avoiding the 'static character' of the period room, Fowler and Lancaster re-interpreted the past to create a distinct, fashionable, and internationally influential style of modern interior decoration. As Wood notes, the style that they created was not confined to the architectural setting of the historic country house; much of Colefax and Fowler's own work of the 1950s and 1960s was completed in London flats and townhouses and was, as Harriet McKay's chapter in this volume indicates, also widely disseminated.

The relationship between modern and traditional architecture and interior design is considered by Christine Lalumia in her chapter 'At Home with Modern Design 1958–65: A Case Study', in which she draws on an extensive archive that records one middle-class couple's experience of home-making in a modern London townhouse in the late 1950s. Lalumia considers their aspiration to live in a completely contemporary setting in relation to their cultural attitudes and European origins (both were born in Germany) and compares their approach to the decoration and furnishing of their home with those of other middle-class home-makers in houses of traditional (cellular) and modern (open plan) design. Her chapter suggests the significance of personal connections with Europe, particularly Scandinavia, in shaping preferences for modern design and perhaps also confidence in design decision-making.

Harriet McKay's chapter 'Conservative Flagship. Interior Design for RMS *Windsor Castle*, 1960' looks beyond Britain to consider the 'politics of representation' and the 'representation of politics' in the design of the passenger accommodation for the

Union-Castle shipping line's flagship, RMS *Windsor Castle*, which operated between Britain and South Africa from 1960. Focusing on the commercial and political interests vested in the *Windsor Castle* at a time of strained British–South African relations, she examines 'the deliberate deployment of a conservative aesthetic' to represent British identity within the ship's public spaces and the different expressions of national identity represented in the first class and tourist class interiors that Jean Monro designed for the ship.

Fiona Anderson's chapter 'Bernat Klein: Colouring the Interior' explores the artistic origins of Bernat Klein's innovative methods of working with colour and his work as a consultant designer of furnishing textiles and carpets. Concentrating on the period from 1966 to 1980, her chapter centres on an important commission to design a complementary textile range for use in a wide range of British government interiors and the *Co-ordinated Colour Guide for Interiors* that resulted from the project. While McKay's chapter suggests ways in which traditional values underpinned the representation of British national identity within a politically charged commercial setting, Anderson offers insights into the interior design choices made by the British government to project a more modern and youthful national identity internationally.

The creation of Britain's seven new universities offered opportunities for architects and designers to re-think educational design from the perspective of contemporary pedagogy. In his chapter 'Ancient Spaces in Modern Dress: Basil Spence at the University of Sussex', Maurice Howard discusses the historical and contemporary sources that informed Sir Basil Spence's design for the core buildings of the new University of Sussex and his sensitive response to local building traditions and the surrounding natural landscape. Seeing in the buildings a 'meeting of Arts and Crafts with modernism' and in their relationships of form and scale a coming together of 'an outstanding contribution to the meeting of townscape with institutional needs', he argues for the significance of the first phase of the university's development as an expression of new directions in higher education.

In his chapter 'Architects Co-partnership Private Practice for Public Service', Alan Powers examines the origins of Architects Co-Partnership and the collaborative, non-hierarchical form of architectural practice that its partners evolved. Positioning the firm as a bridge 'between the ideals of the 1930s at their most ideologically insistent and the realisation of those ideals in the climate of social democracy after 1945', he considers a number of notable public projects completed by the firm in the 1950s and 1960s and the ways in which they responded to work by an emerging generation of modernist architects, who, in the face of extensive and anonymous public sector patronage, sought more personal forms of architectural expression.

The design of the Albert Sloman Library at the University of Essex, by Kenneth Capon of Architects' Co-Partnership, is the subject of the chapter 'Something Fierce: Brutalist Historicism at Essex University Library', in which Jules Lubbock explores the social and academic ethos for the university and the way in which the design of the Library and its symbolic location within a complex of university buildings expressed a new educational vision. As Lubbock notes, 'Capon's rhetoric of the tough modernist architect is belied by a range of allusions both to the architecture of the past as well as to nature' and demonstrates 'how the most original brutalist architects were drawing upon traditional sources, both classical and gothic, eastern and western, to enrich emotional experience and meaning'.

The relationship between architecture and pedagogy is the subject of Catherine Burke's chapter 'Hidden Internationalisms: Tradition and Modernism in Post-war Primary School Design 1948–72', in which she discusses the international context for innovations in educational design by British architects Mary Crowley and David Medd. The Medds' evolving philosophy of practice, in which progressive educational ideas were to form the starting point for the planning and design of school buildings, placed them at the centre of educational developments in Britain. Burke considers the evolution of their thinking with particular reference to the extensive research that they conducted into the design of schools in America in the late 1950s.

Owen Hatherley's chapter 'Clean Living under Difficult Circumstances: Modernist Pop and Modernist Architecture—A Short History of a Misunderstanding' looks at the relationship between pop and modernism in three post-war urban contexts: the London of punk and post-punk, Manchester's Hulme Crescents and Sheffield's deck-access housing estates. Hatherley suggests an ambiguous relationship—'a curious kind of bad faith, where on the one hand the dehumanising effect of these places was lamented, but on the other, the vertiginous new landscape was fetishised and aestheticised'. Re-considered as productive environments, whose social and spatial organization, visual, material and acoustic qualities provided diverse resources for a musical avant-garde, he asks whether 'pop was actually in many ways the grass roots equivalent to, not the repudiation of, the modern movement?'

'Edinburgh on the Couch' by Richard J. Williams is also concerned with the wider urban environment, specifically with responses to modern architecture within a historic urban setting. His chapter considers two significant post-war developments in Edinburgh, the re-building of George Square (from 1949) and the development of the new Scottish Parliament building (2004). Viewing both projects from the perspective of a longer history of urban discourse in the city, he suggests that attitudes to the past, resistance to modernization, and a collectively imagined future of decline have helped to shape Edinburgh's 'peculiar' and 'aristocratic' design sensibility.

In the concluding chapter of the volume, Abraham Thomas interviews Thomas Heatherwick about Heatherwick Studio's new bus for London. Heatherwick discusses the aspirations behind its design, the contemporary and historical context for commissioning public transport and infrastructure projects and the impact on design quality of the artificial distinction that has been made between architecture and infrastructure. His discussion of Heatherwick Studio's ambition to re-capture the excitement of the golden age of London Transport, by placing passenger experience at the heart of the new design, expresses a desire to humanize urban circulation that is also evident in the firm's proposed garden bridge project.

Notes

1   M. Daunton and B. Rieger, *Meanings of Modernity: Britain from the Late-Victorian Era to World War II* (Oxford and New York: Berg, 2001), 14.

2   David Kynaston, Keynote Lecture, 'Modernity Britain: Reflections on a Right Little, Tight Little Island, 1948-2012' presented at 'Spaces and Places: British Design 1948–2012' at the Victoria and Albert Museum, London, May 2012.

3   Daunton and Rieger, *Meanings of Modernity*, 1.

4   Ibid., 5.

5   P. Sparke, *Elsie de Wolfe: The Birth of Modern Interior Decoration* (New York: Acanthus, 2005) .

6   Talbot Hamlin, 'The Place of Tradition in Modern Design', *College Art Journal*, 16/4 (Summer 1957): 307–16, on 307.

7   Hamlin, 'The Place of Tradition', 308–09.

8   M. Augé, *Non-Places: An Introduction to Super-Modernity* (London and New York: Verso, 1995 [1992]), viii.

9   Augé, *Non-Places*, ix.

10   See, Yi-Fu Tuan, *Space and Place: The Perspective of Experience* (Minneapolis: University of Minnesota Press, 1977). *Key Thinkers on Space and Place*, an anthology edited by Phil Hubbard, Rob Kitchen and Gil Valentine, introduces a range of theoretical approaches from within and outside the discipline of geography. See, Phil Hubbard, Rob Kitchen and Gil Valentine, eds., *Key Thinkers on Space and Place* (London: Sage, 2004).

11   Kynaston, Keynote Lecture, May 2012.

1

The Primavera Story: 1946–67

Janine Barker and Cheryl Buckley

Introduction

Writing in 1946 in *Modern English Pottery*, W. B. Honey, Keeper of Ceramics at the Victoria and Albert Museum in London, contended that the well-informed collector, benefitting from breadth of knowledge, would be able to understand 'the new and creative styles appearing in his own time' due to familiarity with change in the past.[1] In this book, Honey demonstrated his knowledge and understanding of diverse ceramic practices as he attempted to identify 'Englishness' in design. Illustrating the work of studio potters Katherine Pleydell-Bouverie, Bernard Leach, and William Staite-Murray alongside those who designed in a variety of industrial contexts, Keith Murray, John Adams, and Agnete Hoy, he argued 'for a living tradition' that drew strength from 'fertilizing contacts from abroad'.[2] In tune with these ideas was the German émigré Henry Rothschild, who in the same year took the bold decision to open a new London shop and gallery, Primavera, to promote modern and traditional craft.[3] As this chapter shows, Rothschild and Primavera perfectly embodied Honey's optimism and forward-looking approach that embraced the future as well as the past and Primavera offered an ideal space for the cross-fertilization of ideas and practices that stretched beyond Britain's borders.

Rothschild was a retailer, collector and patron, but he began modestly with the opening of Primavera at an inauspicious moment, a year after the end of the Second World War [Fig. 1.1]. At 149 Sloane Street, it was around the corner from where Muriel Rose's Little Gallery had been until its closure in 1940 and only a few streets from Elspeth Little's Modern Textiles shop in Beauchamp Place. Slightly further afield in Grosvenor Street was the modern design shop Dunbar Hay. Along with Ethel Mairet's New Handworkers Gallery, originally off Tottenham Court Road, then later in Fitzroy Square, and Dorothy Hutton's Three Shields Gallery in Holland Street, such outlets were places where discerning and comfortably off clientele could buy modern crafts from Britain and abroad in the inter-war years.

FIGURE 1.1 *Window display at Sloane Street (undated).*
Courtesy of Elizabeth Rothschild.

Although many of these shops and galleries closed during the war, some remained. At 22 Knightsbridge was Joyce Clissold's second Footprints shop, which was along from Betty Joel's design shop at number 25, while Heal's Mansard Gallery on Tottenham Court Road, under the management of Prudence Maufe, continued to exhibit art, craft, and design.

It was this latter gallery and shop that Primavera's owner, Rothschild, saw as his principal competitor when he opened in February 1946. Atypical of this predominantly middle-class group, Rothschild was a Jewish German émigré who had arrived in Britain in 1933. Out of place in the rarefied atmosphere of Cambridge, where he read Chemistry prior to joining the British Army in 1938, he later said that he felt most at ease in the craft community that he came to know so well.[4] As an Ordnance Officer during the war, he toured Britain and Italy, which allowed him to study rural crafts and folk art. At Primavera's opening, he determined to promote the 'best things whether hand-made or machine-made'.[5]

This chapter examines Rothschild's role as an entrepreneur and a patron of modern design and craft through the development of Primavera during its original incarnation at 149 Sloane Street. Starting out as a retail outlet, selling traditional and modern crafts from Britain and abroad, by 1953, the date of its first exhibition 'Baskets for Town and Country', it had become a new venue for exhibitions of contemporary and traditional crafts. As part of a network of galleries and shops, Primavera played an important role in providing a space where new and existing craft could be exhibited. Showing the work of established craftsmen and women such as Bernard Leach, Michael Cardew and Katherine Pleydell-Bouverie, it also proved important for the newer generation whose work increasingly questioned the nature of craft, such as fellow émigrés Lucie Rie, Hans Coper and Ruth Duckworth. A different enterprise to those pre-war ventures of Muriel Rose, Elspeth Little and Ethel Mairet, Rothschild said Primavera was 'anti-snob', at odds with the usual practice of the trade, and as he put it, 'I was very anxious for people of all classes to come in—not necessarily to buy but to see, to comment [...] this is where [Primavera] differed from the established galleries.'[6] In part, his attitude stemmed from his outsider, émigré consciousness, his grasp of German modernist art and design, and his growing appreciation of indigenous crafts, whether in rural Italy or Britain. Primavera provided the discerning consumer with an eclectic mixture of the old and the new, the traditional and the avant-garde; although economically precarious, it proved vital to the post-war craft scene in Britain.

Henry Rothschild: Early years

Henry Rothschild was born in 1913 to Albert and Lisbeth and was the youngest of four children. His father, who ran the family business in scrap metals, enjoyed a privileged position in wider German society and was frequently absent from the family home in Offenbach, just outside Frankfurt. His son Henry was close to his mother and she helped to shape his developing artistic and aesthetic sense. The family home in Offenbach was large and grand—Henry Rothschild later described it as 'ugly'—and many of the downstairs rooms were rarely used except for formal occasions.[7] Considering the degree to which both Primavera and his own home housed carefully selected objects, the family home in Frankfurt was the opposite— apparently oppressive and unreflective of his developing tastes. Nevertheless, while his formative years were spent in a context of severe economic and political turmoil, it was also a period of cultural and artistic innovation. Rothschild recalled it as a time of 'cultural flowering' for Germany, during which he attended some important exhibitions in Frankfurt, notably 'From Realism to Symbolism', which included paintings by Van Gogh, Nolde and Kirchner.[8] Despite Albert Rothschild's position as a valued industrialist and a loyal German, the rise of Nazism resulted in him being viewed as the only thing that counted: Jewish. In his journal, which runs sporadically from 1923 to 1934, Albert commented on the anti-Semitism rife in German society as he dissected the cultural idea of 'being a Jew'. In April 1934 he wrote: 'In the new dogma, the Jew is a stranger in Germany, doesn't belong to the Aryan race and is therefore inferior [...] I wake up in the mornings and see the lovely German countryside [to think that...] I should now not be a German.'[9]

By this time Henry Rothschild had left Germany, having been advised in 1932 by a lecturer at Frankfurt University that there would be no place for him there as a Jew. His older siblings had left already, his brother Hermann to England and his two sisters, Margaret and Karin, to America. Rothschild arrived in England in 1933.[10] Despite speaking limited English, he did forge some friendships at college but on the whole found it difficult to establish a place in which he felt comfortable. On the one hand, he was a German who felt out of place with the English upper classes who made up the student body of Cambridge. On the other hand, being a Jew in these circles put him on the outside, as anti-Semitism was not only confined to Germany. He later commented that although he would have been welcomed by the Jewish community, he felt just as ill at ease there.[11]

Émigrés in post-war Britain

Rothschild was one of a growing number of Jewish émigrés arriving in Britain in the mid- to late 1930s, and as Louise London argued: 'Jews leaving Europe were seen by British policy makers as problematic immigrants rather than refugees with a claim to asylum; as transmigrants—"birds of passage"—rather than permanent residents.'[12] Indeed as was the case with many of these Jewish émigrés, Rothschild was 'inbetween' both Germany and Britain, and as Blasch, Schiller and Blanc have argued such, 'Transmigrants take actions, make decisions, and develop subjectivities embedded in networks of relationships that connect them simultaneously to two or more nation-states.'[13] Fortunately, Rothschild had both monetary means, coming from a family that had considerable wealth, and support, and contacts in Britain including his older brother Hermann and Harold Stannard, who helped him gain a place at Cambridge University. He was naturalized in 1938 following a five-year period of settlement.

Louise London gives a figure of some 60,000 refugee Jews remaining in Britain in 1945, but it is unclear if Rothschild and others like him who had become British citizens are included in this figure. Increasingly assimilated into British society and contributing to the war effort, the post-war 'social absorption' of those such as Rothschild went beyond the final confirmation of his British citizenship, as issues of identity and acceptance were far more complex in actuality. Marion Berghahn's study of German-Jewish émigrés found that there was frequent comparing and contrasting of German culture and British culture, or more accurately, English culture, regardless of whether they identified more with one nationality or the other.[14] As a capital city, London was unquestionably at the centre of émigré activity in Britain. Many German and Austrian refugees moved into middle- and upper-class areas of London, primarily in the north and north-west where, 'their meagre incomes notwithstanding, the German refugees maintained their middle-class lifestyle as far as possible'.[15] Towards the west of London, Jewish communities were focused around the West London Synagogue in Upper Berkeley Street and the Central Synagogue in Great Portland Street, both of which were within easy reach of the upper-middle-class area of Sloane Street in the Kensington-Chelsea district. It was here that Rothschild, having enjoyed a middle-class milieu in Frankfurt, felt most at ease.[16]

Many respondents to Berghahn's study remarked that acceptance in Britain was marked by the willingness and ability to fit in with the British way of life. Official publications, such as the German Jewish Aid Committee's *While You Are in England: Helpful Information and Guidance for Every Refugee*, encouraged this deference to an 'English' lifestyle, but as Berghahn has argued, this push for enforced assimilation only further exacerbated feelings of loss. As one respondent explained: 'to be told, this is no longer your country, that is bad and it makes you slightly ashamed [...] When we came we could not speak German, one had to whisper; one was an enemy, one was treated as an enemy [...] Then, later, it made a lot of difference as a grown-up not to feel that there was a place really that fully accepted one for what one was.'[17]

To feel as disregarded and maligned in a country that one hoped to make a home would have undoubtedly left a mark on the psyche of émigrés including Rothschild. What is difficult to measure is the level of anti-Semitism in Britain during the 1933–48 period and whether that altered as more Jewish refugees entered the country and as the atrocities in Germany became more widely known. Louise London has argued that although the official stance of the British government was that it considered prejudice against Jews as unacceptable, anti-Semitism did exist in varying degrees not only in the wider society but also within the governing classes.

> moderate indulgence in social anti-Jewish prejudice was so widespread as to be unremarkable. Hostile stereotypes of Jews were accepted by law-abiding citizens. [...] But how did the widely diffused anti-Jewish prejudice within the governing classes condition the government's broad approach to Jewish refugee policy? What we can say is that British stereotypes of Jews were significant in marking them out as members of a group that was difficult, even dangerous, to help. Such prejudices helped to cast the image of the Jewish refugee in a problematic mould and thus to strengthen support for policies of restriction.[18]

Significantly, at its opening, two key trade journals *Silk & Rayon* and *Furnishing* reported on Primavera and although both mention Rothschild by name, neither gives an indication that he was a German-born national.[19] It would be naive to think that this was accidental or that it was considered insignificant; rather more likely is that it was deliberately excluded in order to avoid anti-German feeling towards the shop and its proprietor.

Craft in the post-war period

In his buying strategies and exhibition policies at Primavera, Rothschild refused rigid divisions between modern/traditional and design/craft. Craft was multi-layered in post-war Britain with certain areas—including ceramics—fundamentally transformed, not least by émigré practitioners.[20] At the same time, there were numerous overlaps between art, design and craft and these were evident in the displays at Primavera.

Prior to the Second World War, craft practice had been dominated by the workshop tradition, supported by practitioners such as Bernard Leach, Ethel Mairet and Eric Gill. Leach, the unofficial leader of this group, felt they had followed their 'artistic intentions faithfully' in keeping with the 'underlying need of their time'.[21] However, in the 1930s, the attitude towards craft and the handmade began to shift:

> The hand-made was increasingly dismissed by commentators interested in design. For them craft practice appeared an inappropriate response to the urgent economic

needs of the 1930s…Despite claims by groupings within the craft world that the crafts functioned as a vital research tool for industry, on the whole makers acted as bearers of dreams rather than as problem solvers. Their role was shamanistic rather than functional.[22]

The decreasing value that was placed on the philosophical side of craft practice persisted into peace time, but this did not spell the end of craft; rather it created a new environment within which craft could develop outside of the constraints of the 'right' way proffered by the workshop tradition. Changes in art education after the war contributed to this. Leach was outspoken against the teaching of craft in an art school setting, believing that techniques were best learned in the workshop. This was further discussed and indeed supported by many at the 1952 Dartington Hall conference. Initiated by Bernard Leach and Muriel Rose, the conference sought to clarify the role of crafts in the inter-war period, the direction that it had taken and what the future held.[23] Support for Leach and the workshop tradition is only one part of the story; the teaching of craft in art schools, such as the Central School of Art, became popular and it was through this route that potters such as Gillian Lowndes, Gordon Baldwin and Ruth Duckworth came to prominence. It also attracted tutors such as Dora Billington and William Newland. The teaching of Basic Design pushed students to experiment with a range of materials and to learn about form and structure through experimentation; this was in direct opposition to the workshop tradition, which trained apprentices in the 'right' way to create. The principles of Basic Design, which had been developed originally in the Bauhaus, are further evidence of the influence of émigrés on British craft. As Peter Dormer argued: 'the Bauhaus invented the foundation course, in which every student would go back to first principles in understanding form, texture, line and colour…. Moreover, what the Bauhaus foundation or basic course demonstrated was an absolute commitment to craftsmanship. The quality of the experimental drawing, paintings, textiles, sculptures, ceramics and metalware is underpinned by craft knowledge.'[24]

As craft began to be taught within the art school environment, its nature was increasingly challenged. Could craft be viewed as fine art? Indeed might it also be design? Dormer has argued that the Basic Design course, as it was taught in Britain, was not carried out with the same level of commitment as it was in the Bauhaus; as a result 'by the end of the 1960s craftsmanship was barely taught at all, nor was it valued'.[25] In consequence, definitions of craft in Britain have become problematic, and to Dormer's thinking the two most common of these definitions are 'sloppy'—'Either craft means "studio crafts" covering everyone working with a craft medium. This includes producers of functional ware as well as abstractionist sculptors working in textiles, clay or glass. Or craft means a process over which a person has detailed control, control is the consequence of craft knowledge.'[26]

When we look at the stock and exhibition pieces selected by Rothschild for Primavera, it is clear that he subscribed to Dormer's first definition, especially from the 1960s onwards. In part this may be attributable to Rothschild's particular interest in ceramics, as ceramics—along with other notable aspects of crafts such as textiles—was craft, fine art, and indeed design as practitioners created functional domestic pieces, largely by hand, abstract sculptural forms (both functional and non-functional), and prototypes for mass production. Perhaps tellingly, Ruth Duckworth, Gillian Lowndes and Gordon Baldwin, all of whom experienced the art schools of the 1950s and 1960s as both students and tutors, have been interpreted as artists working within crafts and as craftspeople working within art.

Primavera: The shop

Rothschild credited his time in Italy during the war as sowing the seeds for what he went on to do with Primavera. In 2001, he stated: '[While in Italy] I started collecting and visiting and seeing workshops…then I suddenly realised that this meant much more to me than the idea of going into the family business.'[27] It was there that he bought a copy of Eleonora Gallo's 1929 book *Arte Rustica Italiana*, which surveyed Italian folk art region by region [Fig. 1.2]. In analysing this volume, it becomes clear that were it not known that the designs and patterns were examples of traditional folk art, the playful and geometric shapes could readily be interpreted within the context of modernism, and indeed this points to the creative overlap and exchange between traditional and modern visual forms within this period. This book, kept throughout his lifetime, demonstrates Rothschild's aesthetic taste and particularly his ability to appreciate the importance of traditional style and its place in modern design.

FIGURE 1.2 *Example of Eleonora Gallo's Arte Rustica Italiana (1929).*
Source: Gallo, Eleonora, *Arte Rustica Italiana* (Italy: Giulio Giannini & Figlio, 1929).

As he established Primavera, Rothschild sought help from the Crafts Council to locate suitable objects for his shop but, after the council refused to give him access to its registers of craftspeople in the United Kingdom, for reasons that he felt were to do with their own retailing ambitions, he turned to the Rural Industries Bureau (RIB), which proved particularly helpful.[28] A central government-funded organization, the RIB promoted traditional rural industries and crafts, such as quilting and basket-making, through its magazine, *Rural Industries*, through education, exhibitions, and via its Country Industries retail outlet, established in 1926. As Christopher Bailey notes: 'Alongside the training and re-equipping of craftsmen the Bureau developed strategies to promote higher standards of design... and to increase sales through the application of marketing techniques for crafts products. Most visibly it also undertook a campaign of persuasion, through its reports on 'revived' industries, its advice pamphlets, and through *Rural Industries*.'[29]

Rothschild relished going out and personally visiting studios and workshops to meet and talk with craftspeople, and to select items to sell through Primavera; this was a practice he continued throughout his life. He remarked that in those early days there was an expectation from the sellers that retailers would take what was offered to them, but even with limited opportunity and availability he insisted that he would not buy items simply for the sake of it.[30] Just after the war, he relied heavily on found items, such as surplus textiles and even fishing nets that could be dyed and altered into wall hangings or partitions. Despite the austerity of those early days in the 1940s and 1950s, Rothschild credits his own success to the fact that 'people were absolutely wanting stuff'.[31] As is evident from advertisements that appeared in specialized journals such as *Furnishing* and the *Architectural Review* as well as in more general publications such as *The Queen* and *House and Garden*, Primavera also sold a wide range of domestic craft wares, appealing to those looking to set up home. As an article in *The Queen* in May 1946 put it, 'You may be one of those lucky people who have found a new flat or house. In that case a visit to Primavera...is indicated. There you will find furnishing fabrics...fibre glass tweed and hand printed linen sheets; the latter two of course are coupon free.'[32] In Primavera's advertising Rothschild employed the talents of artist Sam Smith, also known as Alan Smith. Smith had been an associate of Muriel Rose's during the days of The Little Gallery and as a graphic designer had produced promotional material for her.[33] Smith brought to Primavera a freshness and a playful quality, suggesting that at Primavera consumers would find items that would not only be useful in their day-to-day life but would also bring pleasure to it [Fig. 1.3].

From archival research it is possible to piece together some of Rothschild's early buying practices. The Michael Cardew archive at the Craft Study Centre at Farnham shows evidence of Rothschild buying through the Wenford Bridge Pottery. The earliest invoices date from September 1949 and show Rothschild buying teapots, lamp boxes, casserole dishes, steamers, bread boxes and flower jars. Such large orders were repeated throughout the 1950s and 1960s, with Rothschild being given discounts of up to 33 percent.[34] Also at the Craft Study Centre, Lucie Rie's archive shows that Rothschild bought from Rie from 18 March 1946, a month after Primavera opened. The initial order included 42 cups and saucers, of varying proportions, jars, coffee pots and handled jugs.[35] These purchases continued on a near monthly basis while Primavera was located on Sloane Street and continued during its other incarnations at Walton Street, London, and at Kings Parade, Cambridge.

FIGURE 1.3 *Advertisement for Primavera by Sam Smith (c.1947).*
Courtesy of Elizabeth Rothschild.

Primavera: The exhibitions

By 1953 Primavera had established a reputation for selling a range of crafts from diverse sources. At the same time, Rothschild had proved himself a willing supporter of post-war craftsmen and women (newcomers and well-known makers) with a discerning eye. It is within this context that he became more focused on the exhibition of crafts, which in many ways made very good business, as by exhibiting new crafts he effectively helped to create a market for them while raising the profile of Primavera. During the period that Primavera was located at Sloane Street, Rothschild staged 54 exhibitions and averaged two to three each year. Recalling his approach at that time, Rothschild commented,

> Of course there would be a conflict because the shop's so small. I don't believe that that's vital really; what's vital is vibrance, vitality and beauty and novelty. Those are the things that bring people into a shop and people are not put off by the fact there's something else on show. If they are then they can always walk out. I think looking back I probably overdid the exhibition side.[36]

Whether or not he 'overdid the exhibition side', it would appear that he felt the day-to-day running of the business had become settled and thus he required the different types of challenges that exhibitions offered. Rothschild began his exhibition programme in 1953 with a show entitled 'Baskets for Town and Country', held at the nearby Tea Centre. The objective of the exhibit was, according to the *Cambridge Independent Press*, 'to arouse public interest in the craft of the basket maker. These craftsmen located all over the country, at one time satisfied the national need for baskets of all kind but cheap imported baskets have now largely captured the retail market especially in London.'[37] The exhibition was a joint effort between Rothschild's Primavera and the RIB and coverage was given in national newspapers and periodicals as well as in regional publications. Emphasis was placed on the revival of a dying craft and the diversity of baskets on display, from all over the British Isles. By putting on an exhibition which displayed what was regarded as something of a lost craft and thereby appealing to a nostalgic public consciousness after the war, and by marrying his efforts with that of the RIB, Rothschild was assured of success with his first exhibition programme. He subsequently recalled that he was congratulated by the then director of the Royal College of Art with a succinct 'Damn fine show you've done there Rothschild, but then you can't go wrong with baskets, can you?'[38]

The majority of Primavera's exhibitions were centred on ceramics; however textiles and folk art were also important to the programme of events. In 1957, Primavera held two exhibitions of Sicilian Cart Carvings [Fig. 1.4]. In April, the cart carvings were shown alongside Sardinian weaving; the prices for the carvings, which were largely religious in theme, varied from £2.12.0 to £9.9.0. For the weaving, small pieces fetched from £2.12.0, with the largest item, a carpet, priced at £70.[39] The second exhibition was focused solely on the cart carvings. Rothschild described these as 'a living example of an artistic folk art', noting, 'the simplicity, directness and force of their carving is closely bound up with the cart—often the sole valuable belonging of the poorer peasant'.[40]

In May 1963, Rothschild staged the 'International One' exhibition consisting of 423 practical and ornamental pieces for the home—paintings, pottery, textiles and carvings—from Brazil, Holland, Japan, Mexico, Venezuela, Greece, Madagascar, Peru, Russia, Italy, Crete, Nigeria, Morocco, India, Egypt, Sardinia, and Poland. His motivation was to show the variance of craft in comparison with the uniform nature of mass-produced items for the Western market. As he put it, 'To find these treasures of today and yesterday, we have to travel on wayward paths and listen to many

FIGURE 1.4 *Invitation for Sicilian Cart Carvings Exhibition (April 1957).*
Courtesy of Elizabeth Rothschild.

people. We have to love what the simple and the complex people make for everyday use, for religion, for their children or for adornment.'[41]

Rothschild's association with Sam Smith went beyond employing Smith to do graphic design work for Primavera, as did Smith's talents. He was an accomplished carver, with a background in engineering, who made puppets and toys and was famous in particular for his dioramas of the seaside [Fig. 1.5]. Such works were demonstrative of Rothschild's range of interests and were held in high regard within his own private collection, illustrating that he was willing to go beyond the exhibiting of traditional ceramics provided the pieces spoke to his aesthetic sense.[42]

FIGURE 1.5 *Three men in a boat by Sam Smith (c. 1956).*
Courtesy of Elizabeth Rothschild.

At the establishment of Primavera, Rothschild had found Bernard Leach unwilling to supply him with pottery as Leach was in high demand from retailers such as Heals, with whom he had already formed a working relationship. When Leach did, eventually, sell to Rothschild there was some tension as Rothschild was not prepared to buy merely what was offered, but rather he wanted to select. As Rothschild put it, 'There were so many who submitted to Bernard, and adored Bernard. I loved Bernard but I didn't ever feel like he had got everything right.'[43] Despite obstinate beginnings, Primavera gave Leach six solo exhibitions from 1956 to 1966. Documentation for the porcelain and stoneware exhibition in 1958 shows there were 162 pieces displayed, with prices ranging from £0.15.0 to £25.0.0.[44] A review in the *Times* newspaper commented:

FIGURE 1.6 *Three vertical forms by Gillian Lowndes (1966).*
Courtesy of Elizabeth Rothschild.

His individual pieces in the present show include some magnificent large pots, bowls, dishes and jugs, and a selection of new porcelain that he is developing, although the promised enamelled porcelain is still awaited. A few pieces from the new salt glaze kiln at St Ives are on view. A series of wash drawings showing his designs for pots and their decoration are noteworthy.[45]

At the same time as buying from Leach, Rothschild, informed partly by European modernism (although he was not entirely comfortable with the 'brutal edge' as he put it) and partly by his instinct to explore design in all forms, was drawn to new developments with the ceramics.[46] Ruth Duckworth, another German émigré, was given a solo show in 1960. The 157 items that she exhibited included pinched and coiled pots, as well as sculptural forms. There also appeared to be a high level of experimentation with glazes, veering away from the browns often associated with the Leach generation.[47]

In 1966, Primavera held a joint exhibition of work by Gillian Lowndes [Fig. 1.6] and Ian Auld; again this demonstrated Rothschild's enthusiasm for more sculptural work, which blurred the lines between craft and art. As he put it, 'I don't take sides in this question [of functional and non functional work] because I think they both need to be… I think it is quite interesting, as well as the battle between stoneware, porcelain and earthenware.'[48]

Conclusion

Christopher Breward and Ghislaine Wood have proposed that through 'an examination of the key places and spaces of production and mediation of objects and ideas', the Victoria and Albert Museum's exhibition 'British Design 1948–2012: Innovation in the Modern Age' offered 'a more situated and nuanced account of how we got to where we are'.[49] This discussion of Henry Rothschild's activities at Primavera from 1946 to 1967 contributes to this account by highlighting a brief albeit important period in the development of crafts in Britain. Primavera was a unique initiative that balanced the exhibition and retailing of craft for both an existing market and a potentially new one, as crafts diversified after the war and responded to new initiatives from Europe, Scandinavia and the United States. In tune with traditional British ways of craft making but also receptive to crafts from Central and South America, Asia and Africa, not just those from the West, Rothschild—perhaps due to his own complex national and cultural identity—was well placed to navigate this shifting terrain.

Retrospectively it can be seen that Rothschild was not typical, and his experience within the post-war crafts was unusual, but he was invested with what W. B. Honey identified as the essential requisites of a discerning collector: 'Trust [in] his own eye and judgment'. As a consequence he was not 'guilty of the habitually backward-looking attitude of the antiquarian, neglecting and even opposing the interests of the creative present in a deluded and sentimental regard for the past'. Rather Rothschild could 'recognise the contemporary effort as the growing point of the living art of the potter, to which he is devoted, and by caring for it… rise in status from collector to patron'.[50] Indeed as a retailer, collector, and patron, Henry Rothschild made a significant contribution to what became a highly innovative and experimental crafts scene in Britain by the mid-1950s.

Notes

1   W. B. Honey, *The Art of the Potter. A Book for the Collector and Connoisseur* (London: Faber and Faber, 1946), 3.

2   Honey, *The Art of the Potter*, 93.

3   Primavera operated from Sloane Street from 1946 to 1967. There was some overlap with the Cambridge premises, situated at 10 Kings Parade (1960–80). Primavera was also briefly situated on Walton Street, London (1967–70).

4   Liz Rothschild, interview by Janine Barker, 17 April 2012.

5   Andrew Greg, ed., *Primavera: Pioneering Craft and Design, 1945–1995* (Gateshead: Tyne and Wear Museums, 1995), 1.

6   Henry Rothschild, interview by Tanya Harrod, 9 and 10 December 2003, recording F14338-F14342, British Library Sound Archive, London.

7   Henry Rothschild, interview by Andrew Greg, 7 July 2001, recording DVC 882–885, National Electronic and Video Archive of the Crafts, University of the West of England, Bristol.

8   Henry Rothschild, interview by Tanya Harrod.

9   Albert Rothschild, diary entry, 1934, private papers.

10   Harold Stannard to Henry Rothschild, April 4, 1933, Liz Rothschild private papers.

11   Henry Rothschild's journal, no date, private papers.

12   Louise London, *Whitehall and the Jews, 1933–1948, British Immigration Policy, Jewish Refugees and the Holocaust* (Cambridge: Cambridge University Press, 2000), 163.

13   Linda Bascsh, Nina Glick Schiller, and Cristina Szanton Blanc, *Nations Unbound: Transnational Projects, Postcolonial Predicaments, and Deterritorialized Nation-States* (London and New York: Routledge, 1994), 8.

14   Marion Berghahn, *Continental Britons: German-Jewish Refugees from Nazi Germany*, 2nd ed. (Oxford: Berg, 1988), 121.

15   Berghahn, *Continental Britons*, 127.

16   Gerry Black, *Living up West: Jewish Life in London's West End* (London: The London Museum of Jewish Life, 1994).

17   Berghahn, *Continental Britons*, 145–6.

18   London, *Whitehall and the Jews*, 276.

19   'Shop window for taste', *Furnishing*, July 1946, and 'Retail venture aims high in quality fabrics', *Silk & Rayon*, May 1946, scrapbook cuttings, Liz Rothschild, private papers.

20   Tanya Harrod, *The Crafts in Britain in the 20th Century* (London: Yale University Press, 1999). This is an authoritative source for the following discussion on post-war craft.

21   Harrod, *The Crafts in Britain*, 29.

22   Ibid., 95.

23 Brent Johnson, 'A Matter of Tradition: A Debate between Marguerite Wildenhain and Bernard Leach', *Studio Potter*, 36/1 (2007–8): 6–15.

24 Peter Dormer, 'The salon de refuse?', in Peter Dormer, ed. *The Culture of Craft* (Manchester: Manchester University Press, 1997), 2.

25 Dormer, 'The salon de refuse?', 3.

26 Ibid., 7.

27 Henry Rothschild, interview by Andrew Greg.

28 Henry Rothschild, interview by Tanya Harrod.

29 Christopher Bailey, 'Progress and Preservation: The Role of the Rural Industries in the Making of the Modern Images of the Countryside', *Journal of Design History*, 9/1 (1996): 39.

30 Henry Rothschild, interview by Andrew Greg.

31 Henry Rothschild, interview by Tanya Harrod.

32 'Editorial Comment', *The Queen*, May 1946, scrapbook cutting, Liz Rothschild, private papers.

33 Henry Rothschild, interview by Tanya Harrod.

34 Invoice books for Wenford Bridge Pottery, 1948–80, Michael Cardew Archive, Craft Study Centre, Farnham.

35 Invoice book for Lucie Rie Pottery, 1946, Lucie Rie Archive, RIE/8/1/3, Craft Study Centre, Farnham.

36 Henry Rothschild, interview by Tanya Harrod.

37 'Baskets for Town and Country', *Cambridge Independent Press*, October 1953, scrapbook cutting, Liz Rothschild, private papers.

38 Henry Rothschild, interview by Tanya Harrod.

39 Primavera exhibition notes for 'Sicilian Exhibition', October 1957, Henry Rothschild Archives, Shipley Art Gallery, Gateshead.

40 Primavera exhibition notes for 'Sicilian Exhibition'.

41 Primavera exhibition notes for 'Primavera International One', May 1963, Henry Rothschild Archives, Shipley Art Gallery, Gateshead.

42 Henry Rothschild, interview by Andrew Greg.

43 Henry Rothschild, interview by Tanya Harrod.

44 Primavera exhibition list for 'Porcelain and Stoneware by Bernard Leach', March 1958, Henry Rothschild Archives, Shipley Art Gallery, Gateshead.

45 'Two Artist-Potters: Masters from England and Japan', *The Times*, 12 March 1958, 3.

46 Henry Rothschild, interview by Tanya Harrod.

47 Primavera exhibition list for 'Stoneware by Ruth Duckworth', May 1960, Henry Rothschild Archive, Shipley Art Gallery, Gateshead.

48 Henry Rothschild, interview by Tanya Harrod.

49 Christopher Breward and Ghislaine Wood, eds. *British Design from 1948: Innovation in the Modern Age* (London: V&A Publishing, 2012), 27.

50 Honey, *The Art of the Potter*, 3–4.

2

Tommy Roberts: From Kleptomania to Two Columbia Road

Paul Gorman

The late Tommy Roberts is an important if under-acknowledged figure in the development of popular taste and the appreciation of design and experimental retail environments in Britain from the 1960s to the 2000s. According to Edinburgh College of Art Principal Christopher Breward, Roberts 'exemplified London boutique culture, subversion and the significance of the art school network as an influence on British design'.[1] It is arguable, however, that during his lifetime—Roberts died aged 71 in December 2012—wider recognition for his audacious innovations in the promotion of street style, furniture, gastronomy, homewares, interiors and collectables was undercut by his refusal to observe the sensitivities of England's post-war design world.

Roberts adopted an ebullient public persona to match his stout physique and broad Cockney accent. 'I'm the most vulgar man in fashion, darlin'!' Roberts proclaimed to the no-less outrageous *Sunday Times* fashion editor Molly Parkin in the heyday of his Pop Art fashion and objects emporium Mr Freedom.[2] Such impudence was combined with a lifelong enthusiasm for the role of the traditional but nevertheless adventurous independent shopkeeper. The beginning of Roberts' career coincided with the great British boutique explosion that centred on his home turf of London in the 1960s. He continued to stoutly champion this calling despite the depredations of the economic recessions of the 1970s—during which decade he was bankrupted—and the formalization and subsequent homogenization of the British retail landscape which occurred in the 1980s and 1990s and was all but complete by the dawn of the twenty-first century.

As long ago as 1987, the design historian Catherine McDermott identified Roberts as representative of 'that part of British creativity which is able to delight and surprise...in Italy he would be an elder statesman'.[3] And the country's most successful fashion retail entrepreneur Sir Paul Smith credits Roberts as his 'inspiration…Tommy was always at the forefront of what was new in retailing, fashion and design'.[4] Smith first encountered the 24-year-old Roberts at the artefacts and clothing shop Kleptomania, opened with partner Charlie Simpson in autumn 1966 in Kingly Street, parallel to the newly flourishing Carnaby Street in London's West End [Fig. 2.1]. By this time Roberts—steeped in family rag trade lore by his father's tie-manufacturing business Roberto Neckwear—had cut a dash across the south-east of the capital after completing a one-year foundation course at Goldsmith's School of Art in Lewisham. His rotund form enhanced by chocolate brown Jacques Fath collarless corduroy suits and emerald green Anello & Davide pumps, Roberts ran coffee bars (one decorated with a plywood portcullis, false arches and Sanderson's *trompe l'oeil* brick-patterned wallpaper) and drove a pink Vauxhall Cresta (during a spell as a car dealer). Roberts' rapidly developing visual sensibilities were expressed in the mid-1960s apartment that he shared with his wife Mary in the young professional enclave of Hyde Vale in Blackheath. Painted white throughout, the furniture was predominantly stripped pine but included a pair of OMK chrome and leather chairs from Terence Conran's recently opened Fulham Road outlet Habitat, a Casa Pupo rug, and a wall decoration consisting of an Andy Warhol limited edition Campbell's Soup can paper carrier bag, acquired at the American Pop artist's first British exhibition at the Institute of Contemporary Arts in London in 1963.

In opposition to this modernist style, Kleptomania manifested Roberts' abiding interest in 'weird bits of junk from the past' accumulated on forays around London's street and rag markets: rather than the Swinging London fashions and ephemera sold by such Carnabetian chains as John Stephen and Gear.[5] On opening, the Kleptomania stock consisted of a selection of Victorian erotic postcards, Edwardian

FIGURE 2.1 *Kleptomania, Kingly Street.*
Paul Gorman Collection.

wind-up gramophones, 1920s candlestick telephones, Gladstone bags and an elephant's foot coffee table.

A decade before the popular growth of the antiques market, Roberts fitted the outlet as an authentic-looking south London junk shop, a 'higgledy-piggledy mess with a stuffed bear dominating the window, flags of all nations hung from the ceiling and Mary's Dansette playing full blast'.[6]

Proximity to Soho proved beneficial; that area's nascent advertising business brought custom in the form of 'the tipsy ad man who would wobble away on a Penny Farthing for £30 after a heavy lunch'.[7] Meantime, the premises next door housed the celebrity haunt The Bag O'Nails, whose nocturnal visitors made sure to drop by during trading hours. The members of the rock group The Who left with a set of pith helmets for stage-wear on an Australian tour, The Yardbirds' guitarist Jimmy Page (soon to form Led Zeppelin) bought a Mutoscope What The Butler Saw machine, and Terence Stamp and Julie Christie arrived together from a film set to pick up knick-knacks to furnish their homes.

Importantly, the popularity of Victorian and Edwardian clothing—frock coats, boating blazers, diplomatic tailcoats, grenadier and drummer-boy tunics—spurred commissions for new garments by young designers, including Paul Smith and his partner Pauline Denyer, Rae Spencer Cullen (later to operate the label and boutique Miss Mouse) and the duo Paul Reeves and Pete Sutch, whose label Sam Pig In Love produced the first wave of Westernized caftans as well as lace frill-fronted shirts (as worn by Jimi Hendrix for stage performances and photo sessions in the Summer of Love).

The success of these lines and Roberts' interest in the West Coast hallucinogenic scene prompted a switch to psychedelia. Kleptomania was refurbished in purple and magenta paint with ultraviolet lights strung from the antique shawl-clad ceiling. Posters by British counterculture's leading graphic artists Michael English and Nigel Waymouth (who traded as Hapshash & The Coloured Coat) were added to the mix, and the hi-fi speakers emitted Love and the Mothers of Invention to the accompaniment of joss stick incense fumes.

As Kleptomania hit its commercial stride, Roberts' partner Simpson forced a move onto Carnaby Street, where the proposition became less esoteric, and specialization in stock flower-power designs meant that a customer could 'enter as an office boy and emerge as a fully paid-up head, decked out in trappings from head to toe without even having to think'.[8] In the teen press, Kleptomania was soon identified for supplying the 'complete hippy outfit' consisting of a green caftan shirt at £4.15s (£4.75) and bellbottoms decorated with illustrations on the outer flare for 7/9d (39p).[9] 'What began as a cult lifestyle became a fashion trend,' said Roberts. 'Coach parties and tourists wanted fun souvenirs: a Union jack tie for Dad, a paper Carnaby Street sign for the home and a bell with matching beads for the youngster.'[10]

In a move characteristic not just of his restless nature but also of his nimbleness in tuning into shifts in popular culture, Roberts bailed out, leaving Kleptomania to Simpson. Roberts and younger fashionista Trevor Myles now formulated a design approach which challenged both the out-and-out commercialism of Carnaby Street and the meditative fustiness they detected in the immediate post-hippy era, as exemplified for Roberts by the earth tones of 'floppy peasant smocks'.[11] Leasing the ground floor premises at 430 King's Road in Chelsea, west London—the most significant address in the story of popular music and fashion, which had previously housed Michael Rainey's dandy peacock Hung On You and was later occupied by Malcolm McLaren and Vivienne Westwood (who still operates her shop World's End there)—Myles and Roberts chose for their new retail outlet the name Mr Freedom, after William Klein's anti-US imperialism movie satire in which the sets and cast costumes drew on a restricted and bright palette, comic strip tropes and exaggerated style.

Opening in September 1969, Roberts later said Mr Freedom's direction in terms of clothing design and shop environment stemmed from a single garment: a cotton jersey T-shirt supplied by traditional sportswear manufacturer Gymphlex and printed by himself and Myles in contrasting tones with a five-pointed star emblazoned on the chest.

> It was exciting to use colour in a vivid way: the star in bright red against a green, yellow or blue ground with alternate trim on the collar and sleeves. It looked like it had popped out of the pages of a comic, and with that I knew the world of fashion would never be the same again. Here was something from which we could build a series of collections of clothes, artefacts, even interiors: a concept. It spoke to me because it wasn't contemplative or cool, but garish, loud, Pop, very upfront ... like me.[12]

FIGURE 2.2 *Interior, Mr Freedom.*
Courtesy of Jon Wealleans.

Fascia, fittings and interior design were commissioned from Electric Colour Company, which had recently been formed by fine arts graduates operating from a studio in Hackney, east London [Fig. 2.2].

This engagement with fresh talent emerging from London's art schools was to be a hallmark of Roberts' career and underscored his ability to harness the skills of a multi-disciplinary team to realize his creative vision. As Mr Freedom grew in popularity, so Roberts was the figurehead/art director, overseeing Trevor Myles, who focused on manufacture, and the clothing design team made up of the textile specialist Jane Wealleans and the wacky menswear designer Jim O'Connor (who had both emerged from the Royal College of Art) and Pamela Harvey (who restyled herself Pamla Motown and had been taught by Peter Blake during the Pop artist's visits to Harrow Art School in north London). Also contributing were new designers from the Kings Road milieu, including Dinah Adams, Diana Crawshaw and Diane Saunders.

Electric Colour Company produced an environment bursting with energy and replete with references to Americana and comic book culture. The shop name was in red and black concertina lettering accompanied by a pole, from which hung a banner featuring Dick Tracy's profile in appliqué and plastic in the style of Warhol's 1960 painting. On the ledge above, they placed a 50 percent life-size hollow resin sculpture of the 1940s Western movie character the Lone Ranger on the back of his rearing steed Trigger. The façade, floor and interior were painted blue with red accents and the sales counter was formed from a Plexiglass vitrine containing plastic jewellery, accessories and trinkets. This curved to the wall to a high Odeon arch in red and blue flashing neon; after six months, the counter was replaced by an oblong unit, into which were cut apertures displaying television screens behind panes of tinted plastic film. The panoply of objects and fittings included an authentic spinning Mecca ballroom glitterball, Pop Art posters and 'fun' shoes—baseball boots and 1950s' brothel creepers in unusual colours—presented in tall, clear Plexiglass pyramids.

Roberts explored his taste for the absurd by installing large wooden facsimiles of 78-rpm vinyl discs from the 1950s at the end of the clothing rails and from design duo Sue and Simon Haynes, also recent products of London's art school system, a series of odd display pieces including an eight-foot-tall blue fun-fur representation of King Kong and a balsa wood plate of egg and chips of twelve-foot circumference. These constructions set Simon Haynes on the path to his participation in the group exhibition 'Ten Sitting Rooms', curated by Jasia Reichardt at London's Institute of Contemporary Arts in December 1970; his environment for that show included a fun-fur bearskin and many references to American retro pop culture.[13]

Mr Freedom clothes, meanwhile, were more than a match for the stage-set Roberts had created; he and Myles became the first fashion label to incorporate Disney characters in their designs after striking a licensing deal with The Walt Disney Company resulting in Snow White smock dresses and repeat prints of Mickey Mouse, Donald Duck et al. on T-shirts and jersey maxi skirts. Roberts also resolved to create a sexy garment for the 1970s which would rival the miniskirt of the 1960s. Experimentation with a pair of trousers with Pamla Motown led to the production of a prototype pair of short shorts. These became known as hot pants when eagerly displayed in the national press the day after the first samples had arrived at the shop, thus setting in train one of the biggest womenswear trends of the decade [Plate 2].

With custom from such notables as Elizabeth Taylor and Richard Burton, Elton John and Mick Jagger, Roberts found a backer to fund an ambitious move to larger premises in neighbouring Kensington. Here footwear and children's clothing were introduced in a multi-storey Pop department store designed by the interiors architect Jon Wealleans, who had cut his teeth in the mid-1960s with Norman Foster and Max Clendinning at UK practice Building Design Partnership. Roberts and Wealleans upped the ante at the second Mr Freedom by drawing on a mutual passion for the consumer engagement of such US artists as Claes Oldenburg and Tom Wesselmann. This was combined with admiration for the contemporaneous experimental approach of European designers Ettore Sotsass Junior and Joe Colombo and produced a range of 'fun furniture', including a chair in pink and white vinyl, which resembled a giant pair of false teeth, and foam PVC-covered seats in the shape of jigsaw pieces which slotted together to form banquettes.

The new shop was populated with more 'monstrous oddities'[14] such as Simon Haynes' mechanical fly, designed to flutter its wings while suspended from the ceiling, and an eight-foot-tall replication of a Daz brand soap box constructed by Electric Colour Company's Jeff Pine. Consequently, Roberts' fashion team pulled out all the stops. Jim O'Connor produced such surreal designs as winged boots and adult-sized romper suits, both worn by Elton John to aid his development as the Liberace of the 1970s. These, along with Crawshaw's velvet two-piece Baseball Suit, Motown's vinyl Bingo Jacket peppered with numbers and Saunders' peaked satin Jockey Cap (worn on Top of The Pops by Mick Jagger), were among the twenty-four Mr Freedom items selected by Cecil Beaton for 'Fashion: An Anthology', the huge exhibition that he curated from the Victoria and Albert Museum's clothing archive, which was held at the museum in the autumn of 1971. It is likely Beaton had Mr Freedom in mind when he wrote in the exhibition catalogue of the 'moment when "good taste" becomes dead; what has been considered "bad" is suddenly found to be invigorating. Fashion today has little to do with *la mode* and the tacky is often accepted as an essential part of the necessary "total" look. It can be fun'.[15]

In the basement of Mr Freedom, Roberts unveiled his most daring assault on British politesse: the restaurant Mr Feed'Em, fitted out by Wealleans with 'Thirties eclecticism and, perhaps, a deep bow in the direction of Oldenburg and other old masters of the Pop movement'.[16] Here, waitresses served tables in hamburger repeat print minidresses and headdresses and wore red leather knee-high platform boots. The graphic identity —including the flying custard pie logo—was realized by another Royal College alum, George Hardie, later to make his mark in the music business with designs for Led Zeppelin and Pink Floyd via the Hipgnosis studio. Each soup serving was garnished with a plastic fly, and green-dyed sausages arrived with blue-tinted mashed potato. Roberts' menu of hearty English fare and American diner staples presaged Britain's 'foodie' craze by at least a decade by pointing out that eating could be fun, that lingering post-war austerity in this sphere, just as in fashion and furniture, was vanquished and the act of food consumption, like shopping, was now a leisure activity to be enjoyed conspicuously.

Not for the last time, Roberts' backer became alarmed by the extravagance of his ambition; the cost of refurbishing the basement of 20 Kensington Church Street rose to a staggering £30,000. Added to this, it soon became clear that the sensory overload in the clothing, furniture and food offers was too advanced for mainstream tastes, so the business closed with hefty debts after fourteen months. One newspaper marked the coincidence of this news with the death of the designer Cristobel Balenciaga with a black-bordered notice.[17] Roberts' life-long irrepressibility was made manifest by his next venture, City Lights Studio, the first fashion business in Covent Garden, the central London district at that time still dominated by a vast Victorian fruit, vegetable and flower market. He took over a second-floor loft in a former banana warehouse and directed Andrew Greaves and Jeff Pine of Electric Colour Company to transform it into a darkly glamorous atelier suitable for the presentation of 1930s- and 1940s-style tailored men's and womenswear. This was designed by two more recent graduates from the Royal College of Art: John Yong, who cut exquisitely fitted dresses, cigarette pants and tops, and Derek Morton (who went on to become Paul Smith's right-hand man and remains the head of PS Japan menswear collections thirty-five years later). City Lights represented an opportunity to reverse direction. 'By 1972 it was mainstream to do Pop and 'fun' in fashion,' said Roberts. 'I was set on going the other way. When I looked down from the minstrels' gallery in the loft, I realized the space had a romantic feel requiring the light touch. Restraint was the discipline.'[18] The wooden floor was stripped, scattered with gold-coloured flake and varnished so that it shimmered in the light. A stage coffin housed a mannequin in the gallery and chunky metal chains were strung from black-painted metal poles, which were also draped with silver lamé curtains. The atmosphere of decadence was bolstered by the gloomy strains of Schoenberg from the sound system, and Roberts eschewed gaudy checks and winged boots in favour of a black beret and a frock coat with striped City trousers. Then a fashion journalist, broadcaster Janet Street Porter wrote: 'You can tell it's a Tommy Roberts enterprise the moment you walk in. There's a table supported by four skulls and the walls are covered in what Tommy describes as GLC lavatory paint.'[19] But only the brave and switched-on were prepared to visit the unlikely locale. David Bowie bought many suits, including one in which he was photographed for his 1973 LP Pin Ups, and models Donna Jordan, Twiggy and Jerry Hall were all customers, but lack of footfall and the advent of the 1974 economic recession—which gave rise to The Three Day Week (the government imperative restricting energy supplies to industry and commerce)—forced the closure of City Lights by the spring of that year.

Within a couple of years, the long-awaited regeneration of Covent Garden had begun with the shift of the fruit and vegetable market to south London and the arrival of restaurants, nightclubs, advertising agencies and boutiques. But Roberts was by then bankrupt and in no position to reap the benefits. After a spell managing art-rock oddballs Kilburn & The High Roads—whose front man Ian Dury went onto make his name in the post-punk era—Roberts focused on antiques trading, first from a stall at the local market in Greenwich and then with an import/export business in Lewisham. Business trips to New York with new partner Paul Jones coincided with the publication of Joan Kron and Susanne Slesin's book *High Tech: The Industrial Style and Source Book for the Home*, which contained a directory of specialist suppliers of the utilitarian hardware that was emerging as a key trend in US retail circles.

After tours around East Coast manufacturers, he and Jones realized that, if handled with sufficient confidence (never a commodity in short supply), High Tech as a product genre would appeal to British consumers. 'High Tech was rooted in engineering rather than fashion, but was soon part of the realm of interior design,' said Roberts. 'We were already being told we were entering the 'austere 80s' and it fitted with the back-to-basics feeling in the air.'[20]

Occupying the lower-ground floors of Richard Seifert's modernist landmark Centrepoint Building, close to London's West End, the duo opened their giant homewares store Practical Styling in the summer of 1981, promoting the sale of Dexion shelving units, chrome dome-topped bullet bins, metal dustbins sprayed Schiaparelli Shocking Pink, and office chairs and desks in speckled Hammerite (a proprietary non-rust metal paint). With coverage in the recently established lifestyle magazine *The Face*, Roberts had once again hit the moment, powered by the new popularity of such lines as Fiestaware (brightly coloured glazed crockery sets which had been manufactured in the United States since the 1930s) and cutlery produced by a Portuguese factory at 25 percent larger than the standard. Such arch flourishes aligned Practical Styling with the growing appreciation of postmodern design; new lines included furniture clad in Formica printed with neo-Classical architectural drawings and a series of rugs and sofas designed in the style of such twentieth-century artists as Picasso, the abstract expressionist Mark Rothko and the minimalist Frank Stella. Among pieces from new British designers were glass sculptures by Danny Lane and furniture and forms created from methods of bricolage and reclamation by Tom Dixon and Mark Brazier Jones. Practical Styling had become 'a haven for the bizarre, the outrageous and the straight kitsch' while Roberts, who listed his mentors as Fornasetti, Gio Ponti and Gaudi, and his favourite object as a plastic poodle dog lamp, was described as 'a man with a clear sense of over-the-top'.[21]

Emblazoned as the cover subject of the sixth edition of British design magazine *Blueprint*, for which he was interviewed by one of his biggest fans, Sir Terence Conran's son Sebastian, Roberts was in fact disillusioned at the absorption of Practical Styling's approach by the mass retail trade.[22] Brightly coloured plastic beakers, speckled resin-handled cutlery and tubular shelving units were by mid-decade the common currency not just of national chains such as Anthony Hawser's Reject Shop but of local high street store operators. After five years, he and Jones closed the business and went their separate ways—Roberts into dealing in art, artefacts and furniture. He soon found that his preoccupations—with the work of Charles and Ray Eames and Scandinavian mid-century designers, for example—increasingly coincided with those of private collectors, among them such high-profile individuals as the musician/producer Dave Stewart.

By the mid-1990s, Roberts had accrued sufficient stock and acumen to fund a return to retail with a new outlet called TomTom, just a block from Practical Styling's base in the Centrepoint Building. Coinciding with the rise in national confidence as expressed by both Britart and Britpop, TomTom's wares as listed in the *Evening Standard* set the bar for high-end eclectic design collection and interiors which continues to this day: a yellow plastic 1969 Wendell Castle sofa; a length of Gordon Russell furnishing fabric; an Ettore Sottsass light-up mirror; chairs by Harry Bertoia, Pierre Paulin and Gae Aulenti; prints by Jim Dine, Richard Hamilton and Eduardo Paolozzi; and a 1960s Alan Aldridge-designed Beatles jigsaw.[23] 'We have to consider Roberts's position as an importer of designs from Italy and Scandinavia into Britain in the '90s,' says Christopher Breward. 'In this way Roberts helped create the current culture of appreciation of furniture as art and furniture as statement.'[24]

This contribution to British taste-making was transferred from the tiny and cluttered TomTom to Two Columbia Road, the larger-scale furniture and object emporium that Roberts opened with his son Keith in 2000. In the same manner as his settlement in the unprepossessing World's End area of west London in 1969 and in Covent Garden in 1972, Two Columbia Road represented a step forward in the establishment of Shoreditch in east London as another centre for the capital's creative activities. A lifetime in design had taught Roberts to avoid fashionability. 'Silhouettes come and go but a piece with inherent quality transcends that: a textile design by Lucienne Day, a piece of Eames furniture, an Arne Jacobsen chair,' observed Roberts towards the end of his life.[25] Such pieces were placed in a calm, gallery-like environment with a deliberately discreet exterior. 'Dad suggested we paint the frontage battleship grey, which was a bit surprising at the time,' says Keith Roberts. 'These days that grey is synonymous with shops selling modern design.'[26]

Ill-health forced Roberts into retirement in the mid-2000s, by which time Two Columbia Road had also established a strong online presence, completing this distinguished individual's journey through design retail which started in the back streets of Soho and continues today in the digital world. A year before his own death in 2010, Malcolm McLaren—another unpindownable figure to whom Roberts may be compared—told an interviewer: 'Tommy Roberts is a character out of an Ealing comedy, a jovial, lovable creature, a really brilliant icon of London.'[27] That spirit remains at Two Columbia Road, one of the most important art and design outlets in Britain, which draws visitors and buyers in pursuit of excellence, quality and quirkiness from all over the world, in testimony to Roberts' brilliance and bravura.

Notes

1   Paul Gorman, *Mr Freedom—Tommy Roberts: British Design Hero* (London: Adelita, 2012), Introduction.

2   'Now This Is Where It's At', *Sunday Times*, 15 November 1970.

3   Catherine McDermott, *Street Style: British Design in the 80s* (London: Design Council, 1987), 122.

4   Gorman, *Mr Freedom*, 7.

5   Author's interview with Tommy Roberts on 12 November 2010.

6   Ibid.

7   Ibid.

8   Nik Cohn, *Today There Are No Gentleman* (London: Weidenfeld & Nicolson, 1970), 124.

9   'Today's Raves', *Rave*, January 1968.

10   Author's interview with Tommy Roberts on 23 June 2011.

11   Ibid.

12   Ibid.

13   *Ten Sitting Rooms at ICA*, catalogue, 1970.

14   Richard Walker, 'The Crazy World of Mr Freedom', *Daily Telegraph*, 26 April 1971.

15 Cecil Beaton, *Fashion: An Anthology by Cecil Beaton* (Catalogue of an exhibition held
    at the Victoria and Albert Museum, October 1971–January 1972) (London: V&A,
    1971), Introduction.

16 Alistair Best, 'Waiter! There's a Pop Movement in My Soup', *Design*, 271 (July 1971):
    64–67.

17 'We Note Their Passing with Regret', *Evening Standard*, 26 March 1972.

18 Author's interview with Tommy Roberts on 6 November 2011.

19 'Witty … with a Strong Whiff of Nostalgia', *Daily Mail*, 24 November 1972, 24.

20 From, Anne Witchard, 'The Aesthetics of Ergonomics', *The Face*, February 1982,
    58–60.

21 Catherine McDermott, *Design: The Key Concepts* (London: Routledge, 2007), 30.

22 'Never Knowingly Understated', *Blueprint*, April 1984, 69.

23 Miles Chapman, 'Shop Talk', *Evening Standard*, 7 July 1995.

24 Author's interview with Christopher Breward on 24 June 2011.

25 Author's interview with Tommy Roberts on 6 November 2011.

26 Author's interview with Keith Roberts on 10 June 2011.

27 Transcript of interview with Malcolm McLaren conducted by Will Birch, June 2009.

3

John Fowler, Nancy Lancaster and the English Country House

Martin Wood

It is often said that Great Britain has contributed three things to civilization: the Common Law, Parliamentary Democracy and the English Landscape Garden. One could perhaps add a fourth: English Country House Taste. Although it might seem the very embodiment of tradition and continuity, English Country House Taste is actually a relatively modern invention. What it sought to do was to create an image of the past that was, in essence, an illusion—an illusion rooted in what might be termed reactionary nostalgia, which was enormously influential on both sides of the Atlantic throughout the twentieth century. Perhaps a more succinct description of the style was that it sought to 'give the elegance of the eighteenth century with the comforts of the twentieth century'.[1] It owes much to the rise of the interior decorator in the early years of the twentieth century and to two remarkable figures in particular: Nancy Lancaster and John Fowler, and their development of the decorating firm Colefax and Fowler from 1948.

Nancy Lancaster (1897–1994) was not actually English—she was a Virginian [Fig. 3.1]. She was skilled at doing up houses and over the course of a long life renovated several and gained a reputation for having 'the finest taste of anyone in the world'.[2] Her influence was immense, and remains so, but she was never a decorator and would have been appalled to hear herself described as such.[3] As she often remarked, 'I'm agin decorating: I'm a percolator of ideas.'[4] These ideas came from many sources. She loved her native Virginia and its old plantation houses, which had a faded elegance that was hard to resist—an atmosphere that could also be found in many English country houses where the family had fallen on hard times. Albert Hadley, of the American decorators Parish-Hadley (who were greatly influenced by Colefax and Fowler's work), remarked that 'it wasn't as if it was decorating at all. It was how houses evolve and develop'.[5]

Moving to England from the United States, Nancy and her husband Ronald Tree took a lease on Kelmarsh Hall in Northamptonshire in 1928. They modernized

FIGURE 3.1 *Nancy Lancaster in the garden at Haseley Court, c.1960.*
Courtesy of Martin Wood/Elizabeth Winn.

the house, installing central heating and several bathrooms, and created a series of comfortable interiors using not much more than decent fabrics and colour. Architectural advice came from her uncle, Paul Phipps, who had been a pupil of Sir Edwin Lutyens, and the decoration was done by Elden Ltd., a Mayfair decorating business owned by the Hon Mrs Guy Bethell.[6] In response to the completed house, the Duke of Buccleuch told Lady Astor, Nancy's aunt, 'your niece is going to cost us all a great deal of money'.[7]

John Fowler's background was quite different [Fig. 3.2]. His father had been a clerk at Lingfield Racecourse and had died at a relatively young age. Fowler held a number of jobs before he began working in the studio of Thornton Smith Ltd.,

FIGURE 3.2 *John Fowler, in the garden of his home, The Hunting Lodge.*
Courtesy of Martin Wood/Elizabeth Winn.

a Soho decorating firm, where he learnt to paint the Chinese wallpapers that were fashionable at the time. He also undertook freelance work for Mrs Bethell and would have gone on to work for her had she not died rather suddenly. Instead, at the instigation of Margaret Kunzer, he established a paint studio for the London department store Peter Jones Ltd. This survived for a number of years until he walked out, taking most of his team with him, to establish John Beresford Fowler Ltd.[8] The business was based at his flat in the upper storeys of 292 King's Road, Chelsea. As it had no shop window, the staff made a sort of glazed display barrow that was wheeled out each morning and also made sure that the building's window boxes were eye-catching to passers-by [Fig. 3.3].

Most of Fowler's work was on a modest scale and almost nothing survived beyond the Second World War, apart from a house in Chelsea and a farmhouse in Devon, completed for the same clients. To the commentators of the scene, it was soon evident that amongst contemporary decorators Fowler was undoubtedly the most gifted. He created an atmosphere that 'was light, airy and elegant, with striped wallpapers against white paintwork, chintz-covered sofas, curtains with Regency drapes, Regency couches and gold-and-white painted chairs, and the bedrooms fluttered with white muslin'.[9] In those pre-war days, Fowler's work reflected the Regency revival—the chairs were dainty and the swags were mean—but an air of

292. King's Road Chelsea about 1939.

FIGURE 3.3 *292 King's Road, Chelsea. The sitting room of John Fowler's London flat just before the war.*
Courtesy of Colefax and Fowler.

originality was already apparent in his work which was to become more Georgian, more classical and more distinctive after the war.

In April 1938, Fowler left his own company to go into partnership with Lady Colefax, but the advent of the Second World War very quickly put a stop to such harmless pursuits as decorating. After the war, Lady Colefax became increasingly ill and frail and in February 1948, she sold the business to Nancy Tree, who married Colonel Lancaster of Kelmarsh Hall later that year. Lancaster knew everyone, from the King and Queen down, and if she did not know them, invariably her aunt, Lady Astor, did. Aside from her superb address book, she brought to the firm an almost imperceptible air of 'chic' from a part of society with which Fowler had little or no connection. He found her fascinating, and there is no doubt that he found her a huge inspiration. He also found her a huge irritation. They had what can best be described as a 'cat and dog' relationship—Nancy Lancaster was as famous for her wit as she was for her charm. It was to be the fusion of these two remarkable and distinctive talents that really crystallized the English Country House Style in the second half of the twentieth century.

During the 1940s the opportunities for decorating anew were few, due to rationing and the fact that all building work required a licence. The first house decorated by Fowler to appear in print after the war was Riverhall in Sussex, the home of Joan Dennis, which was featured in *Harper's Bazaar* in 1948.[10] The interiors show Fowler's creativity. Fabric was rationed, so he would buy second-hand curtains, cutting them up and sewing them together with stripes of plain twill (that was un-rationed), usually specially dyed. Georgian panelling was painted and old dresses were used to make loose covers. Old Damask tablecloths, which could be dyed a myriad of colours, were also used for this purpose [Fig. 3.4]. Fowler was often at his best when forced to be inventive, doing great things with virtually nothing. Aside from Riverhall, he worked for members of the Astor family in the 1940s, at Bruern Abbey and at Bletchington Park, a house that he was to decorate twice. He also began to work at Boughton House in Northamptonshire for Molly Buccleuch (Mary, Duchess of Buccleuch), who was a great friend of Nancy Lancaster. Re-opening that enormous house after the war, Fowler helped the Duchess to sort and re-arrange the furniture and showed the estate staff how to touch up the paintwork, and to repair and re-upholster furniture.

FIGURE 3.4 *Riverhall, one of the bedrooms. Decorated by Fowler in 1944. The house was published in Harper's Bazaar in 1948.*
Colefax and Fowler/English Heritage, Millar and Harris Collection.

The 1950s and 1960s were Fowler's heyday, but in reality his productive years were relatively short. One of the most significant houses that he decorated in the 1950s was Nancy Lancaster's own home, Haseley Court in Oxfordshire, which she acquired for a pittance in 1954 after her marriage to Colonel Lancaster of Kelmarsh ended. It was virtually a wreck and her land agent thought it would have been cheaper to have it torn down and rebuilt—the place was riddled with dry rot. It was, in addition, a challenging project simply because Lancaster, like many clients, changed her mind every five minutes and she and Fowler argued about virtually everything.

In his book *English Decoration of the Eighteenth Century* (1974), Fowler talked about the decoration of the Haseley Court Saloon.

> Chintzes and silk were freely mixed; and there was an avoidance of materials and colours matching and of sets of furniture that would give a static character, or indeed of a 'period' feeling in the normal meaning of the term. And yet none of the original decoration of either room [referring also to the Yellow Room at 39 Brook Street, Colefax and Fowler's Mayfair showroom] was disturbed. Indeed at Haseley the plasterwork was most carefully restored. Thus history was respected but re-interpreted to meet the needs and tastes of a particular person.[11]

This was classic Fowler; he would 're-interpret' and adapt, but he was never a slave to history, even though he was passionate about it. He had no interest in recreating period rooms, a practice that could be found on the continent and in the United States at that time.

When completed, Haseley was photographed by Horst P. Horst, who was bowled over by it and described it as 'the ideally comfortable English country house of everyone's dreams'.[12] As Lancaster entertained incessantly, Haseley's fame spread amongst the sort of people who would become clients of the business. Just as Ditchley and Kelmarsh had before the war, Haseley captivated people's imaginations and became hugely influential. Perhaps the secret was one of 'studied carelessness', for as 'Bill' Paley (chief executive of CBS, the American broadcasting corporation) recalled, Lancaster 'had a knack of making a room look old or used … which is very, very difficult to do' [Fig. 3.5].[13]

During the Second World War many country houses were requisitioned, often with disastrous results; Haseley Court was an example. With the arrival of peace, some were in such a poor state that they were simply demolished. After the war, the 'old rich' assumed that the pre-war world would return, but few wanted to exchange their new jobs in factories for life in domestic service. Gradually people began to adapt their houses and their lives to the modern reality. Taxation also had a devastating effect, particularly the taxation of foreign trust income, which compelled Ronald Tree to sell Ditchley Park and Lawrence Johnston to give up Hidcote Manor. Lancaster continued to live more or less as she always had. Others were, alas, not so fortunate.

Jill Chandos-Pole was dismayed by the state of Radburne Hall in Derbyshire when she went to live there in the early 1950s. On her second morning in the house, she began scrubbing the hall floor. The butler was appalled. The next morning he got down on hands and knees and scrubbed along with her. By a stroke of good

FIGURE 3.5 *The sitting room at Haseley Court, decorated in 1955.*
Courtesy of Colefax and Fowler.

fortune, money was found to put the hall in good order and Mrs Chandos-Pole insisted that her husband engage John Fowler. Fowler went on to decorate the entire house, which remains one of his finest and most elegant houses. The usual entrance to Radburne Hall was via a side door opening on to a passage running the length of the house. Poorly lit and perhaps a little gloomy, Fowler chose to paint it a strong terracotta colour—the inspiration probably came from Italy, which he had visited in 1955. Rising to the *piano nobile* the single-storey great hall was decorated in a shade of aquamarine blue and all the mahogany woodwork, such as the tabernacle, was painted in shades of white. Continuity was found in the suite of furniture originally made for its Jacobean predecessor and wherever he could Fowler retained the original upholstery. To complete the effect, he copied the curtains that had been designed by Mrs Bethell for the saloon at Kelmarsh Hall and had them made up in red Mohair velvet.

The great hall opened into the saloon, which Fowler contrasted by painting it 'Rushbrook Pink' with ivory damask festoon draperies and curtains. In his selection of colour, he was following a familiar pattern—blue in east-facing rooms, but not pink. Although Fowler is known for his use of chintz, in this house it was used sparingly. For example in the drawing room, hung with cinnamon silk, the loose covers were of plain green linen, the chintz merely being an accent used for cushions and an odd chair. Radburne Hall shows Fowler's colour sense and his use of colours working with one another in harmony, not only within a room but between rooms so that the whole house had a sense of rhythm and progression.

It was not just his colour sense, but how the colour was created that was important. Rooms were seldom just flat painted and Fowler inspired many fashions in paint finishes. He would quite often use techniques such as dragging and stippling, both of which allow the undercoat to show through. The object was to give the paintwork a translucent quality, a little like porcelain. Invariably he would mix the paint himself or one of his assistants would do so using tubes of artists' colours and he would often add a tiny spot of black to 'smoke' the colour, stopping it being too brash, too bright. He was famous for his use of numerous tints and tones. He would never paint a door with a single colour, for example, but would use several tints— one for the stiles and rails, another for the mouldings, possibly with a highlight, and yet another for the panels. He was also known for his use of many shades of white within a single scheme and employed this formula regularly. He painted Sir Hardy Amies' Salon in Savile Row in such a manner, and as Sir Hardy remarked, 'when John was alive there was no question of having anything other than three whites ... but once he was dead, we just painted it white. Having it three shades, you know, never sold another f****** frock!'[14]

These ideas came from Fowler's observations. Modern paint analysis techniques have revealed that the Georgians did not use as many varying tints as he supposed, but what he sought to do was to create an image of the past, the romance of a bygone age. Although he had known a number of significant figures in the field of decoration, among them Mrs Bethell and the decorative historian Margaret Jourdain, Fowler was largely self-taught.[15] He spent hours studying furniture, *objets d'art* and costumes in the Victoria and Albert Museum. Many of his early curtain trims, for example, were derived from eighteenth-century dress design. He also acquired knowledge and practical skills by buying old draperies that he would carefully unpick, study, and re-make. In his early work, he was heavily influenced by the theatre and would use slipper satin in quite bold colours such as sharp yellows and intense pinks. He also created a number of stage designs and would probably have done more had he not been so imprudent as to steal one of Binkie Beaumont's boyfriends.[16]

Fowler had an assured eye for proportion and a unique way of dressing windows so that his draperies seemed effortless and natural. They were, of course, worked out with the utmost care, and were quite often elaborately trimmed. Indeed, he virtually kept Clarke's the trim makers near St. Paul's Cathedral in business. Again, just as in paint finishes, he inspired fashions in window decoration and towards the end of his life he remarked to the decorator Jean Monro that they had 'certainly started something with the curtains at Clandon and Bath: a lot of unfortunate customers will be made to have them [pull-up curtains and festoon blinds] where they are not suitable'.[17] He could have said the same of swag and tail draperies, for which he is justly famous, and which were, in far less skilful hands than his, used inappropriately, often with disastrous results.

Becoming a client of Fowler was not for the faint-hearted. Before being accepted, potential clients had to pass an interview. Fowler would expect them to be able to describe their houses and to provide a sketch plan of the room that they wanted to have decorated (these were always hopelessly wrong) and maybe a few photographs. If the project was of interest, he would arrange to see the place. He would walk from room to room, his assistant Imogen Taylor fighting with a tape measure and note pad, following in his wake, trying to take notes. Summoned once more to Brook Street, the actual scheme would then be discussed. Fowler never produced elaborate written proposals with fabric samples (except on the one occasion when he worked for Her Majesty the Queen), and his designs for curtains were in essence 'sketches' that would be more accurately and formally drawn up by assistants. In his room, behind his desk, was his 'colour wall' made up of hundreds of bits of fabric, wool and so on—anything that gave a good definite colour. If walls were to be painted blue, for example, Fowler would pull blue samples from his 'colour wall', which would then be hurled on to the floor with a 'this blue, or maybe this one'.[18] Over the back of an armchair might be a large fabric sample, possibly two, which had already been selected and around which the scheme would gradually be assembled. Clients were invariably regarded as children—to be seen, do as they were told, and sign the cheque. Although a great deal of money was often spent, Fowler was never driven by his own profit. He would often say, 'you should do right by the house,' and this was his guiding philosophy.[19]

Fowler was rather more than a decorator: he had an eye for architecture and architectural details. Visiting a job with the architect Philip Jebb, who raved about a chimneypiece he had bought for the dining room, Fowler dryly observed, 'Nice chimneypiece, but what a pity it was intended for a library'.[20] On another occasion Jebb earned the stinging rebuke, 'Why have you put the switches at council house height?'[21] One hates to think what he would have made of modern building regulations with the sockets halfway up the walls. In fact very often he forgot where he had learnt something or why something had to be done in a certain way. It was not only about the aesthetic but also about making the house function and work.

Fowler may have been a successful decorator, but he was a hopeless businessman and Nancy Lancaster was equally useless with finances, so it is hardly surprising that the business lost money every year. Imogen Taylor, who was Fowler's assistant for twenty years, remembers Lancaster remarking, with a degree of indignation: 'I've lost a £180 this year!'—she covered the firm's losses by writing a cheque—at a time when Taylor recalls that she 'only earned a £120 a year'.[22]

By 1960 it was clear that a re-organization was required, so the Tree family invited Tom Parr to take a stake in the company.[23] Parr was a good businessman who recognized that the fabrics that Colefax and Fowler created for individual clients would have a wider appeal. Fowler would perhaps have a chintz fabric printed for a job, but a manufacturer would have a minimum order of two pieces (a piece being sixty yards). He might use all of one piece and a bit from another, so the cellar at Brook Street was full of rolls of fabric which might or might not 'come in' eventually. The client had, of course, merely been charged for the used yardage, so this way of working was a financial disaster. The company had sold fabrics in a rather limited way from the outset. One textile, 'Bowood', was produced in the 1930s and is still in production today. The fabric patterns created before and after the war were often based on eighteenth- and early nineteenth-century designs, sometimes re-coloured and re-scaled. As Fowler's work expanded after the war, he created a number of fabrics of his own, often small geometric weaves which were based on eighteenth-century carriage cloths. As a result, Colefax and Fowler began to retail fabrics through Brook Street and at the specially created 'Chintz Shop' in Belgravia. This was an instant success.

During the 1950s and 1960s, the backbone of Colefax and Fowler's work was the decoration of London town houses and flats. These seldom fired Fowler's imagination and when someone would telephone to ask if he would decorate a new London flat he would invariably remark, 'I'd pay not to do it'![24] He loved country houses. His last, for a private client, was Cornbury Park in Oxfordshire. The house, in a mix of architectural styles, was partly the work of Nicholas Stone and partly by Hugh May. Fowler loved this gutsy architecture for, as he remarked to a friend, 'I'm so bored with all that late-eighteenth-century stuff. I long for some architecture again.'[25] He and Philip Jebb adapted the house for its new owners and Fowler created some very sumptuous interiors for it. The drawing room curtains were a *tour de force* of the curtain maker's art and seemed to incorporate every possible trim and detail imaginable. The bedrooms were just as polished, with magnificently dressed four poster beds, the simplest of which was the Tudor bed in which the Earl of Leicester, Queen Elizabeth the First's favourite, had died.

Throughout most of the 1960s, Fowler was an ill man. He officially retired from Colefax and Fowler on the third of September 1971 and although he remained a consultant to the company, he was to devote the rest of his life to the National Trust. He first worked for the Trust in 1956, at Claydon House in Buckinghamshire—a project which came about through his friendship with St John (Bobby) Gore and James Lees-Milne. Resources were meagre to say the least, but Fowler brought a sense of life to what were in effect 'dead houses'. Other than Claydon, his most important schemes for the Trust were for Clandon Park in Surrey and Sudbury Hall in Derbyshire, where, denuded of their contents, he created an experience for the visitor based on the architecture, highlighted by colour.

His finest work was at Sudbury Hall, where the most controversial thing Fowler ever did was to paint the staircase. The magnificent carved balustrade was stripped of its brown Victorian varnish and painted in shades of white. The decision was based upon historical evidence, but recognizing contemporary tastes, he made the balustrade slightly whiter than it had been (it had been a stone shade) and the walls a stronger, clearer yellow, instead of their original slightly drab yellow ochre.[26] This gave a more striking contrast. James Lees-Milne was impressed: 'Went round the house, which I can truthfully pronounce perfect. I can find no criticism at all of this uninhabited house, sparsely furnished. The walls, floors and ceilings are so self-sufficiently beautiful and so beautifully renovated by John Fowler that they convince me he has as certain a genius in leaving well alone as in decorating anew.'[27] Even today, forty years later, the effect is breath-taking.

Following his retirement, Fowler lived permanently at his country home, The Hunting Lodge near Odiham in Hampshire, which he had bought in 1947. This triple gabled folly was the perfect house for an old romantic like Fowler and he decorated it with great style and panache. As he remarked, it was what he did for everyone else, just on a diminutive scale. With the advent of the 1970s Lancaster was forced (following a disastrous fire) to sell Haseley and retreat to the Coach House. It is perhaps a great irony that two figures who did so much to create the English Country House Style should have passed the rest of their days in cottages. John

Fowler died in October 1977 and Nancy Lancaster, who was slightly older, lived on and died in August 1994.

During the course of his career some of Fowler's work was published, but it was his work for the National Trust that brought his style to a wider public and to a new generation of professional designers. Just before he retired, Laura and Bernard Ashley opened their first shop in South Kensington, catering to a different clientele to that of Colefax and Fowler—the aspiring middle classes—people who had perhaps bought their first home, a good solid Victorian house that they wished to modernize and decorate. The myriad of small patterns, for which the Ashleys were to become famous, drew inspiration from great Victorian designers such as Owen Jones. Of course Laura Ashley was not a designer: she was an editor, and she was very adept at identifying a trend or a fashion and catering to that trend by drawing on the past—by adapting and updating that past for the present. Gradually Laura Ashley's taste and style evolved, particularly after she went to live in France and became slightly grander, more English Country House, undoubtedly inspired by Fowler and Lancaster, both of whom she knew.

John Fowler decorated dozens of country houses over the course of his career, most of which were not open to the public and are little known. Little of his work survives today, but he was able to influence how virtually every country house is decorated and arranged, even if that influence is not immediately apparent. You can see it in the small things—when you sit down is there a convenient table for your glass and an ideally placed light so you can read a book? Is there a good definite colour and charming pattern, which makes you want to linger? And yet, for the most part, the care with which the interior was created belies the first impression. Russell Page used to say that a garden should appear 'inevitable', its design such that it could not have been any other way. In many ways, this is what John Fowler did with his interiors. There was an air of inevitability about them, but there was also great skill, panache and understatement. What John Fowler and Nancy Lancaster actually did was to crystallize a style that has come to represent an entire way of life.

Notes

1   Author's interview with Jill Chandos-Pole on 5 June 2006.

2   Sally Bedell Smith, *In All His Glory: The Life of William S. Paley* (New York: Simon and Schuster, 1990), 206. The remark is often, incorrectly, attributed to Bill Paley. The source is actually anonymous.

3   Nancy Lancaster was married twice before she married Colonel Lancaster. Her first husband was Henry Field (died in 1917), the younger brother of Marshall Field III, heir to the Chicago Department Store fortune. Her second husband, Ronald Tree, was their cousin. Brought up in England, Tree stood for parliament and was elected to the seat of Market Harborough in 1933. Through his political career and Lady Astor (Nancy's aunt), the Trees were famous for their hospitality, first at Kelmarsh Hall in Northamptonshire and later at Ditchley Park in Oxfordshire. Through this, Lancaster's style and sense of taste spread within society, so much so that people copied her ideas.

4   Nancy Lancaster cited by Nancy Richardson in 'The Amazing Nancy Lancaster', *House and Garden* (New York), November 1983, 179.

5   Author's interview with Albert Hadley on 23 March 2010.

6   The Hon Mrs Guy Bethell (c.1865–1932) founded Elden Ltd. in around 1904 in partnership with Alice Dryden (c.1867–1956). Mrs Bethell bought out her partner in 1913. After her death in 1932, the business was bought by Herman Schrijver (1904–72), author of *Decoration for the Home* (F. Lewis, 1939), who closed it in 1940. Lancaster regarded Mrs Bethell as 'by far the best decorator I have ever known', a sentiment with which Fowler concurred.

7   Nancy Lancaster, Private Papers.

8   Fowler did freelance painting for a number of decorators including Margaret Kunzer, who ran a painting studio from her parents' house in Grosvenor Road. She sold a huge amount of her output to Peter Jones Ltd. and to decorators such as Dolly Mann and Syrie Maugham. In 1929, Peter Jones asked her to open a Decorative Furniture Department, which she did with John Fowler as its head. He left in 1934.

9   Anne Scott James, *Sketches from a Life* (London: Michael Joseph, 1993), 76. Anne Scott-James (1913–2009) worked on *Vogue* from 1934 and on the outbreak of war joined *Picture Post*. Subsequently, she worked on *Harper's Bazaar*, where she commissioned work from figures such as Cecil Beaton, John Betjeman, and Elizabeth David.

10 Joan Dennis had been a 'Cochran Girl', a noted dance troupe of the period. She is reputed to have had an affair with Sir Harold Wernher, of Luton Hoo, who showered her with gifts and a flat in Grosvenor Square. She and John became great friends and he went on to decorate all her homes, including one of his finest works, Hay's Mews in Mayfair.

11 Nancy Lancaster, Private Papers.

12 Horst P. Horst, 'Guest Speaker: A Reminiscence of Memorable Interiors', *Architectural Digest*, date unknown.

13 Smith, *In All His Glory*, 206.

14 Martin Wood, *John Fowler: Prince of Decorators* (London: Frances Lincoln, 2007), 123.

15 Margaret Jourdain (1876–1951) was a leading authority on English furniture and decoration. She ghostwrote the famous books on English furniture by Francis Lenygon of the antique dealers Lenygon & Morant. For many years, she shared a flat with the novelist Ivy Compton-Burnett.

16 Hugh 'Binkie' Beaumont (1908–73) controlled H. M. Tennant Ltd. and was the most powerful figure in West End theatre. He was not a man to be crossed and when crossed had a reputation for being unforgiving.

17 Jean Monro was the daughter of Mrs Geraldine Monro and took over her decorating business, Mrs Monro, at 11 Montpelier Street. She was one of the leading decorators of the period and a friend of John Fowler. See Jean Monro, *11 Montpelier Street: Memoirs of an Interior Decorator* (London: Weidenfeld and Nicolson, 1988), 152.

18 Author's interview with Imogen Taylor on 11 March 2006.

19 Author's interview with Imogen Taylor, George Oakes, and Michael Raymond on 11 March 2006. The phrase was one of Fowler's often used maxims.

20 John Cornforth, *The Inspiration of the Past: Country House Taste in the Twentieth Century* (London: Viking, 1985), 162.

21 Ibid., 163.

22 Author's interview with Imogen Taylor on 11 March 2006.

23   In 1950, Nancy Lancaster had been forced to sell her home in Virginia. Following her
     divorce from Colonel Lancaster in the mid-1950s, he sent her a cheque for £100,000,
     which she contemptuously tore up. Thereafter, her financial affairs were managed
     by her two children, Michael and Jeremy Tree. Tom Parr (1930–2011) had been
     in partnership with David Hicks (1929–98), but as he was about to marry Pamela
     Mountbatten the partnership was to be dissolved. Parr took a 49 percent stake in
     Colefax and Fowler with the Tree family retaining a controlling 51 percent.

24   Cornforth, *The Inspiration of the Past*, 158.

25   Author's interview with Michael Raymondon 12 March 2006.

26   George Oakes, who worked at Sudbury with John Fowler, remembered that paint
     scrapes had clearly revealed that the balustrade had been painted two shades of white
     and that the walls had been a dull ochre yellow. Author's interview with George Oakes
     on 11 March 2006.

27   James Lees-Milne, *Through Wood and Dale: Diaries 1975–1978* (London: John Murray,
     2003), 129.

4

At Home with Modern Design 1958–65: A Case Study

Christine Lalumia

This chapter examines ideas about modernity as it was perceived in terms of domestic design and decoration by focusing on one middle-class couple and their home in Highgate, north London, which was built and furnished in 1958. It draws on extensive archival information, spanning many years, held by The Geffrye Museum of the Home in London, and is supplemented by a personal interview with the home's owner in 2013.[1] The chapter considers the cultural context and personal circumstances surrounding the design choices made by this couple in order to see how much can be learned from this specific experience about the wider tastes of the middle classes and investigates whether their European background significantly influenced their design tastes.

This focus on one particular family also permits some wider issues to be addressed. How common was it amongst the middle classes to desire a new-build home? And how modern were the middle classes at home—why were some particularly drawn to and open to a non-traditional style for their furniture and domestic spaces? Was it mainly confined to those moving to or living in a modern house, rather than in older building stock, such as pre-war, Victorian or earlier? Was it a specific type of person who inclined towards it and is it possible to identify a 'type' of homemaker who did? Were there any restrictions to achieving a home of good design? Was it a purely aesthetic choice or equally to do with lifestyle? And how easy was it to acquire modern design for the home? Clearly, it is impossible to answer these questions categorically for a whole swathe of the population. However, by studying in depth the choices of a particular couple establishing a home in the late 1950s and early 1960s and comparing their experience to that of others setting up home at the time, some interesting themes begin to emerge.

To preserve their anonymity, the couple in focus will be referred to as Mr and Mrs H. An art historian by training, Mrs H was a housewife/mother and Mr H, a toyshop owner; both were born in Germany.[2] They met in England in 1939 and married. Despite being from educated and well-off backgrounds, their refugee status in England effectively forced them to 'start from scratch' without inherited possessions and they were thus able to give free rein to their own tastes.[3] It is clear from their testimony that Mr and Mrs H made a conscious and very definite decision to live in a new-build, modern house. When asked directly about this taste for the modern, their openness to new design and, by extension, their desire for a modern home, Mrs H replied quite simply that each period in history has its own form and idea of the 'new'. She elaborated by stating that both her own and her husband's families in Germany had 'new' furniture made for them when setting up home. In the case of Mr H's family, this early twentieth-century furniture was made to suit a new-build house in about 1904. As such, in her eyes, the decision she and her husband took to buy and furnish a modern house with mainly contemporary items was both logical and natural.[4]

They first visited the site upon which their home was eventually built in 1953; they were accompanied by the architect Ernö Goldfinger, who, in Mrs H's words, very much 'wanted to build, à la Corbusier, a block of flats'.[5] Goldfinger's designs for the site never materialized and the Hs, who knew that they wanted to live at this location, had to wait several years until a scheme proposing a development of architect-designed townhouses was approved by Haringey Council.[6] The Hs bought 'off the plan', fully confident that the aggressively modern style of this new housing was right for them.[7] As Mrs H recalls, 'we were the original, first people to move in. And we knew the site before... we bought on plan only because we liked it...the architecture suited us.'[8]

The north London location which they chose was ideally placed for quick access to the centre of town and appears to have been favoured by middle-class couples or families. The professions of the incoming residents included an actor, a publisher, and many 'young but very enterprising' people. According to Mrs H, 'the most amazing people bought these houses'.[9] She felt that 'the houses appealed to architects' and those engaged in liberal arts fields because the development was less conservative than other building stock in the area.[10] Yet interestingly, despite resounding endorsement from the newly ensconced residents, its aesthetic qualities were not universally admired. Mrs H and her daughter 'JR' remember that at the time the Mayor of Highgate called the houses 'the chicken coops or rabbit hutches'.[11]

The Highgate development comprised '43 houses, round this very beautiful big park with a ruin of a Georgian house' that was itself surrounded by nineteenth-century terraced housing and mansion flats [Fig. 4.1].[12] This leafy pocket of town was well suited to the new style of snug, low-lying domestic development that was cropping up around London at this time, which featured small houses with flat fronts and large expanses of plate glass windows front and back. One of the most radical aspects of the design of these houses was the placement of the kitchen at the front, leaving the main living and dining area completely open to the garden view.[13] The architects and developers of many new estates—both private and local authority— adopted this modern idiom for the style and layout of their housing developments, various of which also boasted both small private and larger communal gardens. Open plan and non-traditional in its detailing, the Highgate development bore many similarities to the Span estates that were being built at this time in more

FIGURE 4.1 *View of houses on a housing estate in Highgate (c. 1958), where Mr and Mrs H had their home.*
© The Geffrye Museum of the Home, London.

suburban locations such as Twickenham.[14] A Span brochure of 1960 envisaged the future inhabitants of the firm's houses as 'Young professional men and their families, with a sprinkling of older couples, or single people, probably retired. You would find people who work in advertising, broadcasting and television, journalism and Law. School teachers, surgeons, executives, architects, surveyors'.[15] The original inhabitants of the fashionable Span estates were memorably described by the critic Reyner Banham as 'Zodiac-to-Jaguar income groups, Observer-reading with an interest in improving public taste'.[16] Although not cheap, these modern townhouses were within the reach of the aspiring middle classes: the houses in the Highgate development originally sold for between £5,750 and £6,250, while those on the Span estate in Twickenham were slightly less expensive in 1960 at approximately £5,000 for a three-bedroomed house.[17]

The contemporary townhouse style carried with it cultural meanings: this non-traditional type of house was part of a new typology, which expressed the aesthetic tastes of their owners and, as importantly, genuinely reflected the way that these people wanted to live. The open plan layout of the main rooms encouraged informality and sociability. At the Highgate home of Mr and Mrs H, the living and dining area was communal and constantly in use, often for listening to music and entertaining visitors. The fact that people dropped by is mentioned several times and communicates a real sense of the social aspect, the feeling of community that emerged in the development.[18] The children considered their bedrooms as their 'own' private space, and in the case of JR, decorating decisions were left to her. She chose a chair from Hille, art for the walls and the colour scheme for 'her space', a place to do homework, to take friends, or to be on her own.[19] The ways in which the Hs interacted as a family indicates a careful balance between individualism and privacy and a quite open and expressive family group.

An emphasis on the open flow of the interior spaces, combined with a generous interface between the rooms inside and the private garden or courtyard beyond (often referred to as a 'room outdoors'), was one of the most appealing features of what were essentially very small houses. One of the reasons that the Hs, a family of four, were able to make this rather compact house work for them is that the architects found clever ways in which to maximize space, for instance with the open-tread staircase ascending into a double-height space in the corner of the dining area, which added a sense of sculpture, dynamism and lightness to the small room [Fig. 4.2]. Yet it took more than architectural solutions to make this type of interior really work and for many success lay in the careful choice of furniture and furnishings. The lack of architectural ornament and the clean lines of the house, both inside and out, contributed to a spare and fresh aesthetic that lent itself quite naturally to modern furniture and furnishings.

Part of the appeal of contemporary furniture related to its size as much its aesthetic qualities. Many designers of modern furniture were also architects who were well aware of the decreasing volumes of many domestic spaces and took into account the small size of the houses in which much of the British population lived after the war. In conversation with Mrs H and her daughter, the size of their house—and by extension that of the rooms—was mentioned several times. Although size itself did not bother Mrs H, she acknowledges that it was not to everyone's taste. As she put it, 'if you lived in a Georgian house in the village then you hated a house like this.'[20]

A desire by owners to move furniture around and to be more flexible with the layout of the interior meant that the design of the furniture had to change: it needed to be more lightweight and also attractive from the back. Unlike Victorian or Edwardian parlour and dining room furniture, in these new houses pieces were often moved away from the wall and were seen in the round. Lighter, more sculptural forms were often the result. Much of this 'new' furniture seems to have come from Scandinavia. The Hs had an occasional table with a removable tray top in teak by the Danish designer Hans Wegner, a Finnish sofa covered in purple upholstery, a Fritz Hansen coffee table sold through Heal's, contemporary armchairs in yellow and curtains from Marimekko.

Another example of a preference for modern design can be seen in a new build at Bromley in Kent, designed in 1956 by Mr J Morison, an architect, and furnished by

FIGURE 4.2 *Partition wall between sitting and dining room, showing staircase, in Mr and Mrs H's home in Highgate (c.1958).*
© The Geffrye Museum of the Home, London.

his wife Betty, a teacher. Betty was an admirer of Scandinavian design and became familiar with it through friends who lived in Sweden and Finland.[21] Across London, at the Fieldend Span estate in Twickenham, a young woman named Margret Cochrane was also attracted to Scandinavian design. Of German heritage, she moved to the Twickenham estate in 1962.[22] Her husband was in the timber trade, with professional links to Sweden and Finland, and Margret acknowledges that this was an influence. Shopping at Trend in Richmond, which was known for its good selection of contemporary furniture, and at Heal's in central London, she too owned a set of six Wegner chairs as well as a birch coffee table made by Vilka in Finland.[23]

At another Span home in Twickenham, MR and her husband acquired modern furniture and furnishings, much from Scandinavia, although it is not clear whether or not they had personal connections with those countries.[24] Readers of *House and Garden*, this nurse and civil servant in their twenties chose for their new home Scandinavian carpets, a Danish ceiling light from Heal's, a Finnish pendant 'Coolie' shade from Harrods, curtains, and blinds from Heal's, a Bertoia easy chair in persimmon and a Hille two-seater sofa on a metal frame.[25] To this, they added wallpaper from Sanderson's and a nineteenth-century rosewood Davenport; like Mr and Mrs H, they were not afraid to mix modern with contemporary. As Mrs H asserted in relation to the integration of choice antiques with their Scandinavian and modern furniture, 'we bought what we liked'.[26] This freedom from conformity and rejection of a rigid way of making decisions about design clearly encouraged an expression of individuality in these homes. Specific pieces, combined by the owner in a way which appealed to them, was a very different approach to that taken in more traditionally decorated homes. As Mrs H said, 'oh no, we never had a three piece suite'.[27]

Finding and choosing modern design for the home was a joint endeavour between husband and wife for all of those considered in this chapter. It appears that purchases were discussed and decided by the couple, even if one took the lead on certain types of furnishings. For the Hs, '... all the art buying was up to him [Mr H]. But, chairs, things like that, I sussed out and then, he approved or didn't... yes, he approved. Curtain material and all the upholstery, I, I went around to look and then he saw, or didn't see and then when he liked it we bought it'.[28] MR also remembers that she and her husband made joint decisions about the furniture and furnishings for their Span house.[29]

In all of these cases a taste for modern design, in particular for furniture and furnishings from Scandinavia, was clear in their decorating choices. Although the acquisition of furniture in the immediate post-war years was very restricted, by the late 1950s those setting up home had quite a wide choice in terms of both where to shop and what to buy. In London a number of retailers sold good, contemporary furniture and these shops were no doubt responding to the boom in public demand for an alternative to traditional designs. These suppliers included, as already noted, Heal's in Tottenham Court Road and Trend in Richmond, as well as Oscar Woollens, Liberty's, and Bowman's of Camden Town. Further afield, Dunns of Bromley and Harris and Gibson at Ilford in Essex also provided modern options.

Not all fans of modern furniture lived in contemporary houses, as interesting examples of period properties furnished with Scandinavian and other modern pieces attest. The home of Alistair Freeborn's parents at Orpington in Kent is an interesting case in point [Fig. 4.3].[30] The home of a photographer and a school teacher, this three-bedroomed semi-detached house, dating from c.1935 (complete with a large bay window at the front and decorative hung tiles on the façade) boasted furniture by Finn Juhl, a sideboard by Finmar and a round table with six chairs designed by Hans Wegner.[31] When Mrs Freeborn moved later in life to another period house, the Wegner set went too and is still in use. As Alistair Freeborn remembers, the family home was 'of the time... quite trendy'.[32] This is a compelling example (which is not unique) of contemporary design being used in a period property. By contrast, there were certainly those who chose to use traditional or even period and/or inherited furniture in contemporary architecture.[33] All of this indicates that part of the allure of modern design at the time lay in its adaptability, both on a functional and an aesthetic level.

FIGURE 4.3 *Dining room at Alistair Freeborn's former home at Orpington, Kent (1956).*
© The Geffrye Museum of the Home, London.

The importance of availability is, of course, essential to understanding the keenness with which many of the middle classes embraced and sought out modern design. Affordability was another key point: like the new houses themselves, modern design was certainly not cheap but it was within the grasp of careful shoppers. Mrs H recalls 'saving up for the furniture we wanted', indicating the planning and thought that went into these domestic acquisitions.[34] But there is also an important factor that relates to personal connections and exposure to modern design. This was clearly a key influence in terms of the choices made by the Hs, through their social circle and cultural background, and for those like Mr and Mrs M and

Margret Cochrane, who had strong connections with Scandinavia. As we have seen, couples such as Mr and Mrs H needed no encouragement to embrace the modern ethos in their home and were explicit in their acknowledgement of, and admiration for, European and Scandinavian modernism. Both Mr and Mrs H referred to the influence of the Bauhaus, saying that it was in their blood.[35] Further to this, their social circle included many 'Continentals of a certain age', to use Mrs H's phrase, many of whom seem to have shared a similar taste for modern design. As Mrs H recalled, 'we were very influenced by the Bauhaus, and the Danish furniture particularly.'[36] Mrs H feels that being 'Continental' naturally inclined both her and her husband towards modernism. When the Hs visited the homes of their close friends and relatives in England, they encountered modern interiors very much like their own.[37] But what about those who had less personal exposure to, and experience of, Continental modernism? From where would they find inspiration?

Modern design was gaining currency in Britain of the 1950s, in part owing to a campaign to promote 'good design' championed by a range of designers, manufacturers, architects, writers, social reformers and government agencies such as the Council of Industrial Design. Their ideas about good design were pushed heavily and well publicized. Mr and Mrs H knew about the efforts of the Council of Industrial Design (through friends and more generally) and frequently visited the design centre in Haymarket.[38] Simple, good quality, value for money, anti-historicist design was presented to the public as a serious alternative to traditional styles and the opportunities for seeing it firsthand increased. Most obviously, the two big exhibitions of the late 1940s and early 1950s had a huge impact on public taste. The first, Britain Can Make It at the Victoria and Albert Museum, opened on 24 September 1946, ran for fourteen weeks and attracted nearly 1.5 million visitors, two of whom were Mr and Mrs H. Organized by the Council of Industrial Design, the exhibition's aims were to showcase British design and to stimulate British industry. The exhibition contained over 5,000 items produced by British manufacturers and included most types of consumer goods—furniture, textiles, carpets, wallpapers, tableware, domestic appliances, household equipment, clothing and toys. One of the most popular exhibits was the Furnished Rooms Section, which displayed a series of room settings (complete with imaginary inhabitants) by leading designers. The exhibition's legacy included three major outcomes: it disseminated ideas and catalysed dialogue about 'good design', it raised design awareness across social groups and classes and, most tangibly, it paved the way for the Festival of Britain in 1951. Britain Can Make It was important to Mr and Mrs H and The Festival of Britain even more so; they found it inspirational: 'We absolutely loved it!'.[39]

Inspiration also came from the popular press, and from glossy magazines such as *House and Garden*, *Homes and Gardens* and even *Woman*. *House and Garden*, in particular, consciously promoted 'good design'. Much of this was modern and, indeed, Scandinavian; September 1960 saw the 'The Scandinavian Issue'. In April 1960, *House and Garden* featured on its cover a contemporary townhouse, not dissimilar to Mr and Mrs H's London townhouse or to Span houses of similar date. With its large plate glass windows giving out to a courtyard, its contemporary furniture, bold use of colour on accent walls and exposed materials, this light-filled house clearly represented the 'good life' that could be possible in a non-traditional home. Also revealing is the heading on the cover, telling readers that inside they will find inside information on 'The Many Faces of Modern'. In other words, modern now came in different flavours—there was 'Architect's Modern', 'Industrial Designer's Modern', 'Swedish Modern', 'American Modern' and more. The implication here is that modern design was a broad church with room for individual taste, not a set of prescriptive dictats as many felt the original wave of German modernism of the 1920s and 1930s had been.

The *Daily Express* offered another example of the promotion of good design with a competition that it ran in 1959. The newspaper asked for designs for a house to be submitted in response to the question 'Is your house your master or servant'? John Prizeman's 'Her House' won first prize.[40] It is notable for its links between inside and outside (reminiscent of the Highgate development and also the Span estate at Twickenham), its open-plan and efficient layout, and the convenient and informal style of living it offered. It was forward looking and not beyond the reach of the middle classes in terms of cost. Above all, it was decidedly modern. All of these were features that the newspaper clearly felt would appeal to the aspirations of middle-class readers.

Modernity was not confined to design. The important relationship between modern art and contemporary design, a key principle at the Bauhaus, was nicely underscored in the house of Mr and Mrs H. When thinking of her childhood home in Highgate in relation to those of her teenage friends, JR remembered: 'I was aware [then] that we had lovely pictures, I mean I was aware that we had *art*....'[41] A print by John Piper was hung amongst other original works of art and appears perfectly in keeping with the modern furniture. Perhaps this, too, is an integral facet of having 'Bauhaus in the blood': this harmonious relationship between the arts was thought natural to Mr and Mrs H.

The aspirational aspects of modern interiors and furnishings should not be underestimated. Neither should the importance of the creation of a home—and all the design choices that entails—in the formation and/or confirmation of identity. Mrs H speaks about the complete freedom of having no inheritance in terms of furniture and furnishings and not worrying about the impression their design choices made. When asked if the home reflected the family, she replied in the affirmative: '... it is us, other houses are different you know. I mean some people who... grew up were... are English, are British, they got a lot of furniture off their families which they have in the house. But as we started from nothing... we could do absolutely what we wanted to do and what we liked.'[42]

For many, the idea that their interior expressed their values was a strong driving force in decoration. A person with strong 'traditional values' might feel uneasy in a room filled with aesthetically modern furniture and objects. This idea comes clearly through the findings of the Register Your Choice exhibition held at Charing Cross Station in 1953. Commuters were asked their opinions on a traditional sitting room ('Room L') and a modern-style room ('Room R') that promoted 'good design'.[43] A survey conducted by the Design and Industries Association showed that three out of five of those interviewed preferred 'good contemporary design'.[44] This finding was challenged by Mass-Observation, which ran a complimentary survey and showed the split to be about 50/50.[45] Regardless of the precise proportion, there is enough critical mass in the results of both studies to show that a preference for modern or traditional design was frequently linked to socio-economic class, with the modern scheme favoured by the middle classes and the more traditional one by the working classes.[46] It showed that for many, contemporary, good design was seen as appealing if idealized and perhaps more significantly, unobtainable.

For some, if not many, the design of a room and its furnishings were indistinguishable from lifestyle and self-image. The testimony of a short-hand typist in her early twenties is illuminating:

> R [the modern room] is ideal—need I say more. Wonderful tones of colour are picked up all around the room. But I would never live in it. For one thing my family would have a fit, they'd think I'd gone quite mad and all arty. You see, I'd have to be a different person, I'd have to read the best books and listen to the third programme, don't you agree? The atmosphere, definitely it's highbrow, because I can't think it is the room of the average person—it's too good.[47]

Clearly this woman was attracted to the modern room and in many ways might aspire to it, were it not for ideas about her own position in society. Somehow, the modern, good design did not seem to correspond with her vision of herself or with the home into which she would fit in terms of her own behaviours and interests. For some, if not many, the design of a room and its furnishings were indistinguishable from lifestyle and self-image. It is telling that Mrs H refers explicitly to listening to classical music in the living/dining room and to having 'the third programme' on the radio all the time.[48]

This chapter has sought to determine the extent to which Mr and Mrs H consciously adopted a modern style of home and furnishing and what might have influenced their choices. It attempted to establish whether their choices were outside the mainstream at the time or fairly typical of their social class and background. The home which Mr and Mrs H created from 1958 onwards in many ways epitomizes what was then and is today still thought of as 'good design'. It is clear that their Germanic background disposed them to an openness and acceptance of modern design. In other examples, one can see that exposure to and familiarity with modern ideas of living bred interest and engagement. But these are only a handful of specific examples—beyond these, can any specific conclusions be drawn? Clearly the Hs were not alone but were living in a period in which modern design was becoming a legitimate alternative for home decoration in Britain. As an originally non-English style, initially brought to a reluctant British population by German émigrés in the 1930s, it took time to take root in middle-class homes. Perhaps its enduring popularity—and the fascination with which we now examine this period in design and home-making—is almost more important than whether or not it was adopted in a large number of homes at the time. Today, it earns its keep as being—like most manifestations of modernism—a continuing option for the contemporary home.

Notes

1   The Geffrye Museum holds extensive material about this home in Highgate in its archive, which includes oral history recordings, transcripts, photographs from 1958 and 1988 and objects owned by the couple. The archive has been amassed over a long period: the first wave of information was collected in 1996, when this home was a key part of the research and the inspiration for a new period room at the museum. A recorded interview with Mrs H and her daughter 'JR' was made in 2009. It is unusual to have such a sustained relationship between a family and a museum formally documented and developed through various stages over such a long period of time.

2   Mr H is now deceased.

3   Author's interview with Mrs H in June 2013.

4   Ibid.

5   Ibid.

6   Haringey Council had, according to Mrs H, rejected Goldfinger's plans for a private development because they wanted to build social housing on this site. These plans never materialized and they accepted an offer from a private developer. Author's interview with Mrs H in June 2013.

7   It was located in a speculative development in the extensive grounds of a large Georgian house; the architects were Andrews, Emmerson and Sherlock.

8   Quote from the transcript of an interview with Mrs H about her home in Highgate, London, object number 1/2013-2, The Geffrye Museum of the Home, London, 1.

9   Author's interview with Mrs H in June 2013. Mr and Mrs H's daughter 'JR' remembered 'lots of architects'. Quote ibid 1/2013-2, 3. See also *Architectural Digest* (May 1962): 228.

10   Quote, Geffrye Museum, 1/2013-2, 3.

11   Ibid.

12   Ibid., 1.

13   Geffrye Museum, 1/2013-2, 3.

14   Lesley Hoskins, *Living Rooms. 20th-Century Interiors at the Geffrye Museum* (London: Geffrye Museum, 1998), 34.

15   Span brochure, 1960, cited in Hoskins, *Living Rooms*, 35.

16   Reyner Banham, 'On Trial, the Spec-Builders. Towards a Pop Architecture', *Architectural Review* (July 1962): 112–6. Amusingly, the home of Mr and Mrs H in Highgate was indeed featured in the *Observer Magazine* in 2003.

17   Hoskins, *Living Rooms*, 35.

18   Author's interview with Mrs H and JR in June 2013.

19   Author's interview with JR in June 2013.

20   Author's interview with Mrs H in June 2013.

21   Questionnaire filled in by Andrew Gordon Biggart about the former home of Betty and John Morison, object number 202/2010-1, The Geffrye Museum of the Home, London.

22 'My father was a Burgomeister', quotation from the transcript of an interview with Margret Cochrane, object number 314/2011-2, The Geffrye Museum of the Home, London, 19.

23 'My father was a Burgomeister', 19.

24 Questionnaire filled in by MR, object number 203/2010-1, The Geffrye Museum of the Home, London.

25 Questionnaire filled in by MR.

26 Author's interview with Mrs H in June 2013.

27 Quotation from the transcript of an interview with Mrs H about her home in Highgate, London, object number 1/2010-12, The Geffrye Museum of the Home, London, 16.

28 Quotation, Geffrye Museum, 1/2013-2, 12.

29 Geffrye Museum, 203/2010-1.

30 Questionnaire filled in by Alaistair Freeborn, object number 36/2013-1, The Geffrye Museum of the Home, London.

31 Questionnaire filled in by Alaistair Freeborn.

32 Quotation, Geffrye Museum, 36/2013-1, 4.

33 Author's interview with Mrs H and JR in June 2013. Both mention two neighbours in Highgate who did not embrace the modern ethos: one decorated with traditional styles and the other had a house filled with inherited pieces. The very fact that these two houses stuck in their memory is testament to their relative rarity within this 1958 development.

34 Author's interview with Mrs H in June 2013.

35 Ibid.

36 Quotation, Geffrye Museum, 1/2013-2, 8.

37 Author's interview with Mrs H and JR in June 2013.

38 Ibid.

39 Author's interview with Mrs H in June 2013

40 The design was published on 15 October 1959. The house cost £3,000. A pen, ink and Letratone design is in the Victoria and Albert Museum's collection [E:1135-1979] and is illustrated in Christopher Breward and Ghislaine Wood, eds. *British Design from 1948: Innovation in the Modern Age* (London: V&A Publishing, 2012), 33.

41 Author's interview with JR in June 2013.

42 Quote from the transcript of an interview with Mrs H about her home in Highgate, London, object number 1/2013-2, The Geffrye Museum of the Home, London, 9.

43 The modern room was illustrated in Noel Carrington, *Colour and Pattern in the Home* (London: Batsford, 1954).

44 Sally MacDonald and Julia Porter, *Putting on the Style. Setting Up Home in the 1950s* (London: Geffrye Museum, 1990), chapter on Traditional Values, no pagination.

45 MacDonald and Porter, *Putting on the Style.*

46 Ibid.

47 Mass-Observation Archive, Mass Observation Bulletin: Furnishing, March–June, 1953.

48 Quotation, Geffrye Museum, 1/2013-2, 10.

5

Conservative Flagship: Interior Design for RMS *Windsor Castle*, 1960

Harriet McKay

Writing in *The South African Shipping News and Fishing Industry Review* in August 1960, in an article entitled 'Cape Town Appreciates Benefits Conferred by Mailships', Joyce Newton Thompson, Mayor of Cape Town and Afrikaner Nationalist, proclaimed her welcome for Union-Castle's new flagship vessel, *Windsor Castle*, due into Table Bay on her first voyage on 1 September 1960:

> It is with full appreciation of the benefits conferred upon this Mother City by the fleet of fast, reliable, well-appointed... vessels which carry our mail, passengers and our cargos to Europe, that I am delighted to welcome the newcomer *Windsor Castle*.
>
> Many South Africans have travelled in the luxury provided by the company's other liners and have identified themselves with these great ships... With the entry of the *Windsor Castle* into the listings of the Union Castle mail ships, we welcome also the belief in the future of South Africa of which the investment of 10 million in her building is the proof.
>
> South Africa, and in particular Cape Town, has a splendid future ahead. From the moment visitors by sea are welcomed at the pleasant new passenger terminal and drive up the Heerengracht into the Mother City, they will appreciate the beauty, the steady advance and the hospitality of Cape Town. On behalf of Cape Town I welcome *Windsor Castle*.[1]

Why was it that the South African mayor's 'Mother City' should welcome *Windsor Castle* as a British envoy with such enthusiasm? Although the inter-war 'golden-age' of the ocean liner was long-passed by the time of *Windsor Castle*'s first voyage, post-war passenger ships were still heavily loaded with ideas around national identity and maritime prowess and pointedly acted as markers of technological and social superiority vis à vis other countries. *Windsor's* launch was celebrated accordingly: that her arrival was the subject of an equal jamboree in South Africa is central to understanding the ship's interior design.

   This exploration of the passenger accommodation of Union-Castle flagship RMS *Windsor Castle* presents a history that cannot be meaningfully written without also tracing the relationship between the shipping line to which *Windsor* belonged, Union-Castle, the line's managing company British and Commonwealth (B&C) and the Afrikaner National Party government (1948–94). Such was the nature of the National Party's hegemony that its political ethos is suggested by the economic historian Geoffrey Berridge, in his work on the political economy of the Cape Route, *The Politics of the South Africa Run* (1987), for example, as having had an impact not only upon the process by which, but also the interiors of the vehicles with which the shipping line conducted business, a state of affairs which is corroborated by British concerns as to South African political sensibilities, as will be discussed.[2] It is this relationship between the South African government, the Union-Castle line and its managing company that provides the underlying discussion of the issues presented here: the extent to which the co-constitutive themes of the 'representation of politics' and the 'politics of representation' informed the interior design of *Windsor Castle*, which as a result offer insight into the deliberate deployment of a conservative aesthetic that could not have been further from a vision of the contemporary British design scene as characterized, for example, by stereotypes of a Carnaby Street-style 'swinging' society.

   Newton Thompson's proclamation came at a particularly tense moment in the twentieth-century history of British–South African relations. The tensions of the late nineteenth century, demonstrated most powerfully by the brutal Anglo-Boer Wars of the 1880s and 1890s, had not necessarily been diminished by the establishment of the Union of South Africa in 1910, and uneasiness between the two countries had continued to grow following the coming to power of the Afrikaner National Party in 1948.[3] By the 1960s, with the policy of 'Grand Apartheid'[4] well underway, relations were strained further as a consequence of the notorious Sharpeville Massacre of March 1960, at which a demonstration against the detested Passbook system resulted in the killing of sixty-nine people, some of them children, by the police.[5] Causing consternation in both black and white communities within South Africa and a wave of antipathy towards the country from abroad, the events at Sharpeville were condemned by the United Nations Security Council, in response to which South Africa voted to become a republic and removed itself from the Commonwealth in 1961.

   This is not to say, however, that it was a straightforwardly anti-apartheid stance that lay behind Britain's uncertain relationship with Pretoria at this time. Although Prime Minister Harold MacMillan's famous 'Wind of Change' speech[6] appeared to recognize the need for African independence and in the light of this to question South African racial policy, as has been noted, Macmillan's government 'seemed to find great difficulty in facing the logic of the Cape Town speech'.[7]

   That B&C was able to negotiate this difficult situation successfully and retain a very strong trading partnership with the Republic is a testament to the extraordinary business acumen of its company chairman, Sir Nicholas Cayzer. Taking control of the shipping company on the death of his uncle in 1958 and made a Life Peer as Baron

Cayzer of St. Mary Axe in 1982 by Prime Minister Margaret Thatcher, Nicholas Cayzer was to remain in charge of B&C until 1987. As a trustee of The South Africa Foundation, a member of the Advisory Board of the Graduate School of Business at Cape Town University and President of the UK-South Africa Trade Association, Cayzer was very much immersed in the South African business community.

Interviewed by the journal *Time and Tide* in June 1976 (at which time he had chaired B&C for eighteen years), Cayzer later provided an account of his personal view of trade links with apartheid South Africa: 'Politics is the art of the possible,' he said, 'but our policy towards South Africa is "The Art of the Impossible"... One must get a sense of proportion about South Africa. One has to look at the situation completely objectively... We trade where we can trade. That is our job. And this is the most civilizing thing that we can do....'[8]

Frequently characterizing this 'business is business' attitude as being one of pragmatic 'flexibility', neither the political circumstances nor the edgy relationship between London and Pretoria was to deter Cayzer from flamboyantly marking the start of his tenure as B&C Chairman with the launch of *Windsor Castle*. Hailed in a 1959 press release as 'the largest vessel ever employed on the Union-Castle mail service to South Africa, and the largest passenger liner ever built on Merseyside', and costing over £10,000,000,[9] it was quite probably in the light of such a demonstration of prowess that Dr A. J. Norval, Director of the South African Board of Trade, attacked Union-Castle's building programme as being too extravagant and worse, not '... in conformity with the modern spirit and in particular with the spirit of this country [i.e. South Africa]'.[10] Such criticism had been a recurring theme in negotiations for shipping rights between the two nations for some time, and although not explained by Norval himself, or by Geoffrey Berridge, who cites the remarks in his work on the political economy supporting the 'Cape run', it seems likely that such a large expenditure on so lavishly British (English) an aesthetic was not commensurate with contemporary South African moves to form a Republic.

From the point of view of interior design, it is highly significant that, according to Berridge, Nicholas Cayzer 'was only able to persuade Norval to retain the Union-Castle mail ships [on the Cape route] by agreeing to give the government a say in the general design of the *Windsor Castle*'.[11] It is frustrating but perhaps not insignificant in itself that documentation providing evidence of the extent of this kowtowing is not in evidence in either London or South Africa. What is certain is that Union-Castle ships were frequently used as venues for hosting diplomatic exchanges, cocktail parties and press junkets when berthed in Cape Town, to which South African businesspeople, politicians and dignitaries were invited. With this in mind, and given the very closely bound relationship between B&C and Pretoria, although it is not possible to corroborate Berridge's assertion as to the nature of South African input into *Windsor*'s interiors, it at least seems likely that the ship's interior schemes might have been vetted for aesthetic suitability as a venue for such activities.

Given the autocratic, if not totalitarian, nature of the Nationalist government's administration, insistence on involvement in the design of the new liners is improbable as a case of a *decoratorly* dilettantism on Pretoria's part. Norval's acrimony no doubt stemmed from witnessing plans for an interior aesthetic that ran entirely counter to Afrikaner Republicanism. A 1960 description of *Windsor Castle*, a ship which by virtue of her name was from the outset replete with royal associations, refers both to her passenger interiors and to *Windsor*'s connection with royalty: 'The 1st Class drawing room, in pink and green, has been designed as a comfortable sitting room in the *country house style* (my italics) with fireplace and window seat. Over the mantelpiece a feature of this room will be a repro by the artist himself of a portrait of Her Majesty the Queen Mother by Denis Fildes' [Fig. 5.1].[12]

If resentment at A. J. Norval's insistence on the South African government's involvement in the design of the new ships was felt in B&C's London office, this is not recorded. Business Cayzer-style had simply to be dealt with and in a highly significant move, the society decorator Miss Jean Monro was appointed to do the job.

Admirer of the British decorator John Fowler (1906–77) and the celebrated American interior designer Nancy Lancaster (1897–1994), Jean Monro's similarly historicist aesthetic was perfectly in tune with B&C's need to play it safe as regards Pretorian diktat while subtly reminding the Republic of the superior longevity of British pedigree, democracy and heritage. Following Lancaster's lead in the creation of the English Country House Style, Monro's design for *Windsor*'s passenger accommodation created a vessel that was every inch the society lady that the designer was herself.[13]

Creating editorial copy reminiscent of the celebration of a royal wedding or coronation, *The Times* produced a souvenir supplement to its daily newspaper, 'Yesterday's elegance, today's comfort', on the occasion of *Windsor Castle*'s first

FIGURE 5.1 *First class drawing room, passenger liner 'Windsor Castle'.*
Courtesy of National Maritime Museum, Greenwich, London.

voyage.[14] Highlighted were not *products*, decorated to attract the attention of design journalists or pundits; instead, the two vessels, and *Windsor* in particular, were created as *personalities*, regal envoys of a particular notion of British class-based pedigree. In his eulogy to Union-Castle on her final sailing from Cape Town, Afrikaner liberal Laurens van der Post wrote of *Windsor*, regarding her earlier departure from Southampton:

> Dressed overall, as we saw her in that long level light of the morning of August 15 [1977], she looked [more] like a débutante waiting to be conducted to her first ball... than a ship charged to perform the last rites over the passing of herself and her entire kind.
> Her colours... the lilac hull and scarlet hem of petticoat, underneath the immaculate white of decks... and funnel scarlet again, but bound against dissolution in the blue of sky and ocean with a broad band of absolute black, sat on her like silk and made jewellery of the fresh morning light. Yet as she eased herself with the grace of a young queen from the quay... she was beginning the end of an era.[15]

To anthropomorphize the ships in this way was also to create an interiority which amplified Union-Castle's Britishness. More specifically, the ship's reflections of sovereignty and national identity were thus well placed to act out this personification in the face of upstart Afrikanerdom. In this way, Union-Castle was able to demonstrate a placatory—and business-essential—adherence to Pretorian politics whilst projecting anti-Afrikaner ideas around the continuing 'pedigree' of Britishness (though with an undoubted emphasis on *Englishness*) and of the country's international status. 'The Drawing Room has been designed to reproduce a comfortable sitting room in a typical English way with sofas and chairs, pale pink walls, green and white marble fireplace, card tables for use when the card room is full, and a large bay window with a window seat.'[16]

The importance of eighteenth-century and Regency furnishing styles for decorating in the 'English way', as demonstrated by *Windsor*'s First Class Drawing and Card Rooms, for example, resonates with the country house style's insistence on combining history with modern comfort. Elsewhere on board *Windsor Castle*, references to England and its monarchy add further weight to the suggestion that B&C conceived of the ship as contributing to, as well as being a marker of, Britain's strength, stability and continuing power on the world stage. The castle, a symbol of the social and land-based permanency of the British upper class—the royal apotheosis of which was the palace at Windsor—was given significant visual space in the First Class Dining Room mural [Fig. 5.2]. *Windsor Castle* was also used as a decorative motif for the Wedgwood dinner service that was used there.

That the leisured sociability of the First Class passenger accommodation should have been inscribed so significantly into Union-Castle's interior design at the start of the 1960s is unlikely to have been accidental. During a period in which the relatively speedy and certainly impersonal process of travel by air was suggesting the end of the age of indulgent, extended sea crossings, Union-Castle appears to have deliberately evoked notions of a bygone and, the assumption was, far more elegant mode of travel.

FIGURE 5.2 *First class dining room, passenger liner 'Windsor Castle'.*
Courtesy of National Maritime Museum, Greenwich, London.

Windsor Castle certainly received a great deal of attention, drawing on her 'society' appeal. In 1977, B&C's journal *The Clansman* remembered the ship's launch: 'Everywhere *Windsor Castle* was received with acclaim, and soon, during the peak booking period her passenger lists began to read like extracts from Debrett....'[17] Given the marked extent to which the ship was emblematic of the British establishment, it was no wonder that A. J. Norval had interferingly criticized both the cost and the tone of her design.

If *Windsor Castle*'s First Class passenger accommodation was sold as an essay in serenity and sophistication, an investigation of the ship's Tourist Class accommodation suggests that the conservatism that underpinned B&C's styling of the First Class rooms was, in fact, also apparent here, the shipping company's traditionalist approach being evident in terms of producing a very qualified modernism and also in its paternalistic assumptions about the lifestyle with which Tourist Class passengers would be most at home. On Monro's appointment, Cayzer had stipulated that her design for *Windsor*'s Tourist areas be one of 'great comfort but with a less formal atmosphere [that is, than First Class] and with plenty of gaiety in all the rooms'.[18] Indeed, descriptions of the Tourist Class rooms all employ this kind of terminology:

> Gaily coloured in pink, grey, and lime, the Tourist Class Lounge will have a recessed dance floor in the middle of the room.

The Tourist Class lido and swimming pool will be a very gay area. The verandah café, with bar and soft drinks kiosk, will have soft furnishings of chintz with a bright fruit and flowers pattern, and a wooden teak floor. Round the pool will be covered Promenade and Dance Decks.

A feature of the 1st Entrance Hall will be the very fine square of shops, whilst a gay shopping area will be arranged in the Tourist Class entrance hall.[19]

Throughout *Windsor*'s Tourist Class accommodation, then, the key decorative themes were cheerfulness, colour, and jollity. This was an aesthetic aiming to deliver a sense of an energetic bonhomie, and whereas First Class rooms were decorated to convey a conservatively modish grace, Tourist Class areas on board ship were concerned with the fostering of vivacious high spirits and light-heartedness. To this end *Windsor Castle*'s Tourist accommodation adopted the modern materials and, to a limited extent, elements of the Googie-architectural forms of Californian coffee shops and hot-dog stands, using bold, chequered upholstery, Formica and close tongue-and-groove panelling [Figs. 5.3].[20] Even so, the temptation to historicize was apparently too great for Monro to resist; into spaces that were making a bid to provide a contemporary key intruded heavily gilt picture frames and the paraphernalia and prizes of traditional upper-class activities such as hunting and fishing: 'the Cockpit Bar will be an essentially masculine room, decorated with birds and fish in glass

FIGURE 5.3 *Tourist class cockpit bar, passenger liner 'Windsor Castle'.*
Courtesy of National Maritime Museum, Greenwich, London.

cases, firearms etc.'[21] Nor was Monro creating a particularly modern environment in stressing the gendered occupational references and social interaction of this area of the ship's passenger accommodation. 'The idea was that in Tourist Class one should make new friends', Alice Herd, from Fish Hoek in the Western Cape, remarked in relation to her experience of sailing to the United Kingdom on the *Windsor Castle* in the 1960s.[22] Informality, youth and partying were the themes that these rooms were designed to engender. Peter du Toit, former curator of the Marsh Maritime Centre in Cape Town, has recalled that, 'in fact', the perennial First Class joke on board *Windsor Castle* was that 'if you wanted a party, you had better go *downstairs*'.[23]

As well as providing an arena for a particular kind of sociability, the styling of *Windsor*'s Tourist Class interiors spoke of an awareness of burgeoning British youth and popular culture. And again, it was with this in mind that in these areas a mediated modernism was permitted which sanctioned the limited use of modern materials, such as Formica, and the inclusion of more modern, though hardly cutting-edge, furniture styles.

Popular culture was also noticeable in a modified form in *Windsor*'s Tourist Class interiors in relation to British youth styles. While the 'Swinging London' of the second half of the 1960s was not to arrive until some years after the ship's first sailing, iconic books such Colin MacInnes' novel *Absolute Beginners* (1959) had engaged with popular culture in its exploration of newly formed concepts of youth style, fashion and music. To what extent did ideas like these provide a cultural context for the decoration of the *Windsor Castle*? Christopher Breward has written of London style that it represented the 'triumph of subcultural style over gentlemanly substance' and that this, in turn, contributed to the production of that 'much-discussed phenomenon: the generation gap'.[24] Not so on board *Windsor Castle*, however. Here, instead, B&C's inveterate conservatism merely nodded towards popular contemporary styling and then modified this through the incorporation of generational, class-based and often gendered historical signifiers.

B&C's prescriptiveness was also inscribed into these rooms: when the culture of the client group was assumed to exhibit a tendency for mass-participation, a diluted modernism seems to have been an acceptable trope for interior styling. Part of the reason for *Windsor*'s rejection of a modern aesthetic as a design device in First Class was because this style spoke of industrial manufacture, as opposed to the bespoke production mode of the antique. In Tourist Class, by contrast, B&C seems to have acknowledged a tacit link with popular culture—the culture of the masses and of mass production—which was allowed to make an appearance through the use of plastics and off-the-peg furniture styles. It was acceptable to employ modern design as long as it helped to give a light-hearted impression in spaces in which, free from the need to demonstrate the historicist gravitas associated with First Class accommodation, a more contemporary idiom might be deployed to create a youthful atmosphere.

In line, as ever, with B&C's desire not to appear *too* modern, however, *Windsor*'s Tourist Class social rooms also contained references to traditional working-class culture and entertainment, another indicator of the conservative scripting of 'decoration-as-lifestyle' by the shipping company: 'At one end [of the Tourist Class Smoke Room] is the Cockpit Bar, which has a masculine flavour, with seats covered in tweed and mahogany chairs upholstered in hide, with the colour of saddle leather, based on the design of chairs used by spectators at cock fights 150 years ago.'[25]

While First Class accommodation retained a sense of history, through which Jean Monro discreetly masked the inclusion of modern technology, in Tourist Class the inclusion of contemporary stylistic notes was acceptable as long as these were not too pronounced. Emblematic of an emerging British youth culture, the creation of a lively, high-spirited ambience became the filtering mechanism through which 'modern' came to represent 'young'. It would be wrong, though, to make too hard and fast a distinction between Tourist and First Class spaces on board according to a modern/historicist axis; the picture, in reality, is more complicated. What has been mapped out here are the *overall* tendencies that these interiors make evident. And at no point did Monro's interior decoration threaten to interrupt or dislocate received British (English) notions of class conformity.

Ultimately, B&C seems to have decided upon and offered its clientele the style of design with which it supposed they would be most comfortable, according to enduring class associations. In this way the company produced interior design that made assumptions about First-Class, Debrett-list passengers' preference for the good taste associated with history, played out in tandem with an appeal to the modern holiday-making, gregarious nature of the Tourist Class passenger. And, whether as a country-house incarnation or by borrowing from the youthful modern style emerging from popular/mass culture, *Windsor Castle* represented a thoroughly British style. In a continuing discourse around restrained refinement, class-associated 'good taste', and the importance of conservative values to a 'correct' way of being British, it also represented the longevity of *decoratorly*—as opposed to *designerly*—taste as a marker of these values.

But there is one further and very significant element to the conservatism of *Windsor Castle*'s interior design schemes. In late 1957, with reference to an entirely different subject for representation, it was minuted at the Union-Castle Managing Directors' meeting on 11 November that, 'Her Majesty's picture should not be screened at the end of cinema performances.' The recommendation had been adopted and it had quietly been agreed to drop the showing of the Queen's portrait on the South African coast.[26]

Given that South African Board of Trade Director A. J. Norval had taken exception to Union-Castle's evocations of British national identity and the subsequent insistence that Pretoria be allowed a say in *Windsor*'s interior decoration, it is likely that Pretoria had an influence over one other crucial aspect of the ship's passenger accommodation: nowhere on board (nor indeed on board any of her Union-Castle sister ships) is there any decorative reference to black Africa. If a representation of a white monarch was deemed to risk causing offence to Union-Castle's clientele, how much more risky would references to black Africa have been?

Bearing in mind B&C's ethos of 'flexibility' towards Pretoria, however, and also the company's acute business sense, it is hardly surprising that Union-Castle was complicit in the exclusion of black Africa from its ships. Whether or not Norval was in fact able to make his mark on the ships' decoration in this regard, it hardly mattered. Under no circumstances was a company with a steady eye for profit, and in an already tricky relationship with the South African government, about to jeopardize this association through the demonstration of any kind of black presence on board ship, and make visible, by extension, those people required to remain invisible within the country of destination itself.

Providing a still greater incentive for B&C to toe the line was the South African marketing of the Union-Castle ships as 'floating hotels' in the 1960s. Aiming to attract white businesspeople—many of whom Pretoria assumed to be sympathetic to its aims—and also politicians travelling between Cape Town and the major eastern South African cities, Port Elizabeth, East London and Durban, it was important that the aesthetic landscape of the ships should not alienate this important South African clientele. *Windsor Castle*'s interior design was predicated, then, around not causing discomfort to a significant constituency of those travelling on board the company's ships and also represented compliance with National Party politics: it meant, in other words, that 'separateness' be maintained on board, as on land. The close ties between B&C and the National Party were underpinned by more than Cayzer's good business sense, however. In his 1976 interview for *Time and Tide*, Cayzer is quoted as saying, 'We shall continue to serve South Africa knowing that we are serving *all* the people of South Africa and helping to create employment and prosperity.'[27]

There was more to B&C's involvement with Pretoria than this version of 1970s British Conservative economic priorities and principles, however, as Cayzer's Presidency of the UK-South Africa Trade Association attests. In his 1979 article 'South Africa's Propaganda War', the political economist Galen Hull discusses contemporary relations between Washington and South Africa, focusing on US lobbyists and the National Party propaganda machine at home.[28] In the article, Hull describes the South African government's Department of Information, the body responsible for the regime's propaganda initiatives and which, he details, had put a great deal of time and money into attempting to woo the world to Pretoria's point of view, into encouraging immigration and endorsing—in the department's own phrase—'unconventional' methods of marketing the country, such as hospitality. As Hull points out, the Department of Information was certainly matched in importance with regard to activities of this nature by another body, the South Africa Foundation (SAF): 'The SAF, established in 1959 as a private non-profit organisation, rivaled the Department of Information in the extent of its influence in the US.'[29] Hull also mentions a Washington lawsuit naming the SAF alongside the South African Sugar Association, both of which had been making secret cash payments to National Party campaigns.[30] In the same vein, Hull's article cited another work, *The Power Peddlers*, whose authors observed that it is 'no secret in Johannesburg or abroad, that the South Africa Foundation is a "front" organisation for government'.[31] As a 'Trustee of the UK-South Africa Foundation', Nicholas Cayzer's involvement with the National Party government in Pretoria was clearly greater than his Thatcherite 'business is business' statements alone betray.[32]

In a sense, brooking Pretorian intervention into the design of *Winsdor Castle* was the price that B&C had to pay for the company's strength and success on the South African route in the 1960s. The fact that B&C was keen to not only co-operate with but, as Cayzer's close involvement with the South Africa Foundation illustrates, actually support the National Party provides an important indicator of the extent to which it was prepared to bend to the South African government's position, a situation in which the inclusion of references to the British Establishment in *Windsor*'s First Class accommodation really only represented a minor misdemeanour.

Clearly, dancing to Pretoria's tune included accommodating ideas which had influenced the design of Union-Castle's ships' interiors. No wonder that Mayor Newton Thompson's welcome to *Windsor Castle* had been so demonstrative. She had not simply been celebrating the arrival of a foreign vessel into port but rather highlighting this particular ship as cementing and signifying the result of an important and, in the early 1960s, highly successful, mutually negotiated partnership: RMS *Windsor Castle* was the perfect envoy for the hand-in-glove enterprise that had been constructed between British and Commonwealth Shipping Ltd. and the National Party government in Pretoria.

Notes

1   *South African Shipping News*, 8 August 1960, 16.

2   G. R. Berridge, *The Politics of the South Africa Run: European Shipping and Pretoria* (Oxford: Clarendon Press, 1987).

3   The creation of the Union from the formerly separately governed, British-owned Cape Colony, Natal, Transvaal and Orange River Colony had been implemented partially as a way of reconciling the English and Boer settlers.

4   Implemented by H. F. Verwoerd, Prime Minister between 1958 and 1966, extreme right-winger and staunch Republican, this cornerstone of Nationalist policy was centred on the wholesale removal of all 'non-Europeans' (non-whites) from white areas in a vast act of social engineering in line with the Afrikaans meaning for apartheid—'apartness'. It was also under Verwoerd that the Rivonia Treason Trial of 1963–64 finally indicted and imprisoned almost all the key opposition leaders, amongst them African National Congress (ANC) activists Nelson Mandela, Walter Sisulu and Govan Mbeke, and Secretary of the Transvaal Indian Youth Congress, Ahmed Kathrada.

5   The Passbook system, a cornerstone of apartheid administration, insisted that documentation be carried by every member of the black population at all times and proved authorization to be in white-only areas where this was needed, for example, by the country's legion of black domestic workers.

6   MacMillan's speech was made to the South African Parliament in Cape Town on 3 February 1960: 'The wind of change is blowing through this continent, and, whether we like it or not, this growth of national consciousness is a political fact. We must all accept it as a fact, and our national policies must take account of it.' See, Treasures of the Bodleian, 'Harold Macmillan's Wind of Change Speech', http://treasures.bodleian.ox.ac.uk/Harold-Macmillans-Wind-of-Change-speech, accessed 9 September 2013.

7   G. R. Berridge, *Economic Power in Anglo-South African Diplomacy: Simonstown, Sharpeville and After* (London: Macmillan, 1981), 115.

8   National Maritime Museum, Caird Library, Greenwich, NMM CL CAY/249.

9   Nearly £52 million in 2013 (CPI Inflation calculator, www.bls.gov, accessed 29 June 2013). NMM CL CAY/220.

10   Berridge, *The Politics of the South Africa Run*, 73.

11   South African Conference Lines private archive, cited in Berridge, *The Politics of the South Africa Run*, 73.

12   NMM CL CAY/220.

13   An invention of the inter-war period, the English country house style depended on creating rooms that appeared to have evolved through generations of (aristocratic) family living. It was highly decorative and through both its lack of formal, as opposed to *decoratorly* design values, and its whimsical poetry provided the antithesis to twentieth-century left-wing avant-gardism in the guise of modernism, for example. See Martin Wood's chapter in this volume.

14   'Yesterday's elegance, today's comfort', *Times*, 18 August 1960, iv.

15   Laurens van der Post, 'Last Liner from the Cape', *Times*, 24 September 1977, 6.

16   NMM CL CAY/220.

17   NMM CL CAY/232.

18   A. Wealleans, *Designing Liners: A History of Interior Design Afloat* (London: Routledge, 2006), 145.

19   NMM CL CAY/220.

20   The futuristic, architectural form originating in southern California in the late 1940s inspired by vehicle design, the space age and jetcraft, for example.

21   National Maritime Museum, Brass Foundry, Historic Photographs and Ship Plans, Woolwich, NMM BF Print Boxes 50.1.

22   Author's interview with Alice Herd in Cape Town on 5 April 2008.

23   Author's interview with Peter du Toit in Cape Town on 5 April 2008.

24   C. Breward, E. Erhman and C. Evans, eds. *The London Look* (New Haven: Yale University Press in association with the Museum of London, 2004), 100.

25   NMM CL CAY/220.

26   NMM CL UCM 3/4 11245.

27   Interview with Nicholas Cayzer, *Time and Tide*, July 1976, 21.

28   Galen Hull, 'South Africa's Propaganda War: A Bibliographic Essay', *African Studies Review*, 22/3 (1979): 79.

29   Hull, 'South Africa's Propaganda War', 94.

30   Ibid., 95.

31   Howe and Trott, *The Power Peddlers: How Lobbyists Mold America's Foreign Policy*, cited in Hull, 'South Africa's Propaganda War', 94.

32   Interview with Nicholas Cayzer, *Time and Tide*, July 1976, 21.

The photographs in this chapter were taken by Elsam, Mann and Cooper. Every effort was made to trace the copyright holders to seek permission for their use prior to publication.

6

Bernat Klein: Colouring the Interior

Fiona Anderson

In the post-war period, Bernat Klein became internationally renowned as a designer of textiles for both fashion and interiors, primarily for his accomplished use of colour.[1] Klein's innovative approach to colour was inspired principally by modern art and his work contributed to the greater embrace of the symbolic and expressive power of colour in British design of the 1960s and 1970s. This chapter extends research on Klein's practice as a consultant designer of furnishing textiles and carpets between 1966 and 1980, an area which has not yet been explored in any depth. It also investigates the visual and technical relationships between his textiles for fashion and those for interiors. In addition, the chapter explores the fact that Klein's career centred on the exchange of ideas, goods and cultural influences between the specific locale of Galashiels in the Scottish Borders region and a range of other British and international places.

The chapter begins with a brief synopsis of Klein's personal biography and career, which helps to place the subsequent examination of his designs into their specific historical, geographic and cultural contexts. That section is followed by an exploration of the core elements of Klein's innovative methods of working with colour and the key characteristics of his design consultancy work in Britain and Scandinavia, which mainly related to furnishing textiles and carpets between 1966 and 1980. An extensive commission to design a colour-co-ordinated textile range for the Department of the Environment, which Klein worked on between 1969 and 1971, is then explored. This case study investigates how key themes within design theory and practice of the 1960s, including a shift towards more pluralistic approaches and a reconsideration of the expressive power of colour, influenced the British government's approach to this project. Research for this chapter draws on objects from the Bernat Klein Collection, which was acquired by National Museums Scotland in 2010. This extensive collection of 4,067 artefacts includes garments, textile samples, fabric lengths, press cuttings books, photographs, retail ephemera, rugs, paintings, Dovecot tapestries and Scandinavian metalwares. The chapter is also informed by a series of interviews with Klein, carried out by the author between 2008 and 2012.[2]

Klein in context

Bernat Klein was born in 1922 in Senta, then part of Yugoslavia, near the Hungarian border. His family owned a textile wholesaling business, which was an important stimulus to his later strong desire to work as a textile designer. In 1936, he was sent to study at a *Yeshiva*, or Jewish Orthodox School, in Czechoslovakia, which was followed from 1938 by further religious education in Jerusalem. In 1940, he halted these studies to join the Bezalel School of Arts and Crafts, in Jerusalem, where he studied art initially and later specialized in textile design.[3] It was during this period that Klein's taste for modern art, design and architecture developed. This was primarily through his studies at the Bezalel, where he recalls being taught by tutors who had trained at the Bauhaus or who had been educated by former pupils of that art school.[4]

In 1945, he came to Britain to study Textile Technology at Leeds University. Klein was one of many Eastern Europeans who studied there, including the renowned designer, Tibor Reich.[5] After graduating in 1948, Klein worked briefly as a designer of woven cotton fabrics at Tootal Broadhurst Lee in Bolton. In 1949, he took up a job with the Scottish tweed manufacturer Munrospun, which enabled him to pursue his interest in designing woven woollen fabrics. Soon after Klein joined the firm, their design studios moved to Galashiels in the Scottish Borders region, which was a leading centre for the production of woollen textiles for clothing.[6] This locale was to become Klein's domestic, professional and manufacturing base for the rest of his career.

In 1951, Klein married Margaret Soper, who soon became closely involved in his first business venture, as she was with all of the succeeding businesses that bore his name. The following year, Klein left Munrospun to set up a new company called Colourcraft Ltd. It initially made furnishing fabrics and rugs, but these did not sell well; so it began to make ladies woollen scarves and subsequently woven textiles for men's and women's clothing. By 1962, the company was successful enough to attract the investment of Robert Sinclair Tobacco Company Ltd., which became a majority shareholder.[7] Klein retained a minority interest in the company which was re-named Bernat Klein Ltd. in 1963.[8]

Following these changes, Klein made his first sale to a Paris couturier, which was a space-dyed mohair to Coco Chanel for her spring 1963 collection. Between 1963 and 1966, Klein's fashion textiles sold to leading couture houses including Chanel, Christian Dior and Yves St Laurent in Paris and Hardy Amies, John Cavanagh and Victor Stiebel in London. Unfortunately, his success in the highly competitive market for couture textiles was not to last. In 1966, under pressure from the majority shareholders in Bernat Klein Ltd. to increase the profitability of the business, he sold his shares and resigned because he was unwilling to compromise his design ideas.[9]

These challenging developments helped to lead Klein to a new phase of his career, in which he pursued his long-held desire to design textiles for interiors. This was initially done through the new venture of Bernat Klein Design Consultants Ltd., which is discussed later in this chapter. Between 1973 and 1981, Bernat Klein womenswear collections, fashion textiles and hand-knitwear were sold through mail order catalogues, concessions in department stores and dedicated shops, including one in London's Knightsbridge. By early 1981, the mail order fashion business and dedicated shops had closed down. The Kleins continued their hand-knitting business which exported internationally until 1992 when they retired.[10] Bernat Klein was appointed to the Scottish Committee of the Council of Industrial Design in 1965 and was honoured with a CBE in 1973 for his services to design.[11]

Colour: Method and innovation

Colour is a central feature of Klein's work and it resonates throughout his creative outputs. For example, an article about his fashion textiles in the trade journal *Wool* of Winter 1962–3 states: 'Bernat Klein's cloths have been described as the first real breakthrough in colour and design for over half a century and Mr Klein is certainly an unusual combination of technician and artist.'[12]

Klein's experimentation with colour has involved two key elements, namely, methods of colour balancing and the development of space-dyeing. When asked in 2009 to describe the essence of his work, Klein stated: 'If I wanted to sum it up, balance, colour-balance'.[13] The theory informing Klein's colour-balancing methods was that if different colours of the same weight or tone are used, they will form a pleasing effect when placed together.[14] These methods lay at the core of Klein's consummate ability to make unlikely or challenging colour combinations work well together. For example, his design 'Festival' of c.1963–7 [Fig. 6.1] features a large range of colours including shades of brown, green, blue, white, pink, yellow and orange, which are skilfully combined to give a pleasing overall effect.

Klein's exposure in the mid-1950s to the work of Georges Seurat, the French post-Impressionist painter, was the main inspiration for his subsequent development of the space-dyeing technique. Seurat had developed a way of 'rendering the motif in the combination of small dots of colour', an approach known as pointillism.[15] This had a profound influence on Klein and he was inspired to try to replicate this effect in textiles, primarily by working with local dyers to develop the technique of space-dyeing. In this method, yarns were dyed with different colours in overlapping sections along their length. This enabled Klein to achieve his aim of producing textiles, which featured a series of distinct thumbnails of colour. It also had the effect of greatly increasing the number of colours that could be combined in one fabric, hence simultaneously encouraging the development of his methods of colour balancing.[16] The distinctive appeal of many of the textiles that Klein sold to leading couturiers in the 1960s derived from space-dyed yarns [see Fig. 6.1].

Klein as Design Consultant

Bernat Klein Design Consultants Ltd., which was set up in 1966, was one of only a small number of design consultancies that existed in Britain at that time.[17] The company was initially based at High Sunderland, the modernist house in the Scottish Borders, which the Kleins had commissioned Peter Womersley to design in the early 1950s. From 1972 to 1992, the design and showroom activities of the design consultancy business and subsequently of Bernat Klein Design Ltd. and Bernat

FIGURE 6.1 *Pattern book, Bernat Klein Collection. On the left is a velvet ribbon tweed sample, 'Trefoil' of c. 1964, made from rayon velvet ribbon, space-dyed brushed mohair and cut gimp wool yarn. On the right is a multi-coloured wool and polyester tweed, 'Festival' of c.1963-67.*
©National Museums Scotland

Klein Ltd. were based at the adjacent Bernat Klein Design Studio, a late modernist concrete building, also designed by Womersley, which won a Royal Institute of British Architects (RIBA) award in 1973.[18] Between the mid-1960s and the late 1970s, Klein's international list of clients included Fiedler Fabrics, Weston Carpets and I.R.A., all of Denmark, Sandnes of Norway, Y.F.A. of Sweden, Barker Textiles of Finland, and Dunlop Flooring, Mohair Board of South Africa and Svenmill, all of South Africa. In Britain, customers included Margo Fabrics Ltd., Tomkinsons Carpets, British Enkalon, Arlington Plastics, James Halstead and Thomson Shepherd Carpets. The vast majority of these contracts were to design furnishing textiles, carpets, vinyl flooring and colour schemes for interiors, but some were related to fashion textiles, enamelled metalwares and toothbrushes.[19] Between 1966 and 1979, most of the firm's commissions came from Scandinavia and in particular from Fiedler Fabrics and Weston Carpets. In the early 1960s, Klein had established a market for his fashion fabrics in Denmark, Norway, Finland and Sweden.[20] There were close connections between Klein's first sale of furnishing textiles in Scandinavia and his fashion textiles. He has, for example, recalled that his initial success with designing textiles for interiors was when he sold Cheviot cloths, which were very similar to those that he designed for ladies skirts, to a Danish firm in the mid-1960s.[21]

One of the main British firms that Klein worked for as a consultant designer was Margo Fabrics Ltd., of Gateshead.[22] In 1969, Klein won a Council of Industrial Design (COID) Award for a group of upholstery textiles that he designed for them. This prompted an article in *Design* magazine, which stated, 'It was perhaps inevitable that Bernat Klein and Margo Fabrics would one day work together, for Klein has won an international reputation as a designer who has pioneered a whole new approach to colour and texture in fashion fabrics, while Margo have played a leading part in introducing a more modern look to British upholstery fabrics.'[23] The fabrics that won the COID award—'Spruce', 'Larch', 'Rowan', and 'Aspen'—were based on meticulously planned colourways and textured yarns that were specially chosen by Klein. When the Klein range was launched in 1968, it attracted substantial international interest, particularly from Scandinavia, where his work was already highly renowned.[24] The Bernat Klein Collection includes a Margo Fabrics Limited folder of c.1967–72, which features a design called 'Sunderland', which reveals that vibrant colour, colour balancing and the use of highly textured yarns, which Klein had previously established as key elements of his fashion textiles, were also important in his work for interiors [Plate 4].

Colour and the British government interior

In 1969, Klein was tasked by the Supplies Division of the Ministry of Public Building and Works with creating a major range of colour-co-ordinated upholstery fabrics and carpets. He worked on this extensive commission between 1969 and 1971, by which time the Ministry had changed its name to the Department of the Environment (DoE). The idea behind this scheme was to design a range of colour-co-ordinated options to make it easier for government staff to order furnishing fabrics and carpets that would work well together. It was to be used in a very wide range of government interiors including offices and residential accommodation for Whitehall, universities, hospitals and the armed forces, as well as art galleries, museums and embassies.[25] The final range was promoted in 1971 through an exhibition held at the Design Centre in London called 'Kaleidoscope: Diversity by Design' [Fig. 6.2].

The project also resulted in the *Co-ordinated Colour Guide for Interiors*, which consisted of three volumes containing text, photographs of sample room settings and groups of colour-balanced textile and carpet samples. All of the designs represented by these swatches were put into production.[26] An article in *Design* magazine of November 1971 stated that the Colour Guide folders would enable 'the directors of Supplies Division depots throughout the world to select an entire scheme at a glance. The catalogues contain 66 alternative design schemes based on the new... range and, as a result, orders—even from the most far-flung embassies abroad—can be processed with speed and efficiency.'[27]

An examination of samples in the *Co-ordinated Colour Guide for Interiors* folders, held in the Bernat Klein Collection, has revealed strong interconnections between the textiles that Klein designed for that range and his fashion fabrics. For example, a core element of the DoE designs is the use of colour balancing, both within individual designs and between the various samples. Another signature feature of Klein's work, which is present in the government range and in many of his fashion fabrics, is the use of either vibrant colours or those inspired by the British rural landscape, such as shades of brown, green and orange [Plates 5 and 6]. Throughout the Guide, bright colours are present within every colour grouping, even if this

FIGURE 6.2 *'Kaleidoscope: Diversity by Design' at the Design Centre, London, 1971.*
Source: Design Council Slide Collection, Manchester Metropolitan University

simply consists of a few samples to be used as accents within an interior. This use of colour would have formed a striking contrast with what *Design* magazine described in 1971 as 'the proverbially grey surroundings of government buildings'.[28] Further connections with Klein's fashion textiles are provided by the knitted polyester prints. He began developing similar stretch fabrics for clothing with British Enkalon from 1968.[29] In the DoE scheme, these were mainly to be used as removable covers for office chairs and also for sofas in the larger residential interiors. The 'Nasturtium' sample illustrates that these fabrics mostly featured random, fluid patterns, which could be 'read' effectively when the fabric was stretched in use [Plates 5 and 6]. Klein was unusual as a textile designer in that he did not draw. His creative processes were instead informed by oil painting, which he took up in 1960. This practice was a very important but usually indirect influence on his textile designs for fashion and interiors from that point onwards.[30] Many of the DoE patterns originated from enlarged photographs of small sections of Klein's paintings. Alternatively, they were designed by George Norwich, a graphic designer who was Klein's main assistant at the time, using colours chosen by him. A further link with Klein's fashion textiles is provided by the upholstery fabrics that are reminiscent of his tweeds in their use of mixed colour effects and textured yarns.

Klein's enthusiasm for colour and distinctive working methods clearly had a significant impact on the DoE scheme. However, the contributions from government staff and industry were also pivotal in shaping its character. The manufacturers involved in developing and producing the range of textiles and carpets included

Bernard Wardle, Blackwood Morton, Firths, Margo Fabrics and McKinnon Jenkins.[31] Howell Leadbeater was a key figure in shaping the government's approach, because he was responsible both for hiring Klein and for the management of the development of the scheme. In the Acknowledgements section of his book *Design Matters* (1976), Klein makes the revealing statement: 'My special thanks go to Howard Leadbeater, Controller of Supplies at the Department of the Environment, and to the executives in that Department. Throughout our work together they proved, with imagination, courage and perseverance that compromise in design is not an indispensable ingredient of success in practical, commercial terms.'[32] Further useful insights into the aims of the Supplies Division in commissioning the range may be gleaned from the Introduction to the Guide, which states:

> Efficient buying on a large scale involves standardisation of products. Standardisation gives a buyer lower cost, better quality control, speedier delivery, more reliable supply, greatly reduced stock-holding and stores costs. For these advantages a heavy price is normally paid in the shape of greater uniformity by a society that is becoming increasingly hostile to the mechanistic aspects of modern industrial life. Does standardisation necessarily mean greater uniformity? Is it possible to provide variety and diversity and still obtain the undisputed benefits of standardisation? Supplies Division of the Department of the Environment has tried to serve both these purposes with its new standard ranges of carpets and upholstery fabrics...The careful co-ordination of design has made possible a wide differentiation in interior environment to suit all kinds of tastes and contexts.[33]

This text shows that the DoE was aiming to respond to the shifting, increasingly pluralistic nature of British society and culture of the era. As Jonathan Woodham has indicated, public attitudes to state-sponsored design in the late 1960s and early 1970s were changing. He states: 'The optimism of the immediate post-war years—when designers, architects and planners strongly believed that they knew what people wanted or needed—was no longer acceptable to the wider British public, who had become increasingly resistant to what was viewed as unwanted paternalism, accompanied by a mistrust of authority, the establishment and notions of cultural leadership.'[34]

The focus in the Introduction to the Guide on diversity, rather than visual uniformity linked to standardization, also reflects sympathies, whether conscious or not, towards the emergent postmodernism of the era. This is further emphasized by the claim that the new scheme will 'suit all kinds of tastes', thus revealing the influence of a shift within design of the period towards a more consumerist-inspired approach. For example, the state-funded COID had come under increasing criticism in the 1960s for continuing to put forward a narrow perspective on design that was based on modernist principles. During that decade, these major debates led to an increased diversity in design and a greater emphasis on choice and individual taste. By the late 1960s, these shifts had begun to be taken on board by the British design establishment, including the COID.[35] Although the above quotation from the Guide emphasizes the continued importance of standardization linked to cost, it also clearly expresses a desire, on behalf of the British government, to respond to these shifts in public and professional attitudes to state-sponsored design.

The claim made in the Introduction to the Guide that the range will 'suit all kinds of tastes and contexts' is an ambitious one, given that it was aimed at such a huge group of end users, of so many different types of interior. An article in *Design* magazine of July 1969 provides some insights into the challenges of creating a textile scheme to engage the tastes of individuals working in a wide range of government jobs, including soldiers, doctors, civil servants and art gallery staff.[36] It reveals that prior to the completion of the DoE range, carpets designed by Klein were included in an experimental office set up by the government, a project that took place in 1969, before the move of civil service departments from Whitehall to a projected new building in Bridge Street. It involved '108 guinea pigs' from the Home Office being temporarily moved to a new building at Ruskin Avenue, Kew. The aim of this project was to try out an office landscaping approach, which is described by Alistair Best in the *Design* article as follows: 'Bürolandschaft—the word means office community—evolved about 10 years ago in Germany. Its chief characteristics are a deep open plan, low acoustic ceilings and integrated services. Desks and other office furniture, tending to be light and transparent in design, are laid out in informal groups separated from each other by pot plants and moveable screens.'[37] The carpet in this new space is described in a rather sarcastic manner by Best, who states: 'the first thing to strike the eye, as in all open offices, is the carpet. This was based on a five-colour design by Bernat Klein, dominated by a rather vivid shade of yellow, to achieve an effect of eternal sunshine... From the carpet the eye travels somewhat gratefully across to the continuous floor-to-ceiling windows.'[38] These comments are useful in revealing that creating a textile scheme to truly 'suit all tastes' was a somewhat over-ambitious claim on behalf of the DoE.

The government's commissioning of designs featuring such an adventurous use of colour can also be seen as a move away from the more restrictive forms of modernism. In the 1960s, the reductivist ideas of early modernists such as Walter Gropius and Marcel Breuer, whereby 'Colour, like ornamentation, was deemed inessential or emotional and so tended to be eliminated', had a lingering influence on proponents of the more austere interpretations of design modernism.[39] However, this was also an era in which there was a reconsideration of the symbolic and expressive role of colour.[40] The receptiveness of the DoE to embracing Klein's bold use of colour can be closely related to these shifts within design of the pop and early postmodern periods. However, it is inaccurate to view Klein's designs for the scheme as simply being related to the aesthetic values of a decade in which modernism was increasingly challenged and rejected. His experimental use of colour had been the key driving force behind his work since the late 1950s and it was principally inspired by modern painting of the late nineteenth and early twentieth centuries.[41] This highlights that the responses to modernity within art of that period, particularly in relation to colour, were significantly more varied and pluralistic than in early modernist design and architecture.[42] An awareness of this complex mixture of aesthetic influences and historical contexts helps explain why Klein's essentially modernist approach to colour meant that he was ideally suited to designing for the DoE scheme. His methodical but visually adventurous approach was perfect for a project where the client required a balance between utilizing the benefits of large volume and standardization but also wanted to respond to more pluralistic currents within design, whereby the expressive potential of colour was embraced rather than suppressed.

The scheme clearly indicated a commitment on behalf of the DoE and the wider Labour government to showcasing and supporting British design and manufacturing. For example, in an interview that appeared in *Design* in 1971, Howell Leadbeater stated: 'The textile project symptomizes the efforts we are making to improve the standard of furnishing and interior design throughout all government property. It has also enabled us to encourage British manufacturers to promote good design on a large scale and at the same time explore new production methods, with a view to supplying the private sector in the future.'[43] The article also noted that the Supplies Division was 'possibly the largest buyer of textiles in this country'.[44] In the post-war period, the British textile industry experienced very significant decline and this led to a move away from large-scale manufacturing. As Mary Schoeser has indicated: 'The "big is beautiful" thinking (which persisted into the 1960s) meant standardisation. It required "safe" markets, capable of absorbing large amounts of cloth while making few demands for changes in design. In retrospect it is clear that these markets were disappearing or being taken over by production from developing countries.'[45] These global industrial contexts meant that large government contracts linked to the DoE project would have provided important business opportunities for British manufacturers.

Many British government interiors, both in the UK and abroad, featured the DoE textile range until the late 1970s.[46] It was therefore important in communicating a particular aesthetic vision of British national identity, particularly in key buildings such as embassies. The textile project began in 1969 and was immediately preceded by the pop movement in art and design, which was highly influential in communicating a new, more youthful, colourful, and pluralistic image of British identity internationally. Klein's profound passion for colour was inspired by early modernist painting rather than by pop design. Nevertheless, his focus on its expressive and symbolic power was entirely in tune with the shifting design climate of the time. Although pop had largely exhausted itself by 1969, it gave Britain an international profile as a bold, creative centre and that is likely to have encouraged the government to adopt a new and more colourful vision of national identity through its own interior environments.[47]

This chapter has revealed that the creative methods that were at the centre of Klein's work, including most importantly colour balancing, resulted in strong visual and technical similarities between his designs for fashion and for interiors. The international reputation and connections that Klein made through his work in fashion textiles also helped him to initiate a successful career working as a consultant designer in Scandinavia.[48] Exploring Klein's education and career has revealed that he was at the centre of cultural and economic interactions between his long-standing base in the Scottish Borders region and a wide range of British and international places, from Jerusalem to Scandinavia. This case study therefore presents a dynamic, transnational example of post-war textile design as well as underlining the significance of a specific British textile-manufacturing centre.

The aim to strike a balance between standardization and visual diversity was at the heart of the DoE textile project. This mediated approach derived from the government's desire to simultaneously address a significant decline in the British textile industry and major changes in contemporary design culture whilst keeping costs down. Given the weight of these conflicting forces at a time of economic, social and cultural flux in Britain, it is surprising that the final DoE range does not represent more of a visual compromise. This was partly due to Klein's strong design signature. It was also linked to the approach of the client, which was clearly influenced by debates within British design culture, which by 1969 had resulted in a concerted shift towards greater diversity and an embrace of the symbolic and expressive power of colour.[49]

Notes

1 'Upholstery Fabrics', *Design*, 246 (June 1969): 53.

2 Further primary sources consulted include *Design, RIBA Journal*, Bernat Klein sales records in the Heriot-Watt University Archive and Klein's self-authored books *Eye for Colour* of 1965 and *DESIGN matters* of 1976. The chapter has also drawn on inter-disciplinary, secondary sources from the fields of design history and textile history.

3 Bernat Klein, *Eye for Colour* (London: Bernat Klein, 1965), 17–32; and Bernat Klein and Lesley Jackson, *Bernat Klein, Textile Designer, Artist, Colourist* (Selkirk: Deerpark Press, 2005), 10.

4 Author's interview with Bernat Klein at High Sunderland on 16 July 2010. Bernat Klein, letter to the author, 19 September 2013.

5 Klein and Jackson, *Bernat Klein*, 10; M. A. Hann and K. Powers, 'Tibor Reich—A Textile Designer Working in Stratford', *Textile History*, 40/2 (November 2009): 214; and Linda Fraser, daughter of Tibor Reich, conversation with the author on 27 October 2011.

6 Klein, *Eye for Colour*, 38–45; and Kenneth Ponting, 'The Scottish Contribution to Wool Textile Design in the Nineteenth Century', in John Butt and Kenneth Ponting, eds. *Scottish Textile History* (Aberdeen: Aberdeen University Press, 1987), 87–92.

7 Klein, *Eye for Colour*, 45–51; and Klein and Jackson, *Bernat Klein*, 11–12.

8 Shelley Klein, email message to the author, 27 August 2010.

9 Jacqueline Field, 'Bernat Klein Couture Tweeds', *Dress*, 33 (2006): 41–49; and Klein and Jackson, *Bernat Klein*, 13–17.

10 Field, 'Bernat Klein Couture Tweeds', 51–52; Klein and Jackson, *Bernat Klein*, 17–22. Bernat Klein Design Consultants Ltd. was incorporated on 20 September 1966 and changed its name to Bernat Klein Design Ltd. on 13 September 1973. Bernat Klein Design Ltd. was dissolved on 30 May 1989.

11 'News', *Design*, 197 (May 1965): 73; Bernat Klein, *DESIGN matters* (London: Martin Secker & Warburg, 1976), back jacket.

12 *Wool*, Winter 1962–3, cited in Klein and Jackson, *Bernat Klein*, 12.

13 Author's interview with Bernat Klein at High Sunderland on 10 April 2009.

14 Ibid.

15 Pam Meecham and Julie Sheldon, *Modern Art a Critical Introduction* (Oxon: Routledge, 2005), 307.

16 Klein, *Eye for Colour*, 117–20; Author's interview with Bernat Klein at High Sunderland on 10 April 2009.

17 Guy Julier, 'British Design Consultancy and the Creative Economy', in Christopher Breward and Ghislaine Wood, eds. *British Design from 1948: Innovation in the Modern Age* (London: V&A Publications, 2012), 313.

18 Robert Elwall, 'Working with nature', *RIBA Journal* (January 2002): 94; Bernat Klein and Lesley Jackson, *Bernat Klein*, 17–20.

19 Bernat Klein and Lesley Jackson, *Bernat Klein*, 17–18; Author's interview with Bernat Klein at High Sunderland on 24 April 2012.

20 Heriot-Watt University Archive, Sales Ledger L-M, 1963–6 GL 4/4/2.

21 Author's interview with Bernat Klein at High Sunderland on 24 April 2012.

22 Ibid.

23 'Upholstery Fabrics', *Design*, 246 (June 1969): 53.

24 'Upholstery Fabrics', 53.

25 Hilary Gelson, 'Colour-Coded Supplies', *Design*, 275 (November 1971): 40; Introduction to volume 1 of the *Co-ordinated Colour Guide for Interiors*, Bernat Klein Collection (K.2010.94), National Museums Scotland.

26 Author's interview with Bernat Klein at High Sunderland on 24 April 2012.

27 Gelson, 'Colour-Coded Supplies', 40.

28 Ibid.

29 Gelson, 'Colour-coded supplies', 41; Klein and Jackson, *Bernat Klein*, 17–20. Bernat Klein, letter to the author, 19 September 2013.

30 Author's interview with Bernat Klein at High Sunderland on 19 December 2008; Author's interview with Bernat Klein at High Sunderland on 24 April 2012; Klein and Jackson, *Bernat Klein*, 12–20.

31 Klein and Jackson, *Bernat Klein*, 19.

32 Klein, *DESIGN matters*, Acknowledgements.

33 Introduction to volume 1 of the *Co-ordinated Colour Guide for Interiors*.

34 Jonathan Woodham, 'Urban Visions: Designing for the Welfare State', in Christopher Breward and Ghislaine Wood, eds. *British Design from1948: Innovation in the Modern Age* (London: V&A Publications, 2012), 91.

35 Nigel Whiteley, *Pop Design: Modernism to Mod* (London: The Design Council, 1987), 225–6; and Woodham, 'Urban Visions', 91.

36 Alistair Best, 'The Kew Experiment: A New Landscape for the Civil Service', *Design*, 247 (August 1969): 44–9.

37 Best, 'The Kew experiment', 45–6.

38 Ibid., 46.

39 Whiteley, *Pop Design*, 24–25.

40 Penny Sparke, *An Introduction to Design and Culture in the Twentieth Century* (London: Routledge, 2000), 53.

41 Klein, *Eye for Colour*, 60–70.

42 Paul Greenhalgh, *Modernism in Design* (London: Reaktion Books, 1997), 19.

43 Gelson, 'Colour-Coded Supplies', 41.

44 Ibid., 38.

45 Mary Schoeser, 'Good Design and Good Business', in Penny Sparke, ed. *Did Britain Make It?: British Design in Context, 1946–86* (London: Design Council, 1986), 71.

46 Klein and Jackson, *Bernat Klein*, 19.

47 Klein, *Eye for Colour*, 51; and Whiteley, *Pop Design*, 87–115.

48 Author's interview with Bernat Klein at High Sunderland on 24 April 2012.

49 Whiteley, *Pop Design*, 160–2; Penny Sparke, 'At Home with Modernity: The New Domestic Scene', in Christopher Breward and Ghislaine Wood, eds. *British Design from 1948: Innovation in the Modern Age* (London: V&A Publications, 2012), 136.

PLATE 1 *British Design 1948–2012: Innovation in the Modern Age, Victoria and Albert Museum, London, 31 March–12 August 2012. Exhibition Design: Ben Kelly Design. Photography: Philip Vile.*

PLATE 2 *Interior, Mr Freedom, 1971.*
Courtesy of Jon Wealleans.

PLATE 3 *The Living Dining Room of MR's home in Twickenham (1962–3).*
© The Geffrye Museum of the Home, London.

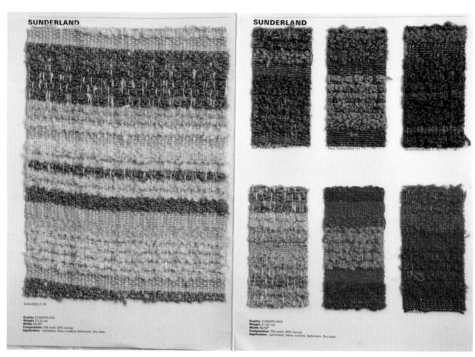

PLATE 4 *Margo Fabrics Limited Folder.*
© National Museums Scotland.

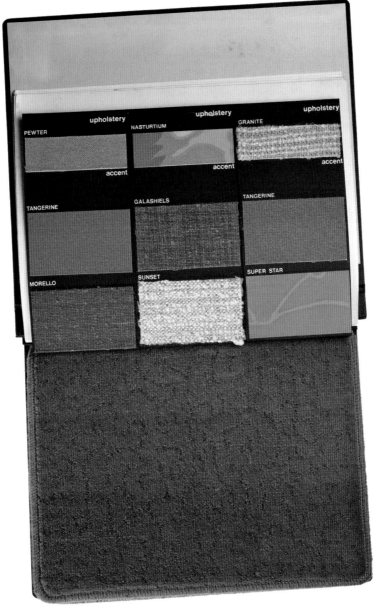

PLATE 5 Co-ordinated Colour Guide for Interiors *showing 'Galashiels' sample.*
© National Museums Scotland.

PLATE 6 Co-ordinated Colour Guide for Interiors *showing 'Sierra' sample*.
© National Museums Scotland.

PLATE 7 *Basil Spence Partnership, model of the Arts Building, University of Sussex.*
© University of Sussex, Special Collections.

PLATE 8 *Peter Winchester, early drawing for the University of Sussex campus.*
© University of Sussex, Special Collections (ref. no. 194DRG).

On the cover, vertical text: CEMENT AND CONCRETE ASSOCIATION: APRIL–JUNE 1952: PRICE TWO SHILLINGS

Concrete Quarterly 14

PLATE 9 *Brynmawr on the cover of* Concrete Quarterly *(April–June, 1952).*
Courtesy of the Concrete Centre.

PLATE 10 *Chaddesden Secondary Modern School, Derbyshire, 1955.*
RIBA Library Photographs Collection.

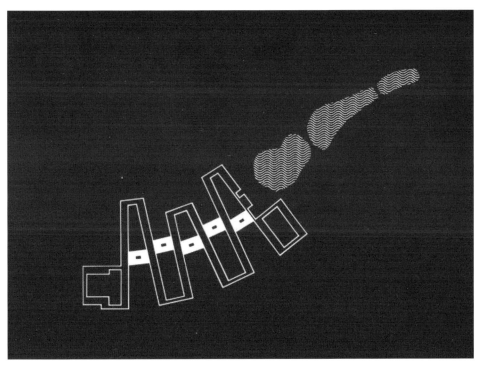

PLATE 11 *Diagram of five squares and three lakes from the cover of the University of Essex Foundation Fund Appeal, October 1963.*
Designer unknown, University of Essex Special Collections, Albert Sloman Library.

PLATE 12 *Finmere School, Oxfordshire.*
Courtesy of David Medd.

PLATE 13 *Model of Eveline Lowe Primary School, Southwark, London.*
RIBA Library Drawings & Archives Collections.

PLATE 14 *Enric Miralles/RMJM, Scottish Parliament Building, 2000–4. View from south, with Queensberry House in the centre.*
© Richard Williams.

PLATE 15 *Heatherwick Studio, New Bus for London.*
© Iwan Baan.

PLATE 16 *Proposed garden bridge across the River Thames in London.*
© Heatherwick Studio.

7

Ancient Spaces in Modern Dress: Basil Spence at the University of Sussex

Maurice Howard

In May 2012, English Heritage announced the Grade II listing of two petrol stations of the early 1960s. As if anticipating criticism that such privilege be accorded to buildings of a period generally tainted with rapid construction, inattention to the needs of people within the space and lack of aesthetic sensitivity, two important factors were put forward as making the structures worthy of special status. One was a sense of their 'cutting edge technology' and the other, a judgement that they represented in a significant way a point in time which was worth preserving; they were said to 'hark back to a time when driving was still an adventure'. Further, with particular reference to the great canopies that make up the petrol station of Markham Moor, Leicestershire, it was said that it survives as a unique example of just a handful of petrol stations constructed to this design at the period, using a hyperbolic paraboloid roof.[1] This combination of technical innovation and a unique match of design to a usage which captures the spirit of the age is something that particularly colours the discussion about the universities of the early 1960s. Seven newly-founded universities in England and one in Scotland were seen as a dramatic expansion of higher education in a way that is hardly recognizable in the early twenty-first century, as the period since the 1960s phase of expansion has seen more than a quadrupling of students in higher education. The core buildings of the University of Sussex, designed by Sir Basil Spence and a series of architectural partners, were the first of these universities to be listed in the 1990s and arguably are still the largest group of individual listed 1960s buildings in the country. Making

---

This paper re-casts some of the material I included in my essay for the book published on the occasion of the university's 50th anniversary, Fred Gray, ed., *Making the Future: A history of the University of Sussex* (Falmer: University of Sussex, 2011).

the case for their unique quality is a complex one because both the character of the individual buildings and their relationship to each other evolved over several years. The key aspects that make the case for statutory listing are worth examining here—the connection to a significant individual (whether architect, patron or later inhabitant), the presence of unique characteristics that demonstrate the best design qualities of the age, and the sense that the building has passed into the nation's history through its iconic status, often proven by its appearance in film, photography and other forms of representation. In addition, it can be demonstrated that certain key writings on buildings, politics and the arts at this period projected no specific influence upon Spence and his team but certainly set the agenda for their reception.[2]

Spence was appointed architect to the new university in 1959. He was already recognized as an architect with sensitivity to the needs of university building and his grasp of master planning an entire site had been confirmed by his appointment to Edinburgh five years earlier. By the time he came to Sussex, he was also architect and planner to the University of Southampton, and it was the commission for a new residential block at Queens' College, Cambridge, that had a crucial bearing both on the design and the nature of a newly-founded university like Sussex. At Cambridge, student protest had led to the rejection of a historicist design by Stephen Dykes Bower and there grew from this a willingness to understand the student experience in its developmental sense—of the university as a place where lives were transformed as learning took place.[3] This influenced a sense of the organic growth of the structures, their open plan and their leaving the door open for change and adaptation.

The major commission of Spence during these years was the rebuilding of Coventry Cathedral, for which he won the competition in 1951 and which was to be consecrated in 1962.[4] The immediate precedents in the design and mastering of problems of site at Coventry for the University of Sussex were the use of a sloping site (prefiguring Spence's sensitivity to the undulating landscape of the eighteenth-century park from which the university campus was taken), the regard for local materials and their traditional use, and something of the way in which certain shapes, especially the circular form, determined some of the buildings' most characteristic forms. The circular form is the motif here—in the case of the cathedral, two almost free-standing chapels; and at the university, a similar respect for the rounded form both externally and internally in the Chemistry lecture theatre and the Arts Centre [Fig. 7.1 and Plate 7].[5] The comparison extends to a sensitivity to site, both natural and in terms of historical context. At Coventry, Spence used the height of the ruins of the old cathedral to determine the limit of the height of the new cathedral's scale, just as the presence of trees from the eighteenth-century landscaped park would determine the heights of buildings at Sussex. The surroundings of downscape at Sussex would also secure sightlines so that the horizon line of the hills was nowhere broken by the new structures. One further aspect of the completion of the cathedral had an impact on the development of Sussex. Spence's work during wartime had included a spell in the camouflage unit of the Royal Artillery, where he met and worked alongside other artists who were to become some of the leading talents in the applied arts of post-war Britain. Some of these people, he employed in the interior of the cathedral. Spence's control of the fittings and furnishings at Sussex was not as paramount and the commissioning of many interior features not at his particular command, but he was influential nonetheless. Coventry had set a precedent for the coming

FIGURE 7.1 *Basil Spence, Chapel of Christ the Servant, Coventry Cathedral.*
© Maurice Howard

together of certain groups of like-minded artists. Neither Spence nor anyone from his immediate architectural practice determined the commission for a John Piper tapestry in the Meeting House, but it was as if it was assumed he would have encouraged and approved this decision.

As Spence approached the commission for a university on a virgin site, how did he envisage the governing principles of such a gathering of buildings? At the moment of his appointment, Spence was President of the Royal Institute of British Architects and was about to leave for a trip to Africa. He left the young Peter Winchester in his studio to draw up some first thoughts for the university and the result was a remarkable series of drawings, the most vivid of them still housed in the university's Special Collections, that present the campus as an urbanized, paved great space [Plate 8].[6] In this vision, buildings are united in style by being fronted with colonnades, said to have been inspired by the unifying use of such a feature at the town of Vigevano in Lombardy, constructed for Ludovico Sforza in the 1490s, bringing castello, church and the provisions of urban life together. Something of the inspiration may also have come from the writings of Gordon Cullen, whose essays in the *Architectural Review* were gathered together in his book *Townscape* in 1961.[7] In these pieces, Cullen discusses the shapes of urban squares, the vistas and surprise approaches to them. Something of the idealism of what the new universities were to be about, bringing the traditional into this new concept of space and anticipating a synergy between them, is seen in Winchester's populating his drawings with figures in billowing academic gowns. Some of the core ideas in these drawings passed into Spence's long-term vision for the university: a circular meeting hall (though this was to be transformed in its intention into a meeting house for all religions), a major square with open arcades on two floors and what appears to be a chapel building fronted by sharply cut-off twin towers. This may have been the origin of what was to become a key motif of the entrance to the Arts Centre—concrete pillars representing the ever-growing patterns of thought—a hope for the imagination of the new paths of learning that the new universities would espouse. But the conception essentially changed from this point onwards to a programme which differentiated the parts of the whole. Spence went on to allow the consistency of building materials, brick, concrete and the highly focused and economic use of the local Sussex flint to create the unity of purpose. But partly to give a different character to each of the major buildings as they went up around the plain of the campus during the 1960s and partly to reflect changing circumstances both aesthetic and financial, the university buildings were individually planned and quite emphatically expressed their different functions.

In this development, Spence was reflecting the development of the Greek *agora*, a gathering of buildings that individually provided the places and spaces for the functioning of the *polis*, the city state in all its provision for people.[8] Historians have stressed how the *agora* cast off the axial planning of cities from earlier civilizations, notably those of Egypt, to create enclosed spaces or squares, though ones which allowed multi-access by wide entrances, alternative narrow alleys creating visual surprise, open arcades that fronted buildings but never in so singular a way as to suggest the autocracy of a single, dominating architectural idea. In 1959, there was published Paul Zucker's influential book *Town and Square from the Agora to the Village Green*, which stressed the idea that the axiality of Mesopotamia or Egypt expressed a dictatorial concept of society, whilst the *agora* 'was based on the potentialities of a gradually growing democracy'.[9] The *agora* as it developed in Hellenistic Greece moved away from a gathering of buildings for administration and government towards something that served the people for trade, education and social intercourse. In the development of Sussex, Spence was anxious to create the right conditions to make 'pockets of completeness' so that the university could not only function as it took shape but suggest a changing use of every space over time. College (later Falmer) House, the key flagship building which initiated the building campaign, at first contained a multiplicity of functions, including that of administration. These were, however, soon hived off as the university expanded to leave a core of structures devoted to learning, social gathering and informed leisure—key buildings for the teaching of Science and Arts, the Library, the Meeting House, and the Arts Centre for performance and display [Fig. 7.2].

As inspiration for his overall idea, Spence drew on a number of sources both deep in his memory of world architecture and from specific encounters with similar academic institutions. From his early life experiences, Spence, born in India of Scottish parents, emphasized the impact upon him of the caves of Elephanta, outside Bombay: 'The vast chambers carved out of solid rock, rich in sculpture in intricate detail, gave a tremendous feeling of size; the cool temperature inside contrasted with the heat outside and the dim lighting revealed features of the interior only after the eye had got used to darkness.'[10] He later claimed that visits to the great English cathedrals persuaded him that buildings had to be of their age and convinced him of an emphatic rejection of mere revivalism; however traditional the concept of an institutional building such as cathedral or university, '[A]rchitecture should grow out of the conditions of the time, should not be a copy of past styles and must be a

FIGURE 7.2 *Basil Spence, drawing of the back of Falmer House, Arts Centre and Library in the landscape.*
©University of Sussex, Special Collections (ref. no. 449DRG)

clear expression of contemporary thought'.[11] For the concept of the university itself, his visit in 1953, fundraising at the time in the United States for Coventry, to the Cranbrook Schools in Michigan was clearly fundamental. Eliel Saarinen's buildings there, the Boys School of which was completed in 1928, prefigure something of the Sussex key motifs, with the use of a warm red brick and different buildings connected by arcades open on both sides. A tall flat-roofed arcade carried on thin brick plinths is reminiscent of the similar motif, in local red sandstone, connecting the new cathedral at Coventry with the ruins of the old. A visit to Aarhus University in Denmark, founded in 1928 and still under construction in the 1950s, also inspired him and he particularly remembered the great hall window and brick terrace beside it raised high in the undulating landscape.[12]

Such experiences gave Spence the essence, the magic, of his conception, but for constructional methods, he drew on his own training in past traditions on the one hand and from the great figures of the age who espoused twentieth century modernism on the other. The Cranbrook Schools are clearly dependent on the English Arts and Crafts movement and Spence's own early years brought him face-to-face with two great architects of the post-Arts and Crafts tradition, Sir Robert Lorimer in Scotland and Sir Edwin Lutyens, in whose office he worked for a short while. The customized appearance of the Sussex buildings with their hand-made bricks inevitably recall the care and exactness of detail that Lutyens brought to his low-lying country houses in the vernacular English tradition but Spence would also have known Lutyens in a different mode at Castle Drogo in Devon, a twentieth-century 'baronial' stronghold completed just at the moment, 1930, when he was working in the Lutyens office. Dramatic internal stairs at Castle Drogo, leading to landings with huge windows lighting them, foretell something of the prominence of great stairs at Sussex.[13] The skills of craft and architectural decorum he learned from these encounters merged with the ambition of modernist architecture that Spence drew from the work of Le Corbusier of the 1950s, especially the Jaoul houses and the Law Courts of Chandigarh. The latter's huge concrete vaults reflected in water are a key precedent for the courtyard of College/Falmer House [Fig. 7.3].

This meeting of Arts and Crafts with modernism also occurred when it came to the issue of compromise over constructional methods. The custom-made quality of Spence's buildings at Sussex, the quality of the bricks and the use of flint are often contrasted with the prefabricated nature of the construction of other new universities of the 1960s, notably the campus at York, built with the CLASP system of concrete cladding on a steel frame.[14] But at Sussex, methods were devised on-site as the project was underway to provide components as quickly as possible: concrete vaults, beams and columns were rapidly made through a form of production devised by Gordon Collins, Spence's associate, and Povl Ahm from the Ove Arup architectural practice. Photographs of the casting yard and of cranes putting these components in place are amongst the most evocative of the university's original site photographs. Brick walls and piers and curved concrete gable beams were engaged into this framework.

The buildings around the plain, known as Fulton Court, began with College House (renamed Falmer House in 1961 though Spence himself still refers to the building as College House throughout 1962), winner of the Royal Institute of British Architects' bronze medal in 1964. This building was designed as the fulcrum of the

FIGURE 7.3 *View of the courtyard of Falmer House, University of Sussex.*
© Simon Lane

university's social gatherings with a large dining hall, a debating chamber, and, in the earliest years, a staff common room and space for a faculty member to reside and fulfil a pastoral role for students. The courtyard has an intentionally 'open' feel with no two of the four ranges alike and with a mixture of open and closed areas that suggest a building with various functions slotted in; Spence once described this effect as 'four chests of drawers arranged around a square space with some of the drawers taken out'.[15] Spence himself noted the inspiration of the Colosseum in Rome, a building of huge vaulted colonnades creating light–dark contrasts and of course in its ruined state asking us to question its own sense of permanence. To challenge the traditional courtyard type of structure, the internal space is paved and has a moat running around it, with a further long and wider stretch of moat (now filled and grassed over) running north from the outer wall before the sheer brick face of the projecting debating chamber. Inside the courtyard, the water in the moat served also to reflect the sharp contrasts of light and dark created in the vaults above it. The architectural language of the building set the pattern for the buildings that followed—concrete arches on brick piers forming colonnades with blank and windowed stretches of wall broken up by voids above. Falmer House was therefore very much the 'gatehouse' to the whole site in the sense that through its materials of brick and concrete, mixed with a staircase tower veneered in Sussex flint, it determines the character, the 'heraldry' of the university as emphatically as any Tudor gatehouse. It announces an entrance point to what has come to seem over time, with the vast expansion of the university northwards in later years, an axial plan. This is still essentially in place, but it is an axial direction that invites the viewer to look from side to side and notice the changes in the rhythm of every architectural feature, never exactly repeated. As for the purpose of Falmer House itself, in the first edition of Ian Nairn and Nikolaus Pevsner's *Sussex* in the *Buildings of England* series, published in 1965 at a point where just a few key buildings were in place, the authors were moved to describe the ensemble of Falmer House as 'exciting in the extreme, in fact so high in its emotional pitch that one may be left in doubt whether the social life in the building will live up to so exciting a visual setting'.[16] In the early days of the university, grand occasions took place here and at the Physics Building; one such, in October 1962, caused Francis S. Mason Junior of the US Embassy to write with enthusiasm to Spence: 'I saw Falmer inside and out, day and night (when it looked spectacular from the road)...The variety one gets outside in the quadrangle as one looks around, not feeling closed in but in a kind of grandly open room with the plash [*sic*] of water, is superb.'[17]

The Physics Building, begun at the same time, equally uses solids and voids and essentially uses the same idea of a block carried on a colonnade but with a different rhythm of spaced elements. Here, the colonnade is effectively the antique *stoa* with deep vaults like an undercroft making for even darker penetrations of the building. The echo, however, of this block with Falmer House makes a significant point about the intellectual aims of the university; whilst the site was planned with Arts Buildings on one side and Science on the other, the creation of Schools of Study rather than traditional university departments underlined the sense that it was hoped that disciplines would influence each other and broaden the experience of the undergraduate. The Physics Building looks quite unlike the science buildings going up at other universities at this period. The Chemistry Building has attached rounded forms, drawing on the experience of Coventry, the larger of the two a grand lecture theatre atop a dramatic staircase, from the summit of which the view back looking west across the university is, on a spring morning before the trees are fully in leaf, one of the great designed expanses of the 1960s.

The idea of the university's largest lecture theatre raised above ground like this had always been an ambition, but Spence's initial plan was for a free-standing lecture hall on arches in the great courtyard. Two further lecture theatres were planned for the Arts Building, directly across the great court from Falmer House, but cost prevented the most dramatic solution, cantilevered halls lifted above ground, the high concrete towers between them giving the appearance of a spring pulling the shapes apart and together. The idea of a raised space was something that was currently sitting awaiting construction among Spence's projects: the British Embassy at Rome, designed in 1959 but not achieved until 1970, is a raised two-storey structure carried on columns to enable free-flow under the building.[18] In the end, the halls simply follow the rising ground but with sawtooth-shaped walls allowing light in to the sides of the buildings, another influence from Coventry, though here they look ineffectual and for many years the light has been blocked for the purposes of darkening the rooms for image projection, the present commonality of which was a rare occurrence half a century ago. Behind the first Arts Building comes the second group, now familiarly known as Arts A and B, comprising faculty offices and small seminar rooms around courtyards. Here, the rising ground suggested a sympathetic mix of path, lawn and pond, with spectacular vistas between the various levels. The side to the west of the great plain is completed by the Library, raised like a temple on a podium, with deep high arches reminiscent of the vaulted remains of the Basilica of Maxentius in the Forum. Another grand flight of steps, echoing that across at the Chemistry Building, provides the ascent.

Two free-standing buildings completed the initial Spence vision, though these were a cost beyond the University Grants Committee's funds for the university and were paid for by benefactors so Spence struck a different note. In these, he worked closely with his son-in-law, Anthony Blee. The communal place of worship, from early times known as the Meeting House (1963–67) to underline its inter-denominational purpose, is a circular structure with brick plinths extending out over a moat on the ground floor and faceted concrete 'bricks' above punctuated with glass openings of equal size and of various colours. Spence had very clear ideas about the setting and basic form, but least to do with the actual building of the Arts Centre (1965–69), where Sean Kenny, architect and stage production designer, took a leading consultancy role. Here is a grouping of circular forms around a core of auditorium and gallery space, brick and solid-walled like the lecture theatre attached to the Chemistry Building and thus providing a contrast with the pierced concrete drum of the Meeting House.

Often forgotten was Spence's hand in the university's completion, his views on furnishing and internal detail. He was instrumental in bringing to the great dining room of Falmer House the gift by the artist of Ivon Hitchens' *Day's Rest, Day's Work*, painted for exhibition in 1960. A correspondence between Spence and the artist, initiated by Hitchens, between March and July 1962, brought the canvas to the university. Spence had strong views on his responsibility for crucial decisions about interiors: 'I cannot stress too strongly the necessity for building and the interior being under one hand. This is, of course, the tradition (e.g. Robert Adam and many others) yet it is by no means a universal practice. In some universities it is thought that the architect's fees can be saved if the Building's Officer thumbs through the catalogue and chooses furniture. In my experience this is a disastrous practice.' Here are his thoughts on colour and fabric:

> In a homogenous background individual splashes of very bright colour are essential to avoid dullness, and we intend to submit a scheme to the university which will include some bright Finnish fabrics woven in wool, which hang splendidly, and do not need lining. We intend to design the furniture in oak of robust but simple design using rough fabrics of purple, lime green and powder blue in the upholstery. Carpets too can be a plain simple weave and bright in colour. A flat overall scheme of lighting will be avoided using glass shades of various colours.[19]

One further aspect of these buildings makes a strong case for their unique solution to the brief the new universities were given. This is the representational history of these structures, since from the beginning they were seen as paradigmatic of the new adventure of re-drawing the map of learning, through photographs of students in green pastures discussing serious things, their background to fashion photography of the period and most especially by Spence's own commissioned projection of their image.[20] The Dutch-born Henk Snoek was Spence's preferred photographer for his buildings, recording Coventry, Edinburgh University, the Hutchestown C project in Glasgow, and most notably Sussex.[21] Here, he captures both the natural backdrop to the buildings and their successful seat within the preexisting landscape and their nigh-perfect otherness, essays in black and white images that provide sharper contrasts than even the brightest summer day can provide, with perhaps just one student referent to the human occupation of these spaces, artfully placed on a projecting edge of stair or a wall. They both complete the photographic cataloguing of modernism in architecture stretching back a few decades and sit perfectly with the sharpness of the early 1960s, a time of drainpipe trousers, piled-up bouffant hair-dos and the contrasts of dark make-up against the pale wall of the face.

Looking around the original university buildings today, the challenge and wit of Spence's command of architectural detail continue to astonish, despite the patina of age (and Spence himself remarked that: 'It is true, of course, that as soon as a building is completely finished, it must begin to die.') and over-zealous conservation is now happily being corrected.[22] The ubiquitous use of side-on brickwork and the repetition of concrete vault and brick piers keep a continuity of material but everywhere façades are variegated and given an interesting asymmetrical treatment: arches of different widths and window openings narrow, wide and segmental.[23] He follows a decorum or appropriateness according to the nature and function of each structure: grand proportions for Falmer House with its vistas through the building and sense of conjuring up public oratory to the more intimate and small-scale Arts Buildings where the emphasis is on grouping and enclosure, on helping the users look inward to courtyard, water and colonnade whilst experiencing small-group teaching within rooms where different widths of brick plinth and therefore window opening create variation from one office space to another. The basic building material of brick has been largely followed in the expansion of the university buildings over time, though the subtlety of Spence's handling is only partly repeated in what has followed. Many of the university's later buildings are raised on what are essentially artificially created platform spaces around them rather than respecting the natural rise and fall of the pre-existing landscape. These create more right angles and controlled access than the speculative, directing the eye left and right, informal approaches that Spence first envisaged for the development of the university. The making of the first phase of the university was, with its changes of shapes and relations of buildings one to the other and with its keeping to a stylistic idiom that allowed for differences of scale and approach to individual buildings, an outstanding contribution to the meeting of townscape with institutional needs and provided a key scenario for the exciting new directions that higher education wished to offer at this time.

Notes

1   English Heritage, list entry number 1402678. See http://list.english-heritage.org.uk/resultsingle.aspx?uid=1402678, accessed 13 August 2013.

2   See Elain Harwood, *England: A Guide to Post-War Listed Buildings* (London: Batsford, 2003).

3   On Spence's architectural biography see Philip Long and Jane Thomas, eds. *Basil Spence, Architect* (Edinburgh: National Galleries of Scotland, 2008); Louise Campbell, Miles Glendinning and Jane Thomas, eds. *Basil Spence: Buildings and Projects* (London: RIBA Publishing, 2012).

4   See Louise Campbell, *Coventry Cathedral: Art and Architecture in Post-War Britain* (Oxford: Oxford University Press, 1996).

5   The idea, however, of the circular form echoing across campus took time to emerge; the earliest layout plans (see Campbell, Glendinning and Thomas, eds., *Basil Spence*, 158) show a single circular building, suggesting that the idea of visual parallels across the space developed in Spence's mind.

6   The university's holdings of Winchester's drawings were displayed at the exhibition 'Sir Basil Spence at the University of Sussex' (University of Sussex, Falmer, 2012) in celebration of the university's 50th anniversary.

7   Gordon Cullen, *The Concise Townscape* (London: Architectural Press, 1961): on squares, 97–102.

8   Spence himself noted the influence of the Acropolis in Athens when describing the initial thoughts for the university: Sir Basil Spence, 'Building a New University: The First Phase', in D. Daiches, ed. *The Idea of a New University: An Experiment in Sussex* (London: Andre Deutsch, 1964), 204.

9   Paul Zucker, *Town and Square from the Agora to the Village Green* (New York: Columbia University Press, 1959) 31. Also influential, A.W. Lawrence's key volume on *Greek Architecture* in the Pelican History of Art series was first published in 1957. See the chapters on 'Town-Planning and Halls before 330' and 'Hellenistic Town-Planning and Halls' in the edition revised by R. A. Tomlinson in 1996, 190–200.

10   Basil Spence, *Phoenix at Coventry: The Building of a Cathedral* (London: Geoffrey Bles, 1962), 7.

11   Spence, *Phoenix*, 8.

12   Louise Campbell, '"Drawing a New Map of Learning": Spence and the University of Sussex", in *Basil Spence, Architect*, 99–100.

13   On Castle Drogo see Bridget Cherry and Nikolaus Pevsner, *The Buildings of England: Devon*, 2nd ed. (Harmondsworth: Penguin, 1989), 245–7.

14   On York see Andrew Saint, *Towards a Social Architecture: The Role of School-Building in Post-War England* (New Haven and London: Yale University Press, 1987), 214–22.

15   Spence, 'Building a New University', 210.

16   Ian Nairn and Nikolaus Pevsner, *The Buildings of England, Sussex* (Harmondsworth: Penguin, 1965), 499–500. The phrase is omitted from the second edition, but there is a much fuller account of the buildings: Nicholas Antram and Nikolaus Pevsner, *Sussex East with Brighton and Hove* (New Haven and London; Yale University Press, 2013), 264–70.

17   Correspondence to and from Spence cited in this essay is in the Basil Spence archive, RCAHMS, MS2329/ENG/52/2.

18   Miles Glendinning, '"Una lezione di civiltà": The British Embassy in Rome', in *Basil Spence: Buildings and Projects*, 172–95.

19   Royal Commission on the Ancient and Historic Monuments of Scotland. RCAHMS, MS2329/ENG/52/2.

20   The cover of *Tatler* of 15 July 1964, showed the Jay twins. See also S. Maclure, 'The "With-It" University?", *The Listener*, 15 February 1965.

21   Henk Snoek, Architectural Photography. RIBA British Architectural Library Photographs Collection (London, 2009).

22   Spence, 'Building a New University', 204.

23   The variation was first expressed in Nigel Llewellyn, 'Building Universities: The 1960s and Beyond', *Bulletin. The Newsletter of the University of Sussex*, 22 March 2002.

8

Architects Co-Partnership: Private Practice for Public Service

Alan Powers

In September 1961, the Pendennis column of the *Observer* newspaper featured 'The men at the back of the buildings'" describing the architectural practices shortlisted for the new St Paul's Cathedral Choir School. Among them was Architects Co-Partnership (ACP): 'Left-wing, public school, they were all students together at the best and most expensive architectural school in the country, the Architectural Association', the paragraph began. 'One can imagine them in those days just round the corner from Bedford Square, lunching at Bertorelli's together, talking Spanish Civil War'.[1]

The practice was founded in the summer of 1939 [Fig. 8.1].[2] The absence of a monograph on its work has meant that it is no longer as well known as it was in the 1950s and 1960s, a period now dominated by studies of slightly younger practitioners of the New Brutalist generation.[3] ACP were in some ways typical of the age group that acted as a bridge between the ideals of the 1930s at their most ideologically insistent and the realization of those ideals in the climate of social democracy after 1945, yet they were exceptional in their dedication to a novel approach to office and staff organization. After explaining the unusual origin of the practice, this chapter will look in particular at the transition in their work in the early 1960s, when they began to operate in a broader range of contexts and building types and were confronted by the difficulty of a younger generation emerging that saw different relationships between design, politics and professional structures.

Sources indicate that Kenneth Capon was the partner who made the first move in the last months before the war to found a practice with like-minded students. The choice of individuals was owed to '75% personal friendship or, at least, tied groups of personal friendships' but also required a level of political and personal commitment.

FIGURE 8.1 *ACP partners and staff, 1956.*
Author's Collection.

During the time we knew the A.A., besides ourselves, there appeared practically no one who felt the frantic social changes to be integral with the architectural problem. It was almost a question of an emotional attitude and perhaps it was for this reason that we found it, in 1939, so hard to convince ourselves intellectually why the Architects' Co-Operative Partnership should comprise some and not others who, in so many respects, seemed suitable.[4]

'If there was a romantic prototype for ACP it was not Tecton in England but GATEPAC in pre-Franco Spain', explained Anthony Cox, another of the partners, in 1984.[5] Tecton, founded by Berthold Lubetkin in 1932, was never a true community of equals, given Lubetkin's dominance as a designer and his seniority to most of his colleagues. GATEPAC, with which José Luis Sert was involved, was a bigger association based in several cities. 'Architects' Co-Operative Partnership', as it was originally called, came somewhere in between, being *sui generis* in its scope and scale, an expression of the ideal of equality shared by the partners and seen by them as the appropriate method for the production of modern buildings. On a more practical level, the eleven founding members, equal in status, could not easily be named individually in a joint title.[6] Cox, who normally acted as the spokesman for the group, later wrote:

'It is not surprising that the notion of working together as a group came naturally to the founders of ACP. It was not only because they rejected the concept of the architect as prima donna dominating the supporting cast, but more fundamentally because they thought a combination of like-minded architects on an equal footing could examine problems more deeply, cover a greater range of expertise and produce more rational and efficient solutions. Small scale individual private practice looked almost impossible without a private income and would never be able to tackle work of any size and complexity; official departments were hierarchical and seemed full of dead wood. The founders recognized that although each of them would make a different contribution none was to be regarded as the leader: hence the anonymous name—the first architectural firm to adopt one since Tecton had coined its almost unprofessional title.[7]

As Pendennis indicated, their Architectural Association (AA) background was significant. Entering the school in 1934, several of them led a successful campaign to maintain a set of changes in the teaching method based on the idea of collaborative working introduced by E. A. A. Rowse, the young principal of the AA. The background to this is complex, but the main contention was less between modernism and tradition as such and more about the principles of educational method. *Focus* magazine, founded by Anthony Cox and Leo de Syllas, two of the future ACP partners, with a contemporary, Tim Bennett, was their mouthpiece.[8] The first issue in the summer of 1938, elegantly produced by the publishers Lund Humphries across Bedford Square at No.12, carried this editorial:

> We were born in the war.
>   Much that follows in this journal can be orientated to that one fact. We were born into a civilization whose leaders, whose ideals, whose culture had failed. They are still in power to-day. But we, the generation that follow, cannot accept their domination. They lead us always deeper into reaction that we are convinced can only end in disaster.[9]

In the battlefield of the AA's premises in Bedford Square, they fought for the students' right to work together in groups and to research real-world problems from sociological and technical angles prior to making designs. The students won their battle by being well organized and writing persuasive reports. The architect H. S. Goodhart-Rendel, recently appointed as Director of Education, was in a difficult position with pressure from opposing directions and in the autumn of 1938 he resigned, Geoffrey Jellicoe being appointed in his place early in 1939.[10]

The ethos of collaboration rested on a belief that architectural form should emerge from design process and never be arbitrarily imposed. Not all the modern architecture up to that time conformed to this ideal of an updated vernacular, expressed by J. M. Richards in *Circle* (1937) as 'The Principle of Anonymity'.[11] To demonstrate his point, Anthony Cox wrote an often-quoted criticism of Highpoint II flats in Highgate, in which he compared the 1938 building unfavourably with its predecessor and neighbour, the Highpoint I flats, completed only three years before.[12] Several future ACP partners worked on a diploma project for a new town that exemplified the ideal combination of social research, regional planning and architecture.[13]

When ACP was set up in 1939, therefore, it was intended to enable a new way of working, continuing the hard-won student experience of collaboration supported by various kinds of research into new but appropriate building techniques in place of the obsession among modernists between 1930 and 1935 with monolithic reinforced concrete and committed to a rather self-denying attitude to style that would avoid the expression of individual personality and aspire to something that looked and felt inevitable. They decided that they would not employ any assistants in the conventional sense but that 'younger architects joining the firm would become an integral part of the firm from the start'.[14] This commitment to anonymity and reality—corresponding to the German definition of *sachlichkeit*—made an impact on older modernists, especially Walter Gropius, who wrote from Harvard to congratulate the editors of *Focus*.[15]

The status of architects within an organization was a wider concern in the 1930s that linked the social thinking of the time to the question of what constituted good architecture and how this was related to its production process. It was felt that the slow pace of change and lack of a coherent relationship between structure, function and form that characterized the majority of pre-war work could only be solved by a radical reorganization, in which architects and other consultants could channel their specialist contributions through teamwork and in which national and local government employment might rise from its low status to become the highest form of achievement both in serving society and in creativity.

While a rather puritanical attitude to design in the pursuit of utopia is attributed generally to the Modern Movement of the 1930s, *Focus* magazine was its most recognizable statement in Britain, ACP being an extension of the magazine's reforming mission into the field of practice. The original 'Co-Operative Partnership' form of the name was abbreviated to Architects Co-Partnership in 1953, partly because they were told that its left-wing implications were putting potential clients off and partly because it led to confusion with the Co-Operative Wholesale Society.[16]

The outbreak of war suspended the development of the firm almost immediately. Strangely, they received their largest and what is still probably their most famous single building commission as their first job after 1945. This was a new factory for rubber production, at Brynmawr in the Welsh valleys.[17] It was a perfect expression of their social engagement and could even be called an expiation of the guilt of being middle class and public school-educated in a world that they wanted to change. There was a long lead-time for the design, and the partners—initially Capon, Cocke and Powers, later Cooke-Yarborough and Cox, who chiefly worked on it—were indeed able to do all the working drawings themselves. With the help of Ove Arup and his partner, Ronald Jenkins, it was a showpiece of shell concrete construction with an extraordinary physical presence, arguably the most spectacular interior of an industrial workplace in the history of British architecture. It also became a place of lost dreams when the company that commissioned it sold it on to Dunlop after a couple of years, although it continued in production as the major employer in the area until the early 1980s. The building survived, listed at grade II*, empty and potentially re-usable, had anyone grasped the opportunity, until 2001.

Brynmawr was exceptional in several ways—generously funded by the state yet constrained and shaped by prevailing conditions, such as the shortage of steel that led to making the wide spans of the factory floor as a grid of nine shallow thin shell concrete domes, achievable at the time with relatively cheap labour. ACP did not follow this project by becoming specialists in industrial building, however, and moved substantially into designing for education, finding in the vision of the 1944 Education Act a perfect vehicle for their social and architectural ideals. When planning their partnership before and during the war, they doubted whether local authorities, which they saw as natural providers of good architecture, would be able to change their attitudes fast enough. One exception was Hertfordshire, where under C. H. Aslin, the schools team quickly became the national leaders in all areas of design and building at the end of the war. Anthony Cox worked there with Stirrat Johnson-Marshall for a spell before rejoining his ACP colleagues.[18] As 'private architects' ACP were among a number of 'approved' modernist firms hired by other County Architects to supplement the work of their own staff when the demand for buildings exceeded their in-house capacity.

The buildings were within the humanist paradigm of the period and the constraints of the Hills 8'3" structural system, often, as they put it in their contribution to the RIBA lecture series, 'Architects' Approach to Architecture' in 1967, 'rather loosely linked together on a functional pattern'.[19] This changed in the mid-1950s owing to economic stringency in the times, combined with 'our own dissatisfaction with these rather amorphous, straggling railway truck assemblies, and a desire for a more positive coherence, social and architectural'.[20] Courtyard forms were favoured because of their economy of circulation space. An alternative constructional system in timber was developed by ACP in partnership with Medway Buildings Ltd., and used between 1955 and 1970. At ACP, as with many architects of their generation, the idea of systems was closer to an ideology than an expedient, objectifying architectural process and modifying the ultimate subjectivity of design decisions in line with the aims of the late 1930s.

ACP moved on from primary to secondary schools and comprehensives, with Chaddesden in Derbyshire, completed 1953 (partner in charge, Leo de Syllas), where they were one of the first firms to build up to four storeys high with their own prototype of the CLASP system. Later came the rather notorious Risinghill School (later known as Elizabeth Garrett Anderson) in Islington of 1960, with a sleek glass skin on a sloping site and the listed Lilian Baylis School in Lambeth (partner in charge for both, Kenneth Capon). Altogether some 40 schools were designed and built, including a group of three residential schools in the 1960s for the National Spastics Society (partner in charge Michael Powers), which were pioneering achievements in design for disability.

In 1954, ACP followed Maxwell Fry in working in the soon-to-become independent commonwealth countries in Africa, setting up a branch office in Lagos, partly to maintain a sufficient workload for the top-heavy management in London. Michael Grice and Leo de Syllas were the partners chiefly involved. Up to the closure of the Lagos office in 1962, several major educational, hotel and infrastructure projects were created with a freedom from high costs and budget constraints unknown in Britain at the time, including the Upper Volta River project in Ghana, a series of smelting works, dams and new towns that must have seemed like a new version of a favourite exemplar of progressive regional planning in the 1930s, the Tennessee Valley Authority.

Did the collective ethos of the partnership result in the production of design by committee? A brief text accompanying an article in *Architecture and Building*'s feature, 'The team in the office' in 1956, questioned how it worked, concluding that the assistants were 'of the group and not merely employed by it', a view corroborated by statements from those concerned, many of whom stayed until retirement.[21] The 'design outlook' was seen as 'sufficiently coherent to permeate the work of their growing staff'.[22] The conventional notion of a partner imposing an aesthetic arbitrarily from above was altered to the extent that there was a shared assumption about what was right, representing a relatively rigid line to be followed, and the article concludes tartly that 'It is the ideal itself that is despotic'.[23]

In a published conversation about office organization in *Architectural Design* in 1958, Leo de Syllas explained that the long friendship and working experience of the partners meant that it was possible for them to share the creative process 'on a terribly personal basis'.[24] Asked whether the structure of the office was horizontal, with interchangeable staff at different grade levels, or vertical, with distinct teams working under the partners, de Syllas replied that, like an egg crate, it was both: 'It really works out that you have got a controlling group horizontally at the top and six operating groups vertically.'[25] While individual partners were involved at an early conceptual stage with every project, some junior staff were taking more active design roles in the cause of job satisfaction. 'We frankly admit', said de Syllas, 'that this is a change which really affects the partners, but doesn't affect A.C.P. as a unit. It doesn't affect our basic premise that designing, which must originate in the individual mind of a person, is improved.'[26] A delicate balance was required between the individual and the group, in which criticism played a vital role, as de Syllas explained, 'I believe that architecture, notwithstanding that it's an art, has to employ a certain discipline to avoid the worst errors of committing yourself to a mistake; and the object of the team is really not to sieve the original conception, even at the "cathedral level", but to see that that conception is carried through with a logic that doesn't contradict the needs of the building.'[27] The anonymity of the products was maintained in the press, profits were divided equally, 'and we just don't argue these issues'.[28]

At Yorke Rosenberg Mardall, a firm with less ideological baggage and a more hierarchical structure, there was a similar principle of anonymity of individuals but with fewer partners. The founders were somewhat older than the ACP founders, and F. R. S. Yorke planned ahead in 1958 by promoting two much younger architects, Brian Henderson and David Allford, to partnership status. As the firm grew through the 1950s, the individual hands of the founder partners were increasingly subsumed in a recognizable range of treatments. White tile claddings were introduced by Eugene Rosenberg, but also widely adopted for projects by the younger partners, while a Miesian steel aesthetic was adopted by Brian Henderson when F. R. S. Yorke gave him primary responsibility for the first Gatwick Airport terminal.[29] Similarly at ACP, individual design personalities began to emerge as the narrow choices offered by systems broadened. Anthony Cox remained the partner most enduringly committed to a minimum of personal expression and a maximum of technical efficiency, in the design of buildings such as the chemistry laboratories at Leicester University, 1961 [Fig. 8.2].

The change in British architecture in the second half of the 1950s has been studied more from the viewpoint of those urging change than in relation to the nature of the preexisting condition. At Yorke Rosenberg Mardall, the promotion of Henderson and Allford influenced their elders who, despite pre-war personal contacts with several of the modernist masters, had dulled their capacity for vigorous forms during the years of making do and luring the public to approve a temperate modernism. At Lyons, Israel and Ellis, there was a succession of young assistants who went on to make names for themselves in a way that seldom happened with ACP and other practices.[30] The term 'New Empiricism', coined in the *Architectural Review* to describe a group of Swedish buildings, was countered by New Brutalism (the use of 'New' being an in-joke against the *Architectural Review*), initially a form

FIGURE 8.2 *Leicester University chemistry laboratories, 1961.*
RIBA Library Photographs Collection.

of secret brotherhood committed to overthrowing the establishment.[31] ACP might occasionally have been guilty of 'New Empiricism' but chiefly in a handful of small brick houses with pitched roofs and some structures on the South Bank in 1951. In other respects, the sublime scale and expressive forms of the factory at Brynmawr, followed by some of the stricter applications of the Hills systems, offered contrasting alternatives to the mainstream. On the other hand, the ethos of the firm, as the Pendennis article made clear, was beginning to seem remote by the early 1960s. According to the received view, ACP would be included among those firms seen by the younger generation as part of the enemy.[32] Henderson himself was the source of Anthony Sampson's Pendennis column in 1961, and the comments on ACP typify the generational gap. Since their early success, Sampson wrote, changes in fashion exposed ACP as 'slightly dated figures in their well-cut suits and homespun ties, dwelling in the houses they designed for themselves in parts of Hampstead and Highgate, and left them ever so slightly behind'.[33]

The young had their own symbolic battles to fight and inevitably turned against those who had fought an earlier architectural war. As the introductory paragraph to an article 'Young Architects' in *Architectural Design*, June 1958, explained, 'the young men trained during or immediately after the war are just beginning to build their first buildings, against a very considerable opposition from the public and their elders'.[34] An accompanying article by James Stirling, 'A personal view of the present situation', complained that the impersonal patronage of the public sector had led to a loss of personality in the work. 'The influence of the client is replaced by that of the 'system', frequently structural, and post-war we have seen the birth of many patent methods of building, including pre-cast concrete and curtain walling... However, without the intervention of the architect's personality, that which is originated rationally may soon become characterless.'[35]

With symbolic appropriateness, ACP was one of two other firms short-listed by Cambridge University for the History Library on the Sidgwick site, for which James Stirling, fresh from the controversial triumph of the Leicester University Engineering Building, was selected (shortly before the split with his partner James Gowan) in May 1963, on the basis that the ACP presentation had failed to show an understanding of the brief. Less commonly noticed are the steps that ACP and other firms of their generation took to catch up with new trends, apparently more with relief rather than disappointment that a broader range of expression had returned and that younger talent was available and in need of encouragement. The openness of the ACP office structure and the continuing idea of collaboration made this a relatively easy process, as de Syllas described, and the external change in architectural climate was soon reflected in their work.

There were yet more factors involved in the change. As Cox explained in 1967, it became easier to use brick after the mid-1950s because bricklayers, a scarce commodity in the immediate post-war years, became easier to find. Compared to the building systems, brick offered a greater flexibility in the positioning and proportioning of windows. Each job brought its own mix of requirements that might influence the choice of materials, and the architects learned new skills in handling them.[36]

ACP began to become known for 'one off' buildings in which the historic urban context was a significant factor. The 'Beehive', a set of student rooms at St John's College, Oxford, completed in 1960 (partner in charge Michael Powers), was one of the earliest modern intrusions into a college quad in either of the ancient universities [Fig. 8.3].[37] It was clad in Portland stone and although the large windows might have been borrowed from a science laboratory, their zig-zag outline, based on a series of hexagonal pavilions, felt more like a traditional architectural language. The Fellow chiefly responsible for selecting a modern firm in succession to Sir Edward Maufe was the distinguished architectural historian Sir Howard Colvin, who requested a shortlist from his fellow historian, Sir John Summerson. While ready to abandon Oxford traditionalism, according to Diana Rowntree, 'the college stood firm on the point that the buildings must be in stone, and in solid weight-bearing stone they are, with concrete floors and one wall of double-glazing to each room'.[38]

The Market Hostel at King's College, Cambridge (partner in charge Kenneth Capon), was faced with precious white bricks supplied from Holland, close in character to Regency brickwork in East Anglia. This project marked a similar shift towards contextualism in 1963, even including a simplified version of a Victorian arcaded shopfront inserted in the adjoining façade, which formed part of the development. On the completion of the Market Hostel, amid a climate of opinion still largely opposed to the insertion of modern buildings in historic streets, Ian Nairn numbered ACP among 'a handful of architects ... teaching the profession what it ought to have learnt at school'.[39] St Paul's Choir School, 1963–7, a competition-winning design by de Syllas, executed posthumously by Michael Powers, was the most challenging of such tasks, selected as a demonstration of modern architecture's

FIGURE 8.3 *The Beehive, St John's College, Oxford, 1959.*
Courtesy of Architects Co-Partnership.

ability to respond sensitively to one of the most famous buildings in London. These buildings represent a line of development akin to the university work of Powell and Moya and to the move by Alison and Peter Smithson into Portland stone cladding at the Economist Building in 1964. The solidity of materials in these buildings and their consequent appearance as monumental architecture conformed to the aspect of New Brutalism that was concerned with rejection of lightweight structures and the universality of system-based solutions.

At St Paul's, Ian Nairn sensed unreleased tension, perhaps brought on by the solemnity of the occasion, writing, 'the Choir School is not over-designed but it is over-serious, in the way that a really responsible senior civil servant can be'.[40] This was always a danger for ACP, stemming from the puritanism of the 1930s and attributable to a group reticence and self-censorship towards the kind of architectural expression available to a single practitioner such as Louis Kahn or Denys Lasdun. The Civil Service ideal of anonymous integrity implied caution, very far from the alluring architectural provocations of an architect such as James Stirling. If any ACP partner was ready to embrace this new turn in architecture, it was Kenneth Capon, a romantic visionary at heart who had been involved in amateur stage design before the war. Unrestrained by caution, he needed a sympathetic client, and it is hard to imagine any of the other partners generating the bold concept of the University of Essex.

Among the projects contemporary with Essex, Dunelm House, the students' union at Durham University, offers a parallel instance of a New Brutalist turn. Michael Powers was the partner in charge, probably because the site, overlooked by the cathedral, was another highly sensitive one like St John's, Oxford. He had already worked on several smaller jobs with Richard Raines, a young American who completed his training at the AA under John Killick and Peter Smithson, and Raines took on the design from the outset. When their design had been accepted, Powers characterized their collaboration over a celebration dinner with Raines by saying, 'Without you I could not have designed the building, but without me you couldn't have got it approved.'[41]

The influence of Peter Smithson's thinking, shared by a younger generation, is apparent in the way that the steeply sloping site was treated as a 'mat building'—an agglomeration of similar parts rather than a single legible form and also in the plan form, which has a descending circulation spine leading from the entrance at the top of the site down five levels to the river below, from which rooms of varying cross section can be reached. Commenting on the building in the *Architectural Review*, John Donat (who was also the photographer for the article) wrote: 'Following the tenuous Smithson link, one could describe the building in terms of love and doorframes: love, because it is lavished on every detail and shows, doorframes because they have all been eliminated and don't show at all.'[42] Donat's article broke with the convention that individuals should not be named as designers of ACP buildings, causing concern among the partners that Raines was given full credit for the design. Donat's pictures captured the uncluttered lightness of the interior with Alvar Aalto furniture, and he was even present to catch the fleeting image of Thelonious Monk and his trio performing at the opening event in the spring of 1965. Ove Arup's Kingsgate Footbridge, opened in 1961, was planned in close association with Dunelm House which abuts it and was started soon afterwards [Fig. 8.4].

The intention was to create a picturesque cascade of roofs that would answer the cluster of buildings around the cathedral in the old city across the river. The window mullions were irregularly spaced, as they are at the University of Essex and John Weeks's Northwick Park Hospital, on each occasion evoking Le Corbusier's convent of La Tourette and the new architectural concern with indeterminacy. Geoffrey Broadbent explained it at Dunelm in terms of providing a variety of window widths appropriate to different room uses and in general for the avoidance of monotony. More generally, the external design shares the aim of avoiding monumentality through the apparently random assembly of similar components, an approach that was explicable in terms of the need to build cheaply with a mixture of in-situ and precast concrete elements. The massive concrete roof tiles, a substitute for the zinc roof originally planned, aroused some adverse local comment owing to their resemblance to coffins, but this passed. Concrete was followed through as a theme, with ashtrays cast into the walls and a concrete base for the billiard table.

Thus Dunelm House and the University of Essex represent a momentary resurgence of concrete in ACP's work, a material not seen in such imaginative use by the firm since Brynmawr. More decidedly, Dunelm, with its photogenic setting and happy but not yet hippy students, showed the practice's ability to move with the mood of a younger generation while containing the contradiction between its Apollonian founding ideals and the Dionysian view of life associated with the young.

FIGURE 8.4 *Dunelm House across Kingsgate Bridge, 1965.*
RIBA Library Photographs Collection/John Donat.

The result was arguably a successful avoidance of the stiffening and ageing process usually found among architects that had been the motive for the rebellions of the 1930s, with a vindication of modernism not as a style but as a particular approach to making architecture.

Notes

1   Pendennis (Anthony Sampson), 'Table Talk, The Men at the Back of the Buildings', *Observer*, 17 September 1961, 5. Sampson was briefed for this article by the architect Brian Henderson of the firm Yorke Rosenberg Mardall (information from Brian Henderson).

2   Architects Co-Partnership went into liquidation in February 2014.

3   *ACP/Architects Co-Partnership, First Fifty Years 1939–1989*, a 44-page pamphlet, was written by Anthony Cox and privately published by ACP in 1989. See also 'Architects' Co-Partnership', *RIBA Journal* (June 1967): 229–38. Anthony Cox's personal papers are in the archives of the Royal Institute of British Architects, uncatalogued, and were consulted for the present work.

4   Introduction by Kenneth Capon in 'Architects' Co-Operative Partnership: Memorandum of a Meeting held by the A. C. P. at 4, Thurloe Street, on the 14 November 1943', 3. ACP Archives.

5   Anthony Cox, speaking at the Architectural Association in 1984 cited in 'The Brynmawr Rubber Factory', *AA Files* 10 (Autumn 1985): 3.

6   The founding partners were Kenneth Capon, Anthony Cox, Peter Cocke, Michael
     Cooke-Yarborough, Leo De Syllas, Michael Grice, Arthur Nichol, Anthony Pott,
     Michael Powers, Greville Rhodes and John Wheeler. Nichol died in a road accident and
     Wheeler was lost flying a Spitfire at high altitude after the end of the war. Pott joined
     the Ministry of Education, and Rhodes left early to start an independent practice,
     leaving a core of seven original partners in the post-war period, up to the death in a
     road accident of Leo de Syllas in 1963. The author is the son of Michael Powers.

7   Cox, *ACP*, 5.

8   See Elizabeth Darling, 'Focus: A Little Magazine and Architectural Modernism in the
     1930s Britain', *Journal of Modern Periodical Studies* 3/1 (2012): 39–63.

9   'Editorial', *Focus* 1 (Summer 1938): 1. Tim Bennett died in action in 1942.

10   The story has been outlined in a number of places, including 'The A.A. Story, 1936–
     1939' *Focus* 3 (Spring 1939): 79–111. See also Alan Powers, 'H. S. Goohart-Rendel,
     the Appropriateness of Style', *Architectural Design*, 'Britain in the Thirties' special issue
     (November 1979): 44–51.

11   J. M. Richards, 'The Condition of Architecture and the Principle of Anonymity', in J. L.
     Martin, B. Nicholson and N. Gabo, eds. *Circle: International Survey of Constructive
     Art* (London: Faber and Faber, 1937).

12   Anthony Cox, 'Highpoint II, North Hill, Highgate', *Focus* 2 (Winter 1938): 71–79.

13   See 'Town Plan, Faringdon, Berkshire' and 'Town Plan: The Unknown Town' by E. A. A.
     Rowse, in *Focus* 1 (Summer 1938): 13–23. The group (Unit 15) included Peter Cocke,
     Anthony Cox, Susan Babington-Smith, Elizabeth Chesterton, Richard Llewelyn-Davies
     Anthony Pott, and John Wheeler. See Elizabeth Darling, *Re-Forming Britain: Narratives
     of Modernity before Reconstruction* (Abingdon: Routledge, 2007), Chapter 6.

14   ACP Memorandum, 1943, 6. ACP was included in Winston Weisman, 'Group Practice',
     Architectural Review 114 (September 1953): 145–52. The article was mainly concerned
     with American practices. In Britain, Tecton and Arcon are also mentioned.

15   Gropius wrote to Leo de Syllas, 'I agree fully with Mr. Anthony Cox about "The
     Training of an Architect" and you may use my name as evidence for this. I think it is
     very wise that you don't mix politics into your paper but are heading towards your
     own aim in a technological way.' Cox papers, Box 1030.

16   It was generally believed that several ACP founders were members of the Communist
     Party of Great Britain in the 1930s. Ann McEwan (née Radford), whose first husband
     was John Wheeler, listed Wheeler, Cox, De Syllas, and Capon as members in a letter to
     Cox of 18 December 1988. Cox Papers Box 1029. She added Rhodes and Nichol as
     other possible members.

17   See Victoria Perry, *Built for a Better Future: The Brynmawr Rubber Factory* (Oxford:
     White Cockade Publishing, 1994), also Alan Powers, 'La manufacture de Brynmawr,
     1946–1951', *Le Moniteur Architecture*, 74 (October 1996): 42–48.

18   See Andrew Saint, *Towards a Social Architecture, the Role of School Buildings in Post-
     War England* (London and New Haven, Yale University Press, 1987).

19   *RIBA Journal* (June 1967): 235.

20   Ibid.

21   'Architects Co-Partnership: The Team in the Office', *Architecture and Building* 31
     (April 1956): 144–5.

22   Ibid.

23 Ibid.

24 'Opinion: Office Organisation', *Architectural Design* (May 1958): 184–5 and 210.

25 Ibid.

26 Ibid.

27 Ibid.

28 Ibid., 210.

29 See Alan Powers, *In the Line of Development, Yorke Rosenberg Mardall* (London: Heinz Gallery, 1992).

30 See Neave Brown and others, *Lyons Israel Ellis Gray: Buildings and Projects 1932– 1983* (London: Architectural Association, 2004).

31 'The New Empiricism', *Architectural Review*, 101 (1947): 199–204.

32 The generational difference ranges over a period of about twenty years between architects such as Yorke, Gibberd, Martin, and Spence (born 1908, all recognized as significant modernist figures before 1939), Lasdun, Cadbury-Brown, Esher and Casson (born in 1913–14 and authors of at least one pre-war building each), the generation of ACP, Sheppard Robson, Gollins Melvin & Ward (born 1915–18, trained pre-war but practising only post-war) and those born after 1920, including Stirling, Alison & Peter Smithson, Colin St John Wilson, Bill Howell and his partners, and others of the 'New Brutalist' group.

33 Pendennis, 'Table Talk', 5.

34 'Young Architects', *Architectural Design* (June 1958): 232.

35 James Stirling, 'A Personal View of the Present Situation', *Architectural Design* (June 1958): 233.

36 'Architects' Co-Partnership', 236.

37 See Geoffrey Tyack, *Modern Architecture in an Oxford College: St John's College 1945–2005* (Oxford: Oxford University Press, 2005).

38 Diana Rowntree, 'Stone to Stone', *Manchester Guardian*, 10 October 1960, 7.

39 Ian Nairn, 'New in Harmony with Old' unidentified cutting in ACP archives dated November 1962.

40 Ian Nairn, 'Something to sing about' *Observer*, 2 April 1967, 32.

41 Information from Richard Raines. See Alan Powers, 'Thoughtful Brutalism: Dunelm House and Kingsgate Bridge, Durham', *Twentieth Century Magazine*, May 2012, 34–7.

42 John Donat, 'Criticism', *Architectural Review* 139 (June 1966): 461.

9

Something Fierce: Brutalist Historicism at Essex University Library

Jules Lubbock

*The International Style is dying … We are going through a foggy crisis.
Let us enjoy the multiplicity of it all.[1]*

In this chapter, I shall explain how the architecture of the Albert Sloman Library at the University of Essex [Fig. 9.1] took shape in the context of the architectural revolution of the 1950s, the perceived failure of International Style modernism and, in particular, the reaction against 'graphpaper' building design and the 'geometry of crushing banality' of Corbusier's Ville Radieuse town planning, which the Smithsons stigmatized as 'a paper tablecloth pattern'.[2] Much of this is familiar territory, *The New Brutalism* and all that; I will focus upon the underlying historicism of the architecture of the period as it is exemplified in the Essex Library.

Of the 'Shakespearean Seven' new universities, Essex was one of the final four granted government approval in 1961.[3] The first Vice Chancellor, Albert Sloman, was selected by the Academic Planning Board chaired by Noel Annan, the modernizing Provost of King's College, Cambridge, in June 1962. Annan also had a large hand in choosing the architect, Kenneth Capon of Architects Co-Partnership, in late September.[4] Capon had produced a development plan for King's in 1961 with four high rise towers opposite King's Chapel, which the Fellows turned down. Just after Christmas 1962, Capon presented Sloman with a draft model of the master plan, made in his son's Lego. It was based upon Annan's blueprint for Essex, entitled The First Report of the Academic Planning Board, printed in February 1962. Sloman and Capon amended Annan's plan as the pair of them corresponded and paced the site many times in the autumn of 1962.[5] Unlike several other new universities, there was, in effect, a written brief.[6]

FIGURE 9.1   *Early photograph of the Library at the University of Essex. Architect:*
Kenneth Capon, Architects Co-Partnership.
Photographer unknown, University of Essex Special Collections, Albert Sloman Library.

Sloman and Annan had three key academic ideas, and one major idea about the
social arrangements: bigness and academic ambition. They were talking of 6,000,
10,000, and ultimately 20,000 students while other new universities envisaged a
maximum of 3,000 students, then the average size of British provincial universities.
Their reasoning was that science departments must be big because of the expense of
equipment and the need for large research teams to produce research of international
standard. In order to prevent the university becoming unbalanced, humanities and
social science departments also had to be big.[7]

There would be a small number of big subject-based departments. Essex would
concentrate upon the physical sciences and their technological applications,

particularly to computers and communications. In the humanities, the focus would be upon the modern world and upon academically unexplored areas such as Latin America and the Soviet Union rather than upon the European postclassical tradition. Sloman's view was that the Social Sciences would form a bridge between these so-called Two Cultures of C. P. Snow's controversial pamphlet.[8] Applied Mathematics would also be a bridge between the physical and the social sciences. But Annan himself had 'eliminated' the humanities almost entirely. His conception was of Essex as a British MIT, an idea which has been mooted since the end of the war but which had run into the sand as a result of the conservatism of British university scientists and of the UGC. There was a strong emphasis upon the employability of its graduates and upon Harold Wilson's 'white heat of the technological revolution'. Essex was to be very modern and technocratic.[9] For several years there was only one humanities department, Literature.

Sloman's premise was that human knowledge was a unity, Wissenschaft, within which subjects and departments were artificial boundaries. The development of knowledge takes place at the boundaries between subjects, so that while subject-focused departments were retained, they would be grouped in overlapping schools of study to encourage cross-fertilization both in research and in teaching. First-year students in each school would take a Common First Year and would not specialize until their second year, in order to counteract the 'premature specialization' enforced by the English secondary school system.[10]

Student freedom was the big social idea. There would be no paternalistic Oxbridge-style colleges or Redbrick halls of residence, no Student Union, no Senior Common Room, no Moral Tutors, no Proctors. Students were adults and must be given the freedom to behave responsibly. They would be housed in communal flats in fourteen-storey towers. The Library was seen as a means of self-education.[11]

The master plan and the architecture arose from Capon's interpretation of how to accommodate these ideas and give them visual expression in the physical context of Wivenhoe Park, a picturesque park of 200 acres outside Colchester, painted by John Constable in 1816. Teaching and administration are accommodated at high density in compact courtyards somewhat sunk in the valley in order to keep the parkland free. These are arranged along a spine of five ascending pedestrian squares forming the high street with high-rise towers placed between teaching buildings [Fig. 9.2]. Far from a style of tablecloth patterns or graphpaper, the window mullions of the teaching buildings are arranged in an irregular non-repeating pattern, the squares are not precisely rectilinear, the site slopes, the spine is not straight but gently curved to follow the line of the valley and continue the pattern of the three lakes, and the towers which were originally to have been cylindrical.[12]

This constituted the fabric of the university, intended 'to create something analogous to the repose and absence of straining after incident' of the Georgian square. But some monuments were also intended which, in Capon's words, could be 'individual and nonconformist ... if they can be jewels, so much the better'. The first three of these were the Library, the Hexagon Restaurant and the Lecture Theatre Block, the latter designed by Jim Cadbury Brown.[13]

Thus we have a densely built and densely populated unzoned, small-scale skyscraper city that could be walked across in ten minutes, intended to provide something of the cohesive community and urbanity of Georgian London or of an

Italian hill city and, like them, surrounded by nature. But the materials—concrete, glass, and dark grey engineering brick—were modern, uncompromisingly so, and defiantly un-English, at first sight anyway. In Capon's words, the English 'love making things shaggy and softening everything up' ... we decided 'to do something fierce to let them work within'. And yet, as my description has indicated, Capon's rhetoric of the tough modernist architect is belied by a range of allusions both to the architecture of the past as well as to nature, which will become clearer when we examine the Library in more detail.[14]

But before doing so we need to summarize how Essex relates to the cutting-edge architectural and planning developments of the time.[15] First, it is obviously part of that reaction against the 'banality' of universal International Style curtain wall building which resulted in offices, schools, homes and hospitals that looked indistinguishable. Architects Co-Partnership had been schooled in this kind of thing at the pre-war Architectural Association and had produced a lot of it themselves.[16] But at Essex they displayed their engagement with Team X, late Corbusier, La Tourette in particular, Japanese architecture by Kenzo Tange and others, and, perhaps most important, Louis Kahn, whose Richards Research Laboratories at the University of Pennsylvania were completed and published in early 1962. To express the power of Sloman's ambitions, Capon developed a sculptural architecture, which I have dubbed the 'counter-modernist sublime'.[17]

In layout or planning, Capon was one of those who abhorred the 'scatter' of private suburbs and public New Towns and preferred 'cluster' exemplified in the work of Sir Leslie Martin, Professor of Architecture at Cambridge, who had drawn up the shortlist of architects for Essex—high-density, low-rise perimeter planning [Fig. 9.2].[18]

Finally, and of lasting importance, the emphasis upon creating a physical community through traditional European planning types—streets, squares, mixed uses—relates Essex not only to Team X but also to Jane Jacobs, whose *Death and Life of Great American Cities* appeared in 1961 and whose ideas, first published in *Fortune Magazine*'s series, the Exploding Metropolis in 1957, were widely disseminated in English architectural journals. Ian Nairn and Gordon Cullen, who had been responsible for the *Architectural Review*'s Outrage series, contributed a section of words and images.[19]

The Library of the University of Essex is the most prominent free-standing building on campus, situated by the new lake on the edge between parkland and buildings, the first building one saw entering from the main car park [Fig. 9.1]. A press release of autumn 1963, drafted by Capon, explains his reasons for placing it in this position. 'Architecturally, its position is as significant as that of Magdalen Tower in the curving High Street of Oxford. The large central Library of the University of Essex symbolizes what the University stands for—the conservation and discovery of knowledge, the importance of self-education, and the inter-relationship of subjects. The location of the Library is characteristic of a Development Plan which is both imaginative and practical.'[20] Within a complex that carries visual allusions to castles, to fortified mediaeval towns, to late mediaeval palaces and colleges, the Library takes the place of Hall, Chapel and College Library rolled into one, particularly since Essex, unlike Sussex, had no religious meeting place. Sloman asserted that 'a library is the university's heart'.[21] There are, to my eyes, clear references to Wren's Library at Trinity Cambridge—Capon himself had worked in Cambridge from 1959

FIGURE 9.2 *University of Essex, looking up from Square 2, through Squares 3 and 4, framing Wivenhoe Park and House. Architect: Kenneth Capon, Architects Co-Partnership, c.1966.*
Photographer unknown, University of Essex Special Collections, Albert Sloman Library.

to 1962[22]—particularly in its location by water and parkland and in its dominance over both built and natural surroundings.

Above all, it is a Temple of Scholarship whose design, while making no *literal* references to classical temple architecture, nonetheless, in its unadorned post and lintel construction with protruding beams, seems to allude to the theory that Doric temples owe their form to the fact that they were originally constructed in wood. This impression is strengthened by the massive concrete piers supporting the coupled cantilevered beams which carry the four main storeys of book stacks and reading space. These piers with their chipped concrete fluting are Doric in spirit and relate to Sir Owen Williams's heroic and very unusual bridges over the M1, opened in 1959, which are more literally Doric. Another significant source is Japan. An *Architectural Review* article in June 1962 entitled 'Eastern Doric' refers to 'an almost Doric exuberance' in a factory by Ichira Ebihara.[23] Essex's twinned cantilevered beams could well derive from Kenzo Tange's Prefectural Office at Kagawa of 1959.[24]

The Library was also described in the press as a 'book palace'.[25] While the exterior is not directly imitative of renaissance palazzo architecture, it does adhere to classical principles of composition: the giant rectangular box is articulated into parts with a rusticated base and the floor plates of the upper storeys are expressed as cornices with the repeated projecting beam-ends [Fig. 9.1].

Finally, when one entered, one was channelled into the book stacks and reading desks through something of an architectural gem, the jewel in the crown both of the Library and of the campus as a whole: a ceremonial entrance staircase divided into three sections. First, there is a ground floor corridor leading one to a second feature, a hexagonal 'spiral' staircase enclosed in a top lit hexagonal pavilion, which leads

FIGURE 9.3 *'The Cloisters', University of Essex Library, corridor leading to hexagonal staircase. Architect: Kenneth Capon, Architects Co-Partnership, 1966. Demolished, June 2012.* University of Essex Special Collections, Albert Sloman Library.

up to the third element, the circulation desk, through which one originally entered the Library [Fig. 9.4].[26]

Perhaps more than any other element of a building, a staircase enables an architect to control the user's aesthetic experience. One enters the ground floor passageway, which is a double cube. It is lit on both sides by eight narrow floor-to-ceiling windows separated by finely detailed mullions twice the width of the windows. This creates a penumbra while also providing one, on one's journey, with glimpses of the park and of the main library building. The stripes of light and shade both in the windows and in the patterns they throw upon floor and ceiling are also suggestive of steps and thereby prepare the visitor for the staircase itself. Apart from a small hexagonal window in the lantern, the stairwell is windowless so that one finally leaves the outside world behind at the same time as being drawn into a small chapel-like enclosure, austere in character, almost Romanesque.[27]

The acts of walking and climbing, and one's movement from the semi-enclosure of the corridor to the absence of external views in the stairwell to the top lit but

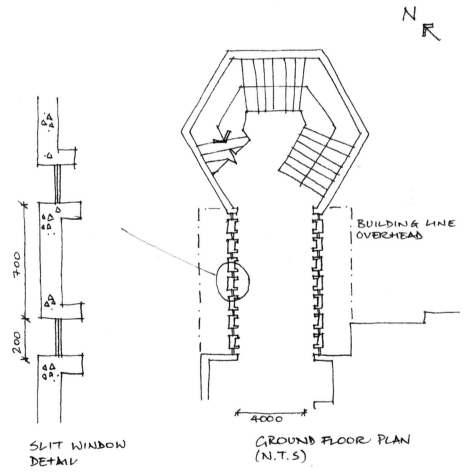

SLIT WINDOW
DETAIL

GROUND FLOOR PLAN
(N.T.S)

FIGURE 9.4 'The Cloisters', University of Essex Library. Architect: Kenneth Capon, Architects Co-Partnership, 1966. Ground plan drawn by Cliona O'Dunlaing.

otherwise windowless issue desk, all serve to imbue the reader with the sense that one is leaving the world of sensory experience and entering a domain of thought and reflection, Sloman's haven for self-education. Indeed Capon explained to the first librarian that his intention had been 'to create a cloistral feeling that would put the reader in the right emotional frame of mind' for entering the Library. The librarians have always called it The Cloisters.[28]

I suggest that Capon's words indicate that he had at the back of his mind the almost free-standing octagonal chapter houses in English gothic abbeys and cathedrals which often lead off the cloister. The chapter house of Westminster Abbey is a good example, being connected to the cloister by a broad, dark and windowless corridor so that one leaves the penumbra of the cloister, passes into the dark, vaulted corridor, up a short flight of steps into the light and splendour of the chapter house.

But in fact it seems that Capon's original concept for the Library was for a central spiral ramp, probably derived from Frank Lloyd Wright's Guggenheim Museum of 1959 and maybe from Wren's Dean's Stair at St Paul's Cathedral, the only previous monumental spiral staircase entrance to a library, a feature which has become ubiquitous since the mid-1960s. This idea was dropped when the founding librarian demonstrated to Capon the physical strain of pushing a loaded book trolley up such a ramp.[29]

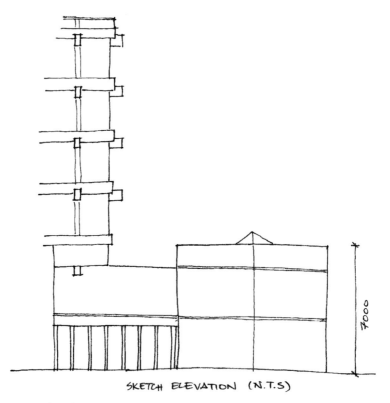

SKETCH ELEVATION (N.T.S)

FIGURE 9.5 *'The Cloisters', University of Essex Library. Architect: Kenneth Capon, Architects Co-Partnership, 1966. Elevation drawn by Cliona O'Dunlaing.*

To conclude: the Albert Sloman Library at Essex, and indeed the campus as a whole, shows how the most original Brutalist Architects were drawing upon traditional sources, both classical and gothic, Eastern and Western, to enrich emotional experience and meaning, which were, in the Smithson's opinion, the most important aspects of architecture and town planning [Fig 9.3].[30]

In June 2012, The Cloisters were demolished to accommodate an extension to the Library after a battle to list the Albert Sloman Library was fought and lost. English Heritage recommended listing the building; however, the Minister of State at the Department for Culture, Media and Sport rejected their advice [Fig 9.6].

FIGURE 9.6 *The Cloisters, University of Essex Library being demolished on 22 June 2012. Architect: Kenneth Capon, Architects Co-Partnership, 1966.*
© Jules Lubbock

Papers:

ASL: University of Essex, Special Collections, Albert Sloman Library

FP ASL: Foundation Papers, University of Essex, Special Collections, Albert Sloman Library

Notes

1   Philip Johnson, 'Where Are We At?', *The Architectural Review*, 127 (1960): 175.

2   'A new generation of architecture must arise—with forms and spaces which seem to reject the precepts of 'Modern' REJECT—curtains—design—history—graphpaper...', *Archigram*, 1961, PAPER ONE—A STATEMENT. For a reproduction of the page see Simon Sadler, 'The Brutal Birth of Archigram', in *The Sixties—Life: Style: Architecture*, eds. Elain Harwood and Alan Powers (London: The Twentieth Century Society, 2002), 120. Alison and Peter Smithson, 'Cluster City: A New Shape for the Community', *The Architectural Review*, 122 (1957): 333–6: '... the plan [of the Ville Radieuse] moves us as little as the pattern on the table cloth at the Vieux Paris...' (on 334). 'The Cluster—close knit, complicated, often moving aggregation' (on 334) was the Smithsons' name for the new, more complex, less geometric ideal. Note the importance the Smithsons place upon emotional experience in town planning and architecture; see page 135 and note 31 below.

3   Stefan Muthesius, *The Post War University: Utopian Campus and College* (New Haven & London: Yale University Press, 2000), 95. The final four were Essex, Kent, Warwick and Lancaster. Sussex was first, in 1958, followed by York and East Anglia in 1960.

4   For Sloman's appointment, see the Minutes of the Academic Planning Board and interview of Albert Sloman by Jules Lubbock et al. February 21st, 1996, FP Box 1(b), ASL. Sloman was interviewed by the APB on January 3rd, 1962 and again on May 18th when he was shortlisted with Richard Hoggart. For Capon's appointment see the 1996 Interview with Sloman, mss. cit.

5   Mss. cit.: '... after dinner Kenneth showed us the model he had made in his son's Lego.' For a photograph of a Lego model see *The Architectural Review*, 134 (1963): 309. This is the model Capon showed the Slomans in 1962. Interview with Lady Sloman, 2013.

6   Muthesius, *The Post War University*, 114 and 142. For Sussex, the Vice Chancellor gave Basil Spence 'a clear idea of the university he wanted to see' and that was all. The Vice Chancellor of East Anglia observed in a 1996 interview with Muthesius, 'Not a college, not a campus, but an Italian hill town, that was Lasdun's brief. Lasdun had no brief.'

7   The Academic Planning Board, established in September 1961, printed its *First Report* in February 1962 halfway through the process of selecting a Vice Chancellor. See University of Essex, *First Report of the Academic Planning Board* (no place, February, 1962), FP Box 1, ASL. Sloman's Reith Lectures, Albert E. Sloman, *A University in the Making* (London: BBC, 1964), were delivered in late autumn 1963. On page 18 Sloman acknowledges that it would be hard to over-emphasize the influence of the Academic Planning Board in establishing 'on the personal initiative of the chairman... the image of a forward-looking university'. For size, see *First Report*, 14, section 35 and Sloman, *A University in the Making*, 9–10 and 24–29. On page 9 he gives the current sizes of British universities. The first page is devoted to the necessity of 'bigness'.

8   C. P. Snow delivered his Rede Lectures at Cambridge in May, 1959. C. P. Snow, *The Two Cultures and the Scientific Revolution* (Cambridge: Cambridge University Press, 1959). F. R. Leavis's rejoinder was delivered as the Richmond Lecture at Downing College in February 1962, F. R. Leavis, *Two Cultures? The Significance of C.P. Snow* (London: Chatto & Windus, 1962). Annan and Sloman wanted to heal the perceived rift.

9   *First Report*, 4 section 9, 10, 6 section 14 and 15, 8 section 20, and 9 section 22 and 23; Sloman, *A University in the Making*, 29–35. Harold Wilson delivered the speech from which that quotation comes on 1 October 1963, around the time of the Reith Lectures. His actual words were: 'We are redefining and we are restating our socialism in terms of the scientific revolution … The Britain that is going to be forged in the white heat of this revolution will be no place for restrictive practices or outdated methods on either side of industry.' http://quotes.dictionary.com/the_white_heat_of_the_technological_revolution#0we8GMfq3bxJrVlB.99, accessed 20 June 2013.

10 *First Report*, 5, section 13, 7 section 18, 8 section 21 mentions a 'common first year course for all students in social studies'. Sloman, *A University in the Making*, 27–28 and 38–41.

11 Sloman, *A University in the Making*, 50–63. He deliberately placed the section on the Library in the lecture about student life rather than in that on formal teaching because he conceived of the library in terms of the student's self-education.

12 Jules Lubbock, 'The Counter-Modernist Sublime: The Campus of the University of Essex', in *The Sixties*, 105–18. Author's interview with James Sutherland of Sutherland & Harris, civil and structural engineers on the first phase, May 22, 2007, FP Box 3(d), ASL. For the original circular towers, see that interview and R. J. M. Sutherland, 'Looking Back on the Essex University Towers', *Masonry International, Journal of the British Masonry Society*, 10 (1996): 36.

13 'Architects' Co-Partnership', *RIBA Journal*, 3rd Ser., 74 (1967): 238. This is based upon a talk at the RIBA given by three of the partners in January. No author is given. I assume that Capon spoke and wrote about Essex. The construction of the first square and the first teaching block began around May 1964 and they were completed in May 1966. The first tower, Rayleigh, was completed in November 1965, the Hexagon Restaurant in August 1966. The Library was completed in September 1966. The Lecture Theatre Block was completed in November 1967. Information based upon dated photographs taken for Sutherland & Harris, ASL.

14 'Something fierce' is quoted in Muthesius, *The Post War University*, 158, who is quoting from John Maule McKean, 'University of Essex: Case Study', *The Architects' Journal*, 156 (1972): 656, based upon his interview with Kenneth Capon on 26 April 1971.

15 Richard Rogers, in a conversation at the opening of the Victoria and Albert Museum's British Design exhibition in March 2012, enthused about Essex, which was being completed when he was just beginning practise.

16 'Schools by the Architects' Co-Partnership', *The Architectural Review*, 118 (1955): 355–61.

17 Lubbock, 'The Counter-Modernist Sublime', 105–18. I coined the phrase to emphasize two things, first that the buildings were, in a Burkean sense, sublime rather than beautiful, and second that they were not anti-modernist so much as a reasoned response to modernism.

18 For 'scatter' see Lionel Brett, 'Universities: Today', *The Architectural Review* 122 (1957): 240–51. On page 242, he speaks of 'the post-war loose scatter of [university] buildings in parkland'. His remedy—'compactness is all', even if that involves twenty-

storey towers for student housing with twelve rooms per floor, which was Capon's solution both for Essex and earlier for the 1959 Churchill College competition at Cambridge as well as for King's College Cambridge around 1960. See also A. & P. Smithson, 'Scatter', *Architectural Design* 29 (1959): 149–50. For their views on 'cluster' see note 2 above. Leslie Martin's courtyard residential building, Harvey Court for Gonville and Caius College, Cambridge, was published in *Architectural Design* 32 (1962): 522–9. Martin's theory of perimeter planning was expounded in *Urban Space and Structures* (London: Cambridge University Press, 1972) edited by Leslie Martin and Lionel March. For a clear explanation of the principle, see Lionel March, 'Mathematics and Architecture since 1960'" http://iisca.files.wordpress.com/2011/05/nexus-iv-march_pp9-35.pdf, accessed 20 June 2013. March claims that they developed these ideas when working on the Whitehall reconstruction plans in 1965, Leslie Martin, *Whitehall: A Plan for the National and Government Centre* (London: HMSO, 1965), but Harvey Court already embodies the concept. See also Patrick Dunleavy, *The Politics of Mass Housing in Britain, 1945–1975* (Oxford: Oxford University Press, 1981), 135–7. At the February 1955 RIBA 'Symposium on High Flats' all the architects supported high-rise flats apart from Martin, who said, presciently, that the problems had not been properly studied. This may have been the point at which he began thinking about perimeter planning as a means of achieving high density without high buildings. See too, *High Flats: Report of a Symposium Held on 15 February 1955 by the Royal Institute of British Architects* (London: RIBA, 1955).

19 Jane Jacobs, 'Downtown is for People', republished in *The Exploding Metropolis*, ed. the Editors of Fortune (Garden City: Doubleday Anchor Books, 1958), 140–68; Ian Nairn and Gordon Cullen, 'The Scale of the City', in *The Exploding Metropolis*, between 138 and 139.

20 'Basic Principles of the University of Essex Development Plan by A. Rowland-Jones, Registrar.' Undated five-page cyclostyled typed document which can be dated to the autumn of 1963 at the same time as the broadcasts of Sloman's Reith Lectures and the mounting of a travelling exhibition of the Development Plan in Colchester, Wivenhoe House, Chelmsford, Southend, and other Essex towns. My grounds for believing that this description was written up from a text supplied by Capon himself is that the text referred to in note 26 below, signed by Capon, was quoted verbatim in a press release issued by the registrar. It seems reasonable that the university authorities would ask Capon to supply such descriptions for the architectural aspects of the promotional material they were issuing in the early years.

21 Sloman, *A University in the Making*, 61.

22 See note 18.

23 'Eastern Doric', *The Architectural Review* 132 (1962): 378.

24 *Architectural Design*, 29 (1959): 211; *Essex County Standard*, University Supplement, 'The Start of the Second Year', 15 October 1965, vi—The Library 'is quite a departure in style from the other buildings in that it will use structural concrete beams in a visually arresting way. It is slightly reminiscent of the Japanese style of timber-frame building where the prominent beams cause deep, shadowed patterns on the face of the finished structure.' This too was probably written by Capon.

25 *Essex County Standard*, Magazine Section, University Special, 13 October 1967, III 'The Making of a Powerhouse', where the £5 million library is described as a 'book palace'.

26 'The connection between the first floor and those above will be mainly by non-stop lift…The access to the first floor, however, is by a wide hexagonal stair only. This

stair has been designed to serve the Library in the future when it is greatly expanded.'
University of Essex Library, cyclostyled typed document signed Kenneth C, black
photograph album amongst FP ASL.

27   Church with béton brut shuttered walls by Carl Nyrén in Vällingby, Sweden, illustrated
in *The Architectural Review* 121 (1957): 404: 'Nyrén couples the concrete's blunt,
almost Early-Christian simplicity, with a chancel-form and lighting that gives the feeling
of a cave or catacomb.'

28   Information supplied orally in 2013 by Jane Long, widow of the founding Librarian,
Philip Long, and other long-serving members of the library staff.

29   Sir Albert Sloman told me the story about the book trolley, but not in the 1996
interview.

30   See note 2; Alison and Peter Smithson, 'The Function of Architecture in Cultures-in-
change', *Architectural Design*, 30 (1960): 149: 'Architecture is concerned with finding
the patterns of buildings and communications which make the community function
and, at the same time, give it meaning.' Peter Smithson, 'Lament for Stockholm',
Architectural Design, 32 (1962): 169: In this rather bad prose poem, Smithson
complains that however well contemporary Stockholm might function, 'the buildings
are mute' in comparison to old Stockholm 'which is "really one big building"'.

10

Hidden Internationalisms: Tradition and Modernism in Post-war Primary School Design, 1948–72

Catherine Burke

Introduction

This chapter will demonstrate the international context for innovations in primary school design during the middle decades of the twentieth century when England was recognized as pioneering in this respect. The architects Mary Crowley (1907–2005) and David Medd (1917–2009), who worked for Hertfordshire County Council Architects' Department just after the war and from 1949 for the Ministry of Education, devoted their professional lives in pursuit of a form of education for children and young people that would be best described as progressive in its values, principles, practices and essential humanity [Fig. 10.1]. They travelled widely: Mary Crowley to Scandinavia, The Netherlands, and Germany during the 1930s and together to the United States, Sweden and Denmark in the 1950s. Attention to these journeys reveals transnational and trans-Atlantic connections and influences that have until recently remained hidden in the story of post-war educational renewal. While the Scandinavian influences have been recognized in commentaries on their school designs, the impact of mid-twentieth-century developments in thinking and practice regarding the relationship between education and architecture in the United States has been less well accounted for. This chapter will therefore dwell on the latter to attempt to tell the story of transnational dialogue and exchange during the post-war period of architectural reconstruction and political realignments.

FIGURE 10.1 *Mary and David Medd meeting with a group of architects to discuss a school plan, Milan, 1975.*
Newsam Library and Archives, Institute of Education, University of London.

Mary Crowley and David Medd were by all accounts pivotal figures among a generation of young architects dedicated to meeting the demographic challenges of post-war reconstruction and renewal through public rather than private practice. Through development, research and practice, they became involved with the fundamental and pressing contemporary design question of how to live well in the modern world. For Mary Crowley, finding design solutions to support modern education was an essential part of the answer. When she eventually began working solely on the design of school environments, she expressed her conviction that education and pedagogy had to be the starting point. The building must be regarded as a vehicle for education and never for architectural showmanship. For David, who by his own admission learned all that he knew about education from Mary, the coupling of education and architecture was a life-long project. He once suggested that the work of architects building schools might become easier were someone to invent a word in the vocabulary uniting the two disciplines. This overriding principle of the indivisibility of education and architecture in school planning characterized the Medds' approach and drew them towards fellow-minded individuals at home and abroad.

During the period of their greatest influence, from the 1940s to the 1970s, through formal and informal international exchanges, close observation, planning, building and writing, the Medds, as they became known, came to be recognized as the centre point of a philosophy of practice shared by an influential group of educationalists and architects in the United Kingdom. To the extent that they are remembered by the architectural and educational professions, the focus has understandably been on their considerable achievements at home. Yet their many extensive international trips took them to visit schools designed by leading modernist architects as well as to establishments constructed by pupils and teachers as part of a radical curriculum.[1] In turn, their schools were visited and studied and the findings disseminated by visitors from across the UK and beyond its shores. This knowledge exchange and engagement around what the modern school should be in the post-war world is an important and often neglected aspect of school design histories.

In 1958–59, the Medds spent the entire year in the United States visiting schools, meeting architects and spending time enjoying the vast country. By this time, they were well known as architects responsible for a new approach to school design in the UK. They had already achieved a great deal through various projects for Hertfordshire County Council and the Ministry of Education—the latter via the Development Group of the Architect and Buildings Branch (A&BB). In the context of their whole career together, one can see the late 1950s as pivotal in that they were at a position of strength, national influence, and some international notoriety but they were yet to proceed to work on some of their most significant school buildings.[2]

In 1958, David Medd was awarded a Harkness Fellowship by the Commonwealth Fund, usually requiring the holder to spend up to one year at an academic institution in the United States. David accepted the fellowship but, seeing an opportunity for Mary and he to extend their knowledge of developments in post-war school renewal, requested that the Ministry of Education allow Mary to accompany him. They travelled by car—Mary drove—roughly clockwise, a 36,000-mile journey, starting from Cambridge Massachusetts, having arrived by ship in New York.[3] Commencing their journey, fresh in their minds were the house they had constructed for themselves at Harmer Green, Welwyn (1954), the now operational Woodside primary school at Amersham (1956), and plans for a new school at Finmere, Oxfordshire. They arrived in America, therefore, after almost a decade of work with the ministry, at a moment of confident authority in knowing what was possible and what was necessary when designing for education. They were hoping to see the most modern developments that united education with architecture. In their terms, this meant that architects would be working closely with teachers who were able to recognize how far institutionalized education had impoverished learning and teaching and who could improvise with their environments. To this extent, teachers were indicating to designers how school buildings might be planned to support their educational aims. 'In seeking the growing points of education ... we found ourselves in the mountains, in the deserts, in the forests, on the plains, in the swamps, in the cities, suburbs and villages, in the pueblos and hogans, among Indian-speaking and Spanish-speaking communities and in fact in the extremes of material wealth and poverty.'[4]

The 1950s was a period of rapid development in educational planning and school building across the United States. The Medds arrived at a significant moment, in the midst of the panic generated by Russia's successful launch of Sputnik.[5] The response was the National Defence Education Act of September 1958, which significantly increased funding for Public schooling.[6] The Medds wrote publicly about the impact of the NDE Act while in the United States, which they saw as compromising the post-war aims of strengthening democracy through enabling education to flourish in an atmosphere of freedom. They talked about the fear and trepidation expressed in the legislation and warned 'that to outsiders it seems that as state and national resources are inevitably and increasingly used for education, so must the opposing forces of freedom and control be resolved'.[7]

The 1950s saw some of the most significant architects from continental Europe developing a presence in the United States through some iconic buildings, including schools. There was also a profound recognition that education would be inevitably changed by developments in technology while talk of 'schools for the future', 'learning laboratories', and 'the disappearance of the classroom' inflected the debate about the form that schooling should take. For some, including the National Educational Association of the United States, improving education was a direct means of meeting the challenge of the nation's military and economic competitors and represented 'defence potential' in the struggle for 'world leadership', a principle the Medds would have understood but would have regarded as a renegade step for the interests of children and young people.[8]

Between socializing and sightseeing, they were subjected to numerous talks and tours of 'uninspiring' public schools. Visiting altogether 200 schools and colleges in forty states, including nineteen from the progressive independent sector, David filled some forty notebooks, Mary generally made sketch plans of classroom interiors, and they both wrote home regularly to colleagues and to family and friends, offering us a glimpse of their experiences during this significant year. Rarely did the school superintendents that they met enquire about the English educational system, so eager were they to explain and describe their own school sites and systems.

The large number of schools visited included nurseries, elementary schools, high schools, schools for 'Negroes', colleges and progressive experiments, the latter providing the closest examples of what they were seeking as 'growing points of education'. Usually they were in the hands of district authorities who wanted to show off what they considered their best achievements, such as the integration of television labs in schools and colleges. Early on, they recorded difficulty in 'finding a technique for making such visits profitable' and were occasionally obstructed by press photographers.[9] Soon, they expressed their disappointment in what they did see and hear and were appalled by what they viewed as 'the general direction away from real things, everywhere', finding most of the high schools 'pretty tedious'. The relationship between architecture and education had produced 'some pretty dreary high schools with photogenic extensions and dismal education'.[10] David acknowledged in a letter home to his father, 'there is much evidence of concern and interesting experiments in school design to meet changing teaching methods, but we have yet to see actual activity in schools which matches the latter, some of which is very glib.'[11] Mary's analysis was that this was 'mostly the fault of a constipated curriculum which is monotonously uniform in spite of lack of central control'.[12] In a letter to Anthony Part, by then under-secretary and head of the Schools Branch at the Ministry of Education, David indicated the need to 'widen our field of enquiry', as limiting the survey to public schools was inhibiting access to the 'growing points' in education, more likely to be seen in the newly founded progressive or experimental private schools.[13] In general, they were 'finding education to be more interesting and more important than architecture—school architecture, anyway'.[14]

However, they were occasionally able to see, in passing, more than was intended by their hosts. Although there was much talk about democracy, 'one wonders whether much of it is a form of selfishness. Personal gain and comfort is implicit in every advertisement and even the verses we have heard recited in an elementary school.'[15] Mary lamented, there were 'vast amounts of money for huge gymnasiums in schools but not enough for 'frills' such as a few trees'.[16] Arriving just as Mies van der Rohe's Seagram Building was opening in New York, they discovered a nation in the midst of great changes, brimming with resources and rich opportunities yet shackled by fears generated by racism and McCarthyism.

Their informal itinerary often took them to schools in the independent sector, some experimental schools that the Medds found to be refreshingly radical and offering a lively alternative to the institutional, conservative and safe environments they were constantly shown. While travelling through Colorado, they visited the Rocky Mountain School, founded in 1953 by John and Anne Holden, originally teachers at the Putney School in Vermont.[17] John Holden, like the Medds, would have preferred progressive practices to be incorporated into public schooling. 'Why not an eight hour day for public schools so that pastoral work could be included?'[18] They discovered at Rocky Mountain, in relative wilderness, a fascinating project where the pupils were constructing their own buildings and where there was a great emphasis on simplicity and respecting nature.[19] The Holdens introduced the Medds to the work of Ed Yeomans, whose book, *Shackled Youth*, they read aloud to each other as they travelled. Yeomans had founded an independent progressive school in Ojai, California, in 1911, based on the principles of experiential learning and understanding of nature.[20] Like many of his generation and social class, Yeomans had found his own education dull and stifling and wanted to establish a school that would emphasize experiential learning and a love for the outdoors. He envisioned a place where music, art, and construction would be equally valued alongside more traditional subjects. Such a school was what the Medds thought should be possible to design given the interest in the UK among educational leaders such as Alec Clegg for such a balanced curriculum.

Yeomans' son, Ed Yeomans (Junior), was at the time principal of Shady Hill School in Cambridge, Massachusetts, which the Medds visited early in their journey.[21] The school for 490 pupils, grades 1–9, had been founded by a group of parents in 1915 and, in modifying some of its principles, had, according to David, become more generally acceptable without loss of some of the values its founders had stood for. Shady Hill was the rare kind of school that Mary and David were looking for. Here was 'an excellent example of a building or buildings following the dictates of an attitude towards education'.[22] In the buildings erected in 1920, they found the appropriate understanding of 'variety' they were searching for. Each grade group had a building distinctively different from the next, being planned for the specific age group, and they discussed the absence of corridors, a feature mentioned by Yeomans. 'First of all, it was decided that the architectural character should be modest and unimposing. Simple materials were chosen and interiors were not to be final and polished architectural compositions. They were to be backgrounds for the school's activities.'[23]

As they travelled from state to state, the Medds met with architects responsible for some of the most noted innovative school plans of the decade. The most popularly admired American schools included Hillsdale High School, San Mateo,

California, with an innovative and flexible loft plan 'prophetic of things to come'.[24] But the Medds found the landscape of California more attractive than the schools as they travelled 'from wonder to despair', and Hillsdale left David with a clear argument to make against an American tendency towards uniformity of character offering an unsatisfactory 'flexibility of the wrong kind—mechanical rather than...'built-in' flexibility, which is better translated as variety'.[25] This provoked an exasperated call to arms: 'How about a school run by educators or teachers and not by administrators? How about libraries run by teachers and not by librarians? How about the great outdoors instead of gyms? How about abandoning text books? How about teaching about the sources of Western Civilization rather than its white projection in the States of Colorado or California? How about accepting the fact that the High School has created Americans who practice loyalty to higher authority? How about the High Schools learning from the better elementary schools... if each person is to go at the optimum pace, groups will be various in size and the standard classroom disappears? How about running a high school on the basis of trust and self sufficiency rather than suspicion and imposed discipline? Are not these the sort of questions upon which the architectural solutions follow? Otherwise, the cart is before the horse and the result—a Californian school.'[26]

By the spring of 1959, Mary was able to reflect on an emergent summary of knowledge gained from their survey, having witnessed the best and the worst of the range of possibilities in American schooling. In a letter to Pat Tindale, carrying out the Finmere project at home, she wrote: 'I suppose we've been inside 80–85 schools by now of one kind and another ranging from a 75' long monstrosity entirely encased in concrete fretwork, with central corridor, in New Orleans and another ditto in Hobbs Texas with no windows at all, to Caudill schools in Andrews (also Texas) which set standards of achievement altogether for us both in the education and design of schools.'[27] William W. Caudill (1914–83) was to directly influence the design of one of the Medds' better known primary school projects—Eveline Lowe School at Southwark in London as we shall see. But first, it is important to pause with the Medds as they visited the public elementary school building considered to be most noteworthy and influential in the United States at this time—Crow Island School, Winnetka, north of Chicago [Fig. 10.2]. The school was designed by two architectural design teams: Eliel and Eero Saarinen, who were based at the Cranbrook Foundation, with the young Chicago firm of Perkins, Wheeler and Will. Completed in September 1940, Crow Island was the architectural and pedagogical projection of a philosophy of education espoused by Carlton Washburne, superintendent of education for Winnetka and a man known to Mary's father, Ralph Henry Crowley, who as medical officer for health at the London School Board travelled widely and regularly in the United States during the inter-war years. Crow Island was the result of bringing together some of the most progressive educational ideas of the time clearly articulated with modern architectural interpretations of school. Like Mary, Washburne had become a Quaker and like the Medds believed that transformation of educational experience could be brought about through the serious recognition of the power of the built environment to inform pedagogy. The Medds had the pleasure of meeting Washburne on their journey through the United States and they visited Crow Island, where they saw in practice what they had known about through Washburne's publications and through reviews in the architectural press.

FIGURE 10.2 *Crow Island School,* Winnetka.
© Cranbrook Archives, 5657–8. Richard G. Askew, photographer

Washburne's philosophical orientation towards the interests of the individual child guided not only his support for individualized instruction but also his belief that children's native curiosity should be harnessed through first hand experience. He accordingly promoted the use of art, music, discussion, play, field trips, and various

kinds of group work as a means of engaging children's creativity while drawing
them into learning about the world outside of school. Crow Island was carefully
planned, after a year of close observation of elementary school practice, as a school
that signalled a new understanding of how to meet the child's developmental needs.
The building gained international fame through richly illustrated articles published
in the architectural press as well as through the inclusion of large photographs in an
exhibition 'The New Architecture in the United States' prepared by the Museum of
Modern Art in New York.[28]

The design process carried out at Crow Island was followed almost exactly by Mary
Crowley and David Medd in later decades. Their attention to scale in the provision
of fittings within the reach of small children and their concern with the quality and
design of furniture and fittings is very similar to what they found at Crow Island. We
know that they met with Larry Perkins during their year long stay in the United States
and they may have talked over the value of close observation, designing for comfort
and function, and working with miniature furniture in encouraging teachers to think
spatially. They found at Crow Island a building and equipment scaled to the pupils'
physical requirements; detailed attention to display and working surfaces; practical
work areas in classrooms; domestic lavatories for each class; modern standards of
heating, lighting and ventilation; and outdoor teaching facilities. Finmere village
school, completed shortly after the Medds' return to England, achieved a similar
spirit and was furnished similarly with a dedicated space for resting (including a
built-in bed) and contemplation (with a built-in fireplace).

The intricacies of design at Crow Island were based on a progressive
understanding of education that was in stark contrast with other schools that the
Medds saw in the United States where: 'The relatively empty and formal scene
encountered in some classrooms, compared with the wide range of activity and
richness and the paraphernalia in others suggests that space and small numbers—
both admirable in themselves—are not the only key to good teaching.'[29] It was
rare to find more examples of public schools designed with a progressive approach
to education as a starting point and where, as at Crow Island, educators and
architects had collaborated and developed a common vocabulary. As David
explained, 'because we believe in diversity rather than conformity, we are trying to
seek out buildings that express an educational ethos rather than an architectural
preconception.'[30] They were to find this in some of the public schools recently
designed in Texas.

One of the architects whose commitment to school work most impressed the
Medds was William W. Caudill. Caudill was also an academic and the author or
co-author of twelve books, the most influential of which were *Space for Teaching*
(1941) and *Architecture by Team* (1971), which argued for interdisciplinary
planning in accordance with the proposed function of the building. His major
reference work, *Toward Better School Design* (1954), focused on flexible use
planning, such as the implementation of movable classroom partitions, storage
space, and indoor-outdoor connections. Progressive and deeply interested in
education, Caudill led a practice with a commitment (familiar to the Medds) to
challenge conventions in school design so that activities associated with 'learning
by doing' which had not yet been properly accommodated in architectural terms

might be facilitated and so that schools could adequately house the 'different kind of curriculum' entailed by the activity-based approach.[31] Mary wrote home, 'In our opinion the combination of a good school superintendent or two and the firm of C. R. & Scott have produced in Texas in the last few years the best schools we've seen yet which put in the shade the luxury jobs of New York and the north east. For the first time we've seen fine architecture interpreting educational thinking and boy its sure good to see it!'[32]

In his 1954 book, Caudill asserted the importance of avoiding too much flexibility by suggesting: 'In all grades provide nooks in classrooms for individual instruction and guidance.' One of the elements of an elementary school that Caudill and partners thought appropriate was a 'kiva', a representation of which was featured in *Life* magazine's article on school design in 1954. 'The kiva, patterned after the ritual huts of the Pueblo Indians is a circular space enclosed by painted concrete blocks where recitals, plays and assemblies can be put on. With folding walls guided by tracks along the ceiling, it can be divided into three separate work areas, or it can be opened up wide.'[33] This may well be where Mary and David realized their idea for a kiva as a central and iconic element of Eveline Lowe school (1966) [Fig. 10.3]. Of utmost importance was a built-in variety of size, shape and character in such spaces, more often found in schools designed for younger children. Without this, they warned: 'An environment uniform in character, however sub-divisible runs the risk of providing, in the words of one American critic, "not flexibility for the future, but poverty for the present".'[34]

Between them, the two progressive architectural practices of Perkins, Wheeler and Will and Caudill Rowlett Scott had built over 204 new elementary schools in post-war United States, all with a commitment to a new form of school design.[35]

On their return to England, David gave a series of talks about their experiences and impressions in America under the various titles of 'Architecture in an Affluent Society' and 'The Aesthetics of Plenty: a dilemma for American architects', the latter an address to the Architectural Association.[36] There was also a radio broadcast for the BBC Third Programme, which was later published in *The Listener*.[37] In the Architectural Association address, David picked out a remark made by Ed Stone at the New Orleans American Institute of Architects' annual conference, which captured the problem he and Mary discerned. 'In this age of prosperity and abundance, we can afford everything but beauty.'[38] Mary's letters home during their trip demonstrate her own view of how David presented his concerns. In one reflection she wrote, 'when you see a couple of rabbits in a monumental architectural structure, it makes you wonder—and an industrial arts shop filled with expensive machines of all kinds, in which boys are making small wooden models of a village pump, or some ghastly knick knack. Really, it won't do! We've yet to find anything to touch the work that is produced by children from West Riding miners' homes in the West Riding schools which have about 0.1 percent of the fittings of these schools.'[39] In this land of 'extraordinary paradoxes', there was 'nothing to match the talk' and they were, over months, subjected to much talk. Mary concluded, 'we have had a year of crowded experiences but I believe it will be the natural wonders of the country, rather than what man has done, that will stay most deeply in our memories.'[40]

FIGURE 10.3 *The kiva at Eveline Lowe Primary School, Southwark, London.*
Newsam Library and Archives, Institute of Education, University of London.

Bringing it all back home

In the United States, the Medds were shown much that they found dull and uninspiring but sought out opportunities to engage with practices in education and architecture that connected strongly with their own principles and values. In a modest way, we can see examples of what they did find of value expressed architecturally in two schools with which they are closely associated —Finmere Primary School in Oxfordshire, which opened in 1959, and Eveline Lowe Primary School in London which opened in 1966.

Finmere was a village school designed to replace scattered and dated older buildings in this rural part of Oxfordshire.[41] The school was divided into three spaces which, when required, could be opened up to be used as one by means of movable walls. The spaces were planned down to the smallest detail including the furniture layout.[42] The two central spaces were further sub-divided into a library, a sitting room (for children) including a 'fire place' and a bed, a cooking area and a general practical area or 'bays' for construction work. There might have been an open fireplace, as was the case at Crow Island, but in adapting the idea to a smaller building, there was instead an electric radiator to sit around. The bed was set in a small alcove, curtained off. All of the spaces had easy access to a shared verandah and an open playing field with a specially constructed mound for play. According to Louis Christian Schiller, Staff Inspector for Primary Education, for the first time ever, Oxfordshire children and their teachers were released completely from the confines of walled boxes and given a planned environment of opportunities.[43]

The influences on the design of the building are clearly Scandinavian, reflecting Mary Medd's early influences and travels.[44] The roof is pitched and the timber beams exposed. However, there are hints of Crow Island about the arrangement of interconnecting spaces and efforts to ensure that practical areas were within easy reach of more traditional classrooms. But Finmere was also influential internationally. It was visited over the years after it first opened and this included a team of teachers and film-makers from Norway. Led by Torvald Slettebø, they spent six weeks in various Oxfordshire schools, including Finmere, to record and study how they operated, paying attention to how the building supported teaching and learning. The results were published in a booklet entitled Åpne Skoler (Open Schools). Slettebø also made a documentary about schools in the West Riding of Yorkshire which was broadcast on Norwegian Television as well as twenty films for national television marketing Oxfordshire ideas. These had a profound effect on the design of Norwegian schools at the time.[45]

Eveline Lowe School was a school without classrooms and was celebrated in the national press as a radical unconventional school (Plate 13). It was cited in the Plowden Report *Children and Their Primary Schools* (1967) and is probably representative of the Medds' most confident assertion of what they believed to be important in designing an effective and modern school. There are several elements to the school that are reflective of international achievements and experiments in school design in Europe and the United States. John Pardey, the architect who carried out a renewal and redesign of the school in 2011, described it as Scandinavian and ensured that its features of wood-clad walls and bays were preserved. The courtyard with many natural features, gardens and a pond were considered essential for a school of this age group, where there should be as seamless as possible a connection between the indoor and outdoor environments. An experimental feature of the school was the integration of five spaces of different character to provide children with opportunities to withdraw from the general work areas to find a place of quiet and calm. These spaces could also be used by teachers for storytelling and other group activities. One space that drew a lot of attention from the press was the kiva, which can be recognized as a design idea that the Medds brought with them from their journey through the United States.

There is no space here to explore further examples of design influences in transatlantic or European contexts but it is to be hoped that this chapter has opened up the question further of the place of international exchange and travel in the post-war design of educational spaces. Certainly, the Medds' influence was profound in the post-war design of school buildings in England and Wales. This brief and partial review of influential visits abroad exposes their interest in a form of education and associated school design that was radical and adventurous. They not only influenced the work of educators and architects in Europe but there is evidence, as discussed here, that they learned from others through their encounters and close observations and introduced what they could towards a freeing up of the institution of school at home. As civil servants working for a government department, they were forced to compromise to some extent. Nevertheless, the principles and values that shaped the schools built under their influence were recognized as valuable across the developed world during their years at the Ministry (and Department) of Education as progressive ideas about education came to the fore. Many such schools designed in the 1950s and 1960s are still operating and a recent research project has shown that teachers continue to appreciate the attention to scale and a child's experience that the buildings exhibit.[46] Today, as school buildings come to be renewed or redeveloped, such principles remain relevant and connect strongly with the expressed needs of pupils themselves.[47]

Notes

1   For examples, see Catherine Burke, *A Life in Education and Architecture. Mary Beaumont Medd 1907–2005* (London: Ashgate, 2013), 178.

2   For an insight into the recognition of the Medds in Denmark, see Catherine Burke, 'Putting Education in Its Place: Mapping the Observations of Danish and English Architects on 1950s School Design', *Paedagogica Historica*, 46/5 (October 2010): 655–72.

3   They made longer stays in Washington, where the national school inspectorate had a representative, Robert Morris, and at Boulder City, Los Angeles, Carmel, Chicago and Maine.

4   David Medd, 'The Aesthetics of Plenty—Dilemma for American Architects', *Architects' Journal*, 39 (July–August 1960): 818–19. Cutting in ME/F/11, Newsam Archives, Medd Collection, Institute of Education, University of London, hereafter NAMC.

5   The first artificial satellite to orbit the Earth was launched on 4 October 1957.

6   Wayne J. Urban, *More Than Science and Sputnik: The National Defense Education Act of 1958* (Tuscaloosa: University of Alabama Press, 2010).

7   David Medd and Mary Medd, 'British School Architects Examine Our Work', *Architects' Journal* (12 May 1960). Cutting in ME/F/11 (NAMC).

8   Statement of the National Education Association of the USA, presented by Dr Lyman V. Ginger, President NEA, Washington D.C. with Walter W. Heller, Department of Economics, University of Minnesota, 29 April 1958. Assorted articles USA ME/F/1 (NAMC).

9   An image of the Medds appears in *Newsday*, 13 September 1958, 14.

10   MBC letter home, 26 November 1958 (NAMC).

11   DLM letter home, 9 September 1958 (NAMC).

12   MBC letter home, 28 October 1958 (NAMC).

13   DLM letter to AP, 19 November 1958 (NAMC).

14   DLM letter to Joan, Stirrat, R and Maurice, 26 November 1958 (NAMC).

15   MBC letter home, 13 September 1958 (NAMC).

16   MBC letter home, 28 May 1959 (NAMC).

17   MBC letter to Ena Curry, 21 June 1959 (NAMC).

18   DLM notes of conversation with Holden, 6 June 1959. USA ME/F/6 (NAMC).

19   Ibid.

20   Yeomans was a member of Winnetka school board who hired Carlton Washburne as Superintendent in 1919 on the advice of Frederik Burk.

21   Visited 11 November 1958: Yeomans was Principal of Shady Hill 1949–62.

22   DLM notes on a visit to Shady Hill School, 17 November 1958. Miscellaneous file USA (NAMC).

23   Ibid.

24   C. William Brubaker, Raymond Bordwell and Gaylaird Christopher, *Planning and Designing Schools* (New York: McGraw-Hill, 1998), 15.

25   David Medd quoted in S. MacLure, *Educational Development and School Building: Aspects of Public Policy, 1945–73* (London: Longman, 1984), 138.

26   DLM letter to Bill (Curry), April 1959 (NAMC).

27   MBC letter to Pat Tindale, February 1959 (NAMC).

28   Cranbrook Archives, Saarinen Papers 2.10. The exhibition travelled to Egypt in the spring of 1944.

29   Ministry of Education, 'Schools in the USA', *Building Bulletin*, 18 July 1961, 39.

30   DLM letter to E. Wickman, 19 May 1959 (NAMC).

31   William Wayne Caudill, *Toward Better School Design* (New York: F. W. Dodge Corp., 1954), 26.

32   MBC letter to Pat Tindale, 3 March 1959 (NAMC).

33   *Life Magazine*, 1 February 1954, 76.

34   'Schools in the USA', 112.

35   *Life Magazine*, 1 February 1954, 75.

36   Later translated into Danish for the journal *Arkitecten*.

37   *The Listener*, 10 August 1961. The BBC broadcast was recorded on 3 July 1961 and
     was entitled 'Affluence and Architecture'.

38   DLM—*AA Journal* (1961): 41.

39   MBC letter home from New York 20 October 1958 (NAMC).

40   MBC letter home, 9 September 1959 (NAMC).

41   Ministry of Education Development Group (job architect David and Mary Medd with
     Pat Tindale, built 1958–59. Enlarged 1973. Listed 1993). *Building Bulletin*, 3, HMSO,
     1961; D. Rowntree, *Guardian*, 25 May 1960; *Architects' Journal* (30 June 1960):
     1005–6; *BOUW*, 133 [Dutch Architectural Journal] (19 August 1961): 1016–17;
     Sunday Telegraph, 21 November 1965; *Education and Culture*, 4 (Spring 1967):
     19–22; *Children and Their Primary Schools, The Plowden Report* (London: HMSO,
     1967), 396.

42   ME/E/18/5 (NAMC).

43   Christian Schiller, 'Changing Needs in the Design Context', *Built Environment* (May
     1972): 96.

44   For details of these travels see Burke, *A Life in Education and Architecture*.

45   An online version of Åpne Skoler is available at http://www.agderkultur.no/
     Oxfordshire-skole/Side1.htm, accessed 29 August 2012.

46   C. Burke, D. Cullinan, P. Cunningham, R. Sayers and R. Walker, *Principles of Primary
     School Design* (Cambridge: ACE Foundation and Feilden, Clegg and Bradley Studios,
     2010).

47   See Burke, *A Life in Education and Architecture*, chapter nine, 'Towards the Future-
     Building School: Lasting Legacies of Design and Democratic Practice'.

11

Clean Living under Difficult Circumstances: Modernist Pop and Modernist Architecture—A Short History of a Misunderstanding

Owen Hatherley

Introduction

Although some like to remember that 'mod' is short for 'modernist', the 'low' art that is pop music and the 'high' that is modernist architecture have not always mixed particularly well. Arguably, the clean lines and optimism of mod and the first mass building of tower blocks in the mid-1960s could have influenced each other, both movements sharing a penchant for what the mod publicist Pete Meaden called 'clean living under difficult circumstances', an aesthetic that prized pride, wakefulness, clarity and a sometimes harsh modernity.[1] One might have taken it largely from Tamla Motown and Italian tailoring, another from Le Corbusier and the Bauhaus; one might have been created by working-class youth and the other by middle-class professionals in early middle age, but the correspondences were obvious enough.

Equally, psychedelia and hippy culture's hostility to modernism is wildly obvious. When former art student and partial creator of English psychedelia Syd Barrett was once asked to explain why he and the rest of Pink Floyd did not get on, he offered the pithy explanation they were 'architecture students'.[2] In fact, one of the more obvious correspondences of pop and architecture comes from here, in the form of Nick Mason's cover for Pink Floyd's *Relics*, a Victorian-Futurist architectural fantasy that has a clear resemblance to the work of Archigram, who, with their ludic visions of free festivals, 'rokplugs' in the woods, and hostility to mere utility were the psychedelic era's nearest architectural analogue. The squatting scene and the back-to-basics, anti-modernist 'community architecture' movement of the 1970s were less visual, more serious outgrowths of the same movement.

By the time of Glam, this hostility has taken a different form—'Hunger City', David Bowie's dystopia in *Diamond Dogs*, is a gleeful description of modernity gone horribly awry, something which is taken up by punk, where interestingly the massive urban rebuilding programmes of the 1960s and 1970s are actually addressed in specific songs.

In this chapter, I will try to explore this complex and often disavowed relationship in three cities—first, the London of punk and post-punk and then, in greater depth, Manchester, specifically its demolished Hulme Crescents housing estate, and Sheffield, with its monumental deck-access housing estates.

London: A neon outline on a car crash overspill

The Los Angeles-based property developer John Lydon recently opined that he had seen what a failure socialism was, because he had lived in a council flat. This squares with the idea that punk was a sort of counter-cultural equivalent to Thatcherism—a movement for individualism, cruelty and discipline against the woolly solidarity and collectivism of the post-war consensus. Council flats were always an emblem of punk, at least in its more socialist realist variants. There was a sort of delayed cultural reaction to the cities of tower blocks and motorways built in the 1960s, to the point where their effect only really registered around ten years later, when a cultural movement defined itself as having come from those towers and walkways, leading to a curious kind of bad faith, where on the one hand the dehumanizing effect of these places was lamented, but on the other, the vertiginous new landscape was fetishized and aestheticized.

The Jam and The Clash were the most obvious exponents of this. The Clash, despite being fronted by a diplomat's son who had been educated at Westminster School, explicitly presented themselves as youth who had been shaped by West London's environment of high-rises and flyovers, a world described in the likes of 'London's Burning' [Fig. 11.1]. Guitarist Mick Jones made the unlikely claim that he had never lived below the nineteenth floor. For The Clash and for the socialist realist strain in punk that they exemplified, tower blocks and concrete serve a strange dual role. On the one hand, they are emblems of the terrible inhumane circumstances of everyday life, the blank consumerism Jones tremblingly recounts in 'Lost in the Supermarket', and on the other, they are just so exciting. 'London's Burning' (1977) attempts to sound sarcastic when it sings the praise of the Westway, but Joe Strummer cannot hide his excitement. Rather fittingly for someone whose entire project entailed reviving mod, only twelve years dead, as a retro gesture, Paul Weller's lyrics mark mod's disassociation from modernism. On The Jam's first album, 'Bricks and Mortar' is evidently informed by the Poulson case, the public discrediting of local councillors, and the modernist architects and developers, all found to be involved in some extensive corruption. Therein, our modernist, offended by the destruction of heritage, asks 'why do we try to hide our past?' Yet on the cover of their second album in 1977, *This Is the Modern World*, the three

FIGURE 11.1 *Erno Goldfinger, Trellick Tower, London.*
© Owen Hatherley, 2007.

band members stand poker-faced in front of the Westway in full mod gear, the lines on the clothes and the lines of the flyover and towers, all evidently complementary. Later, on The Jam's last album, *The Gift* (1982), Weller delivers a much more direct commentary on 'The Planner's Dream Went Wrong'. Over a curious calypso backing the story is told of how naïve but sincere modernists 'were going to build communities' but ended up creating only anomie. The song is a mixture of grievances both concrete (recalling the 'piss-stench hallways and broken-down lifts' that had become notorious by the early 1980s) and faintly ridiculous, as when he grumbles, in true pub bore style, 'if people were meant to live in boxes...'

The ambiguity of punk in its relation to modernism becomes in many cases a much more direct engagement in post-punk. This is partly visible at the level of record sleeves and clothes—most post-punk bands looked like they had leafed through a copy of John Willett's mid-1970s Weimar Republic study *The New Sobriety*, and their sleeve designers, like Peter Saville and Malcolm Garrett, certainly had, borrowing motifs from Jan Tschichold, El Lissitzky and Piet Zwart. Because of this, the architectural writer Mark Owens, in his essay 'New Brutalists/New Romantics', has written of a 'delayed reaction'[3] that caused the aesthetic effects on inhabitants of the New Brutalism, as the most extreme of the various modernist currents, to have only really become apparent in the pop of the late 1970s, where after a time they were able to produce something as strange, inhuman and futuristic as the architecture. The bastard technologies and deadpan dystopianism of Cabaret Voltaire and the early Human League are New Brutalism in pop, much as the latter was pop in architecture: the rough synth textures, the bastardized technologies and outlook caught between technological optimism and urban paranoia. Japan, straight out of Catford, a suburb heavily redeveloped by the notorious commercial Brutalist firm of Owen Luder, sang of the romance of 'concrete squares', and perhaps most of all, John Foxx's Ultravox, from Stockport but based in London, drew heavily on J. G. Ballard to evoke a London landscape that had been completely recreated in a manner that, however horrifying it might have been to Paul Weller, could and should be embraced. Their 1977 'My Sex' declared that 'my sex is invested in suburban photographs/skyscraper shadows on a car crash overpass...my sex is an image lost in faded films/a neon outline on a car crash overspill'. Foxx's 1980 solo album *Metamatic* was practically a Brutalist concept album, with 'Plaza', 'A New Kind of Man' and most of all 'Underpass' working as convulsive anthems to the new artificial cityscape. This comes out especially strongly in the onrush of concrete in the video to 'Underpass', where punk's sociology has been stripped of all its moral concern, reduced to a high-speed awe. For many post-punk currents, Brutalist imagery was not so much source for socialist realist critique as a spur to new conceptions of surface and space. This was especially true in the north, in Sheffield and Manchester.

Sheffield: In the shade of crumbling concrete bus shelters

Sheffield's most famous modernist (or any) building, Park Hill, was an early response to what were considered, even in the 1950s, to be modern architecture's failures [Fig. 11.2]. Empty spaces, isolation, a lack of street life, a middle-class 'this is good for you' ethos—all were fiercely critiqued by its planners and architects. Unfortunately for its advocates, the style of these buildings—reliant on 'béton brut', unpainted concrete—was christened 'the New Brutalism'. The New Brutalism's chief propagandist and associate pop artist with the Independent Group, Reyner

FIGURE 11.2 *Jack Lynn and Ivor Smith, Park Hill, Sheffield.*
© Owen Hatherley, 2010.

Banham, pondered in a 1966 book whether the idiom was an 'Ethic or Aesthetic', so firmly marked was it by social concerns. He claimed that the Brutalists were the architectural equivalent of the 'angry young men' of the 1950s, of Arnold Wesker or Alan Sillitoe. Banham wrote that these architects were of 'red brick extraction', products of post-war class mobility, usually Northerners, like its main theorists and occasional practitioners, the fiercely self-promoting Stockton-on-Tees and Sheffield-born intellectual couple Alison and Peter Smithson, whose Golden Lane scheme for a deck-access block of council housing defined Brutalism, and added a pop art touch, when the architects added images of Marilyn Monroe and Joe Di Maggio to the drawings for the unbuilt structure.

'In our zeal to erase the evils arising out of lack of proper water supply, sanitation and ventilation, we had torn down streets of houses which despite their sanitary shortcomings harboured a social structure of friendliness and mutual aid. We had thrown out the baby with the bathwater,' claimed Jack Lynn, co-designer of Park Hill, Sheffield, in 1962.[4] Reading the above quote, you have to remind yourself that Lynn is not talking about the building he designed at all but the orthodox slum-clearance modernism he and his colleagues were setting themselves against. Park Hill was an early response to what were considered, even in the 1950s, to be modern architecture's failures. Park Hill was, along with London's slightly larger but contrastingly affluent Barbican estate, the largest scale application of Brutalism's ethic and aesthetic. It cleared a notoriously violent slum by Sheffield's Midland Station nicknamed 'little Chicago', but rather than rehousing the residents in isolated towers, the architects—Jack Lynn and Ivor Smith with Frederick Nicklin, selected by Lewis Womersley—attempted to replicate in the air the tightly packed street life of the area. Associates of the Smithsons, Lynn and Smith, were enthusiasts for the close-knit working-class life supposedly being broken up by the new estates and new towns. As in the Smithsons' mythical, unbuilt Golden Lane scheme, claustrophobic walk-ups or corridors were rejected in favour of twelve-feet-wide 'streets in the sky'. These 'streets' were almost all connected with the ground, on steeply sloping land. Street corners were included where the winding building twisted around, with the spaces around the blocks filled with shops, schools and playgrounds. Park Hill was closely monitored to see if it succeeded in its aims and had its own tenants' magazine, the laconically named *Flat*.

Meanwhile, the architectural aesthetic was shaped by a rejection of the clean geometries of mainstream modernism, in favour of roughness and irregularity. The marks of concrete shuttering were left, in the fashion of Le Corbusier's Unité d'Habitation. Yet the use of multicoloured bricks, gradated from scarlet to yellow, in abstract patterns aided by the artist John Forrester, connected it with a specifically English, Northern idiom. The blocks rose from four storeys at the highest point of the hill to thirteen at the lowest, giving a continuous roof line visible from much of the city: at the highest point they looked out over the expanse of the city centre and the postindustrial Don Valley and at the lowest, they mingled unassumingly with Victorian terraces. Despite—or because of—Park Hill's aesthetic extremism, early responses to the blocks were very positive indeed. *Romancing the Stone* features much footage of children and pensioners praising the place's modernity and community. Over old footage of the playgrounds, a South Yorkshire voice intones 'there's no stopping this collective thinking. It's the future'. Encouraged by these responses, the architects designed a 'Park Hill Mark Two' built just behind the site— Hyde Park, which rose to an eighteen-storey 'castle keep'. Later, a mark three, Kelvin Flats, was designed by other architects west of the city centre.

In 1962, the book *Ten Years of Housing in Sheffield*, documenting Lewis Womersley's tenure as City Architect, was published in English, French and Russian, rather extraordinarily. It is a curiously sad book, an object from what now seems a completely alien culture but which makes clear just how tentative the planners and architects actually were—no grandiose declarations of success here. Park Hill was presented in there as an experiment, albeit one about which the writers were cautiously optimistic. Noting that there was a huge risk in such a development of 'creating a vast inhuman building block', Womersley was at pains to point out how much they had attempted to lessen this effect, from the public park created between the estate and the street to the way the courtyards opened out further as the storeys rose—though he noted that 'it must be left…to the occupants to judge to what extent the architects have been successful'.[5] Meanwhile, along with the expected shops and schools, Park Hill and its sister scheme Hyde Park were unpretentious enough to include no less than four pubs.

Streets in the sky were only one facet of Sheffield's housing programme. The less futuristic but equally remarkable suburban counterpart to Park Hill's urbanity was Gleadless Valley, a collection of houses and flats making breathtaking use of the hilly landscape, resembling a strange socialist South Yorkshire version of 1950s southern California. Park Hill makes sense best when seen as part of a larger project in total city planning, aligned with other estates also placed on prominent hilltop sites, such as the more straightforward tower block and maisonette modernism of Woodside and Netherthorpe. By the end of the 1970s, over half of Sheffield's housing was council-owned, and they were still building Brutalist deck-access housing, albeit on a warmer, smaller scale that can still be seen in suburban Gleadless Valley. This is a reminder that council housing was never intended to be the emergency measure it is now but something which was genuinely 'mixed'.

Park Hill was not utopia nor was it intended to be. It had too few lifts, and the concrete on the taller sections was spalling by the 1980s. More arguably, it might have been excessively successful at recreating the space of the old rookeries— like them, it was full of escape routes and shadowy spots. The notion that it could have single-handedly preserved a working-class communal life being obliterated everywhere else is unsurprisingly unconvincing. Nonetheless, there is little evidence that it ever became a 'sink' estate until at least the mid-1990s. However, the other two schemes were always considered less successful, and in the 1990s, Hyde Park was partly demolished, while Kelvin Flats were levelled completely.[6]

But while conventional architectural opinion was turning against the streets in the sky, popular music told a different story. The Human League were keen to have it on record, on the sleeve, that their shimmering, proto-techno instrumental 'Dancevision', described by Simon Reynolds in terms that portray contemporary Sheffield rather well as an 'ambiguous alloy of euphoria and grief', was recorded in front of Kelvin Flats. The group staged a deck-access romance in the video to 'Love Action' and their 'Blind Youth' reprimanded punks for their anti-modernism, insisting with tongue only slightly in cheek that 'you've had it easy, you should be glad/high-rise living's not so bad'. In fact, it could be argued that, when Sheffield City Council was no longer prepared to create an image of the future and a new way of life, Sheffield's electronic producers did so instead. At the same time that Hyde Park's modern, cubist terraces were being given pitched roofs, Warp Records, and Sheffield producers like Richard H. Kirk or Rob Gordon were creating an art form that formed a continuation of the streets in the sky's vertiginous sense of new space and their Brutalist, low-end rumble. Nonetheless, it is almost certain that Park Hill would have suffered the same fate as Kelvin Flats and Hyde Park had it not been listed in 1998. Practically inescapable in Sheffield, it is an overwhelming reminder of what it once wanted to be—the capital of the Socialist Republic of South Yorkshire—rather than what it wants to be now, a local service and cultural industries centre. Yet like all British cities, it spent the following decade undergoing the dubious ministrations of regeneration. This too was done with reference to pop music.

The estate was transferred—for free, not sold—to Urban Splash, the Manchester-based property developer best known for turning derelict mills, office blocks and factories into city centre 'lofts'. It grew out of a pop poster stall run by founder Tom Bloxham, a former Labour Party Young Socialist, and is an interesting amalgam of two New Labour fixations—the 'creative industries' and property speculation, as opposed to Old Labour's heavy industries and social housing. Urban Splash has always stressed a link between its work and the Manchester of post-punk and acid house, and its brochure for Park Hill was elegantly rendered by Warp Records and Pulp's sleeve designers, the Designers Republic, themselves a recent casualty of the recession. Full of quotations from Sheffield bands like the Human League and ABC, the whole document is written in infantile music-press clichés that contrast tellingly with the popular but non-patronizing language of *Ten Years of Housing in Sheffield*. '*Don't you want me Baby?*' it asks, and proceeding through numerous factual errors, it promises to restore 'the love' to Park Hill. 'Make it a place', it says. 'Make it a special place. Make it an EXTRA special place', although at least they are honest enough to admit 'we're in this to make a profit'.[7]

For all this, the group that most thoroughly fixated with the built landscape of Sheffield was Pulp, whose name was also traduced in the marketing of Park Hill to media professionals. Long after the demise of post-punk, starting with the tour-de-Sheffield in their 1990 single 'My Legendary Girlfriend', Pulp would return again and again to the ambiguous post-war landscape of their hometown, seeing it alternately as utopia and dystopia. In their 1992 'Sheffield: Sex City', Jarvis Cocker intones a series of Sheffield place names, with luridly sensual relish—from 'Intake' onwards, each one of them emphasized for any possible double-meanings—Frecheville, Hackenthorpe, Shalesmoor, and *Wombwell*. The next voice you hear is Candida Doyle, deadpan and Yorkshire, reading—of all things—from one of the sexual fantasies in a Nancy Friday book. Here, the city itself is the focus for all libidinal energies. 'We were living in a big block of flats ... within minutes the whole building was fucking. I mean, have you ever heard other people fucking, and really enjoying it? Not like in the movies, but when it's real ... .' Then, the 'sun rose from behind the gasometers at 6.30 am', and we are on a tour of the carnal possibilities in a postindustrial city.

The most important sounds in it (aside from Jarvis' own increasingly astonishing groans, howls, gasps and ecstatic squeals) are hers, too—the banks of synths, taken from the same jumble sale ransacked at the same time by Stereolab, interspersed with some more recent artificial instruments. It is these smears of indistinct, tinny keyboard atmospheres, the arpeggiated stutters, the repetitive house vamps, and Russell Senior's queasily treated violin which simulate the vertiginous feeling of nervousness, anticipation and mania which underpin the ridiculous, magnificent lyric, an obsessive, clammily sexual ambience. Underneath, a metronomic kick drum pounds and deep, relentless, low-end throbs which the group got Warp Records' in-house engineer to lower to sub-bass levels. As it pulses, the whole city is 'getting stiff in the building heat', and Jarvis walks through its entire extent trying to find his lover. So overwhelmed is he by the sheer sexuality of Sheffield that he finds himself 'rubbing up against lamp-posts, trying to get rid of it'. The places made sexual are exemplars of non-utopian everyday life, as we traverse the semis, the gardens, and hear 'groans from a T-reg Chevette—you bet ... you bet ... ', and in a particularly memorable moment stop to penetrate 'a crack in the pavement'. This transfigured space is cut with moments of frustrating mundanity, 'crumbling concrete bus shelters' and tedious nights indoors watching television. The pursuit is interrupted, because 'the fares went up at seven'; our protagonist loses his lover while 'sentenced to three years in the housing benefit waiting room'. The frustration and fascination builds and builds and builds to the point of explosion, leaving the city's topographical extremes as location for the final consummation, with the city abstracted below them. 'We finally made it, on a hilltop at 4am. A million twinkling yellow street lights. The whole city is your jewellery box. Reach out, and take what you want…' The city has not survived its orgy, and our lovers survey the wreckage left over. 'Everyone on Park Hill came in unison at 4.13 am, and the whole block fell down. A tobacconist caught fire, and everyone in the street died of lung cancer.'

A 'Guide to Sheffield' that Pulp compiled for the *New Musical Express* (*NME*) in 1993 partly concentrates on its role as the centre of the 'Socialist Republic of South Yorkshire', when the red flag famously flew above the town hall. This comes out in a particularly quotidian way through these songs, where the all-but-free public transport is recalled as a way of seeing the city as a totality, only to be destroyed with deregulation and privatization: 'I remember when the buses were only 10p to go anywhere. That's why buses are mentioned quite a lot in our songs. Anyway, it all stopped in the mid-'80s. There are about six different bus companies now, like Eager Beaver, Yorkshire Terrier…it's ridiculous—if the driver sees the stop they're supposed to be going to hasn't got any people at it, they change the number and go to one that has. People came from Japan to see our bus service—it was the end of the Western World.'[8] As much as Pulp's Sheffield songs were the voyeur's view into an interior, they were an all-surveying view from the top deck of a bus.

More particularly, their gazetteer is about the city's failure to become the modernist metropolis that it once promised to be. Of all provincial cities, Sheffield went furthest towards becoming some sort of viable modern city, reconstructing itself after the Blitz in a markedly dramatic form, using its topography—this is a city practically built into the Peak District—as an advantage. At one end, there was the slickness of Sheffield University, designed by Gollins Melvin Ward (in a style completely in hock to Mies van der Rohe) in the early 1960s, the first wholly modernist university campus in the UK. This series of precisely engineered, machine-tooled, glass-and-steel pavilions and towers, recently renovated to their post-war splendour, is closer to the high modernist aesthetic of Warp rather than Pulp's more Heath Robinson pop modernism. To find the possible inspirations for that, you have to look elsewhere, first to the Castle Square 'Hole in the Road', an underpass-cum-shopping-centre, whose early 1990s demolition was lamented by Pulp in the music press as an attempt 'to make everything like Meadowhall', the postmodernist out-of-town mall constructed on the site of a former steelworks, or you could find it in a series of montage-based modernist edifices designed under Womersley, constructed as assemblages of walkways, multiple levels and almost kitsch details. There is the Castle Market, for one, where Cocker worked on the fish stall in his youth, the subject of a short local television item where he held it up as an example of what makes Sheffield unique and specific. Then there are the housing estates, the monumental, interconnected collective housing blocks placed on the city's hilltops. Park Hill, we know about; but there are also its successors, Hyde Park and Kelvin Flats, the latter of which gets a markedly less ecstatic Pulp song devoted to it. The suburban version at Gleadless Valley was the place where Russell Senior was raised.

Read another guide, any Shell Guide or Pevsner from the 1960s or 1970s, and it is this which they will tell you to look for—aside from a single Georgian square and a couple of Victorian civic buildings, they all point the traveller to that visionary series of housing estates and markets or to a new town hall designed as a concrete honeycomb and soon nicknamed 'the egg box'. This vision was propagandized in *Sheffield: City on the Move*, a confident, convincing, if undeniably clunky, vision of civic futurism that was sampled as a 'what were we thinking!' joke at the start of the 'dance, prole, dance' genre's most noted product, *The Full Monty*. Many schemes were shelved for lack of money—at one point, the council were making plans to run street decks and walkways across the entire Sheaf Valley. By the 1990s, buildings that had a life span of barely twenty years, whose futurism was suddenly dated—the aforementioned Town Hall, the 'wedding cake' registry office next to it, the concrete housing estates of Broomhall, Hyde Park and Kelvin Flats—began to be demolished, leaving huge scars across the city which have not fully healed two decades later.

Another early 1990s *NME* interview makes it especially clear just how much of an effect this construction and destruction had on the future members of Pulp: 'Sheffield's full of half-arsed visions of cities of the future that turn into a pile of rubbish', Russell Senior reflects, standing on the biggest traffic roundabout in Europe. 'We grew up reading the local paper and seeing "Sheffield, city of the future", with a map of how it's going to be and pictures of everyone walking around in spacesuits, smiling. But we're the only ones who took it seriously ...' 'When I was younger I definitely thought I'd live in space', says Jarvis Cocker ruefully. 'But when you realise you're not going to, it colours your life; you can't think, "It's alright if I'm signing on because I'll be on Mars soon", you have to try and get it down here.'[9] What runs through all of this is the lament of true believers in modernism, holding the present to account for its failure to create a viable future, and the pinched vision of the possible that then instils in those born after the future; as Cocker would yelp in 1998, obliquely apropos New Labour's workfare schemes, 'we were brought up on the space race—*now they expect you to clean toilets*'. *Intro* opens with a song that confronts this directly, 'Space', where an ambient drift of indeterminate hums and flutters imagines the previously longed-for journey above the earth's surface, where all the trash of bedsit life is left behind—'this is what you've been waiting for', he whispers, 'no dust collecting in corners or cups of tea that go cold before you drink them ... it doesn't matter if the lifts don't work or the car won't start. We're going to escape'—and then suddenly rejects the reverie, stiffening into a determination to 'get my kicks down below'.

It is this that lies behind all the obvious retro sounds and signifiers—the Farfisas, Stylophones and Moogs, the jumble sale clothes, the tower blocks, space hoppers and luridly bright artificial fabrics that pervade Pulp's music videos—a sense of being cheated out of the future, responding by fetishizing the last time that a viable future appeared to exist. Yet Pulp's songs did delve into 1970s nostalgia, not least as a way of talking about the stripped-pine compromises and bland conformities of the 1990s.

'Deep Fried in Kelvin' (1993) is like a ten-minute reversal of 'Sheffield: Sex City'. Like the latter, it centres on one of the three huge collective housing blocks designed by Jack Lynn and Ivor Smith for Sheffield City Council. Kelvin Flats, which were, as we have seen, approvingly mentioned in the Human League's sleevenotes for the sublime 'Dancevision', were demolished in the 1990s and replaced by low-rise, low-density Barratt Homes, the sort you could imagine housing the soap-on-a-rope sagas of 'His & Hers'. In marked contrast with 'Sheffield: Sex City', there is little interest in the utopian possibilities of Brutalist megastructures in 'Deep Fried', which instead depicts a people congenitally unable to live in anything other than houses with gardens, centring on a man destroying his flat by filling it with soil, trying to turn it into a garden, walking 'on promenade with concrete walkways, where pigeons go to die'. It's a vision of a consumerist, barely literate proletariat destroyed by Thatcherism, where children are 'conceived in the toilets of Meadowhall', the huge 1980s postmodernist shopping centre on the site of a former steelworks. It has equal disdain both for the 'fizzy orange and chips' youth of this 'ghetto' and for those who might improve it (memorably, 'we don't need your sad attempts at social conscience based on taxi rides home at night from exhibition openings. We just want your car radio and bass reflex speakers. Now'), and eventually the contempt seems to be aimed at the narrator himself and his social concern.

Similarly bleak as a portrayal of a modernist environment is 'Mile End', palatably translated into genial space-skiffle. Here it's the old East End of London, repository for Blur's proleface sentimentality, which is, when surveyed from the top of a tower block as the 'pearly king of the isle of Dogs', 'just like heaven, if it didn't look like hell', and where maintaining your difference, rather than blending in, is the only way to keep sane. 'Nobody wants to be your friend, cos you're not from round here, oh no—as if that wasn't something to be proud about!' They are all songs that appear, to the untrained eye, more or less autobiographical, tales of dole life when you could still get a council flat without having to lose an arm or a leg or have a family in double figures. Sometimes, these London estates become neither utopian nor dystopian but have a more everyday romanticism; Jarvis Cocker and Martin Wallace's elegantly self-deconstructing 1992 video to 'Babies', for instance, takes place in Southwark Council Architects' Department's Sceaux Gardens Estate, Camberwell, where Jarvis and Steve Mackey were living at the time, and like Park Hill, somewhere with much architectural reputation when it was built. Its low- and high-rise curtain-walled blocks, with their elegant, cubic green panels and their Francophone names, were spread across green space taken over from former back gardens and overgrown bomb sites. Ian Nairn wrote of Sceaux Gardens in 1966 that because of this, 'the magical transformation has happened, an estate transformed into a place'.[10] The block named 'Voltaire' gets a particularly wry shot in the video, as do the patches of green and swaying flowers in front of the towers, creating a place perfect for the song's rum, giddy nostalgia. One of the blocks caught fire in 2009, killing several people. The recent investigation blamed the council for installing as-cheap-as-possible uPVC panels on the whole block, which melted in the heat, spreading the fire. These council flat dystopias are, for all their justified bitterness, the correlate of the failed utopia that is longingly re-imagined in 'Sheffield: Sex City', indicators of what has happened to the working class and the places it lived in after (then only fifteen years of) Thatcherism.

Manchester: Up the tenth floor down the backstairs, into no-man's-land

The perception of post-punk as the music of concrete and piss, grim towers and blasted wastelands, is best exemplified in the imagery of Joy Division. Take for instance the poster to Anton Corbijn's woeful Ian Curtis biopic *Control*, in which Sam Riley, fag dangling from mouth, looks wan and haunted below gigantic prefabricated tower blocks (which were shot in Nottingham, not the gentrified-out-of-recognition Manchester—although there are certainly parts of Salford that could still do the trick). Decades ago, when asked by Jon Savage why Joy Division's sound had such a sense of loss and gloom, Bernard Sumner reminisced about his Salford childhood: 'there was a huge sense of community where we lived…I guess what happened in the '60s was that someone at the Council decided that it wasn't very healthy, and something had to go, and unfortunately it was my neighbourhood that went. We were moved over the river into a towerblock. *At the time I thought it was fantastic*—now of course I realise it was a total disaster. [My italics.]'[11] This is often quoted as if it is obvious—well, *of course* it was a disaster. This is the narrative about modernist architecture that exists in numerous reminiscences and histories: we loved it at first, in the 1960s, then we realized our mistake, knocked them down, and rebuilt simulations of the old streets instead.

This is symbolized perhaps by the poet and architecture conservationist John Betjeman's journey from the 'Hates' list on the 1975 'Loves/Hates' T-shirt that future Clash manager Bernie Rhodes, Sex Pistols Svengali Malcolm Maclaren and Vivienne Westwood put together for the 'Sex' shop in the King's Road to the 'Loves' corner on a remake Rhodes put together in 2008. But the Situationist International, who lurk in the background of both punk and post-punk, had different ideas about the city of the future. While it certainly had an interest in those areas untouched by renewal, regeneration or prettification, the Situationist International in the 1950s dared to imagine a *new* urbanism, an entirely new approach to the city which was not based on two-up/two-downs or on spaced-out, rationalist tower blocks. To have an idea of what the Situationist City would have been like, you could read Ivan Chtcheglov's 'Formulary for a New Urbanism', an elliptical prose-poem imagining a self-creating world of grottoes and Gothic spaces, which, through the declaration 'You'll never see the Hacienda. It doesn't exist. The Hacienda must be built', inadvertently found its way into the annals of Manchester history.[12] Tony Wilson and Factory Records were not entirely joking when they gave this name to their Manchester nightclub; the irony of its current incarnation as 'Hacienda Apartments' is grimly fitting.

Chtcheglov's city divided into pleasure-driven quarters is not as unlike contemporary Manchester as one might assume, and a travesty of it can perhaps be found in the Green Quarter, Salford Quays or New Islington. There is, however, no trace of another Situationist proposal in the contemporary landscape for a new urbanism, New Babylon. This was a proposal for a genuinely new city, designed by the Dutch architect, painter and early Situationist Constant Nieuwenhuys. A ludic city dedicated to play, where 'creativity' becomes its own reward rather than a means for the accumulation of capital, New Babylon is a blueprint for a city that might exist in a future in which automation has eliminated the problem of work. Here, there are no Le Corbusier tower blocks, Constant's 'cemeteries of reinforced concrete, in which great masses of the population are condemned to die of boredom'.[13] But then neither will you find here any homilies on behalf of back-to-backs, redbrick mills or outside privies nor on the glories of the entrepreneurial city. If punk obsessed over the realness of the streets, New Babylon does not even have streets, in the old sense—it is a construction based entirely on multiple levels, walkways, skyways. It is a city in motion for a population in motion, 'a nomadic town' that functioned as a 'dynamic labyrinth' entirely through means of modern technology and construction.

Models of New Babylon show tentacles of elevated bridges above the existing city, linking together megastructures sometimes the size of a whole town in 'a continuous spatial construction, disengaged from the ground'.[14] The most important part of it seemed to be this element of circulation, the walkways and bridges themselves, designed to create accidents and chance encounters.

Manchester may have had a fragment of New Babylon within it without really noticing, in the form of its major example of the New Brutalism. The idea of the multi-level city, which Constant and the Situationists were arguing had the potential to create a new urban landscape based on chance and on play, was very much in the air in the 1950s, particularly through the international architectural group Team 10. Though, as practising architects, none of Team 10 was ever likely to be accepted by the Situationists, there is evidence that they had some contacts with Dutch members of the group such as Constant. Team 10 set itself up in opposition to the mainstream of modernist architecture and planning, and the structures which it championed, opposed to the serried ranks of tower blocks that mainstream modernism was erecting en masse, were based on walkways and the elevation of the street above the ground, based on the urban theories of the British architects Alison and Peter Smithson. The nearest built equivalent to this in Britain, though no 'Pro-Situ' or psychogeographer would dare admit it, is Sheffield's Park Hill, a building whose Mancunian offshoot has a decidedly complex history.

After leaving his post as Sheffield's City Architect, Lewis Womersley set up a private practice with another architect, Hugh Wilson. Together, the pair designed two enormous structures in Manchester at the turn of the 1970s. One of them, the Arndale Centre, swallowing up a huge swathe of the inner city and sucking it into a private shopping centre under one roof, is the antithesis both of New Babylon—dedicated as it is to work and consumption—and of Womersley's work at Park Hill, with montage and walkways replaced by a lumpen, grounded space topped by a lone office block, while its multiple levels benefit the car rather than the pedestrian. The other structure designed by Wilson and Womersley was the comprehensive redevelopment of the inner-city district of Hulme. The most notorious part of this, the Hulme Crescents, were a shadow, a memory of Park Hill, a series of labyrinthine blocks accessed by street decks. The relative conservatism of the Crescents can be ascertained from their names—John Nash, Charles Barry, and so on, all taken from architects of the Regency period, to whose work in Bath and London this was intended to be the modern equivalent, and their prefabricated concrete construction was markedly less solidly built than Park Hill. Nonetheless, in the context of Greater Manchester, where dozens of blocks from Pendleton to Collyhurst rose out of the Victorian slums, gigantic spaced-out tombstones that amply made Constant's point about the boredom of post-war redevelopment, the Crescents provided a modernist labyrinth, with its street decks winding round and interconnecting four vast, semicircular blocks enclosing a no-man's-land of indeterminate pedestrian space. Within a couple of years of its 1971 completion, it was vermin-ridden and leaky, as a result of costs cut during the construction.

Hulme Crescents and its surrounding area were demolished in the early 1990s [Fig. 11.3]. Apparently yet another example of the failures of British modernism, its demise was seen as being nearly as pivotal for Manchester's regeneration as the Hacienda, the Commonwealth Games, and the IRA bomb. '*Now of course I realise*

FIGURE 11.3 *Site of Hulme Crescents, Manchester.*
© Owen Hatherley, 2010.

it was a total disaster.' There is another story about what went on within the street-decks, a story which suggests that post-punk was not so conservative in its urbanism. After its initial failure as a housing estate for working-class families, Hulme started to become something else entirely. Manchester City Council, which had at that point a surplus of council housing, was implementing a policy of rehousing the families that found Hulme unnerving or unliveable on housing estates with gardens in Burnage or Wythenshawe, leaving many empty flats. The Russell Club, which was home to the Factory nightclub, opened in 1978 by the embryonic record label, was surrounded by the estate's concrete walkways—and the club's clientele would follow suit.

Liz Naylor, fanzine editor and scriptwriter of the Joy Division-soundtracked film *No City Fun*, remembers how after running away from home in 1978 at the age of 16 she asked the council for a flat. First of all, she was housed in Collyhurst, then an area with a heavy National Front presence. She asked for a flat in Hulme instead, because it had already acquired 'a population of alternatives', but 'by then the Manchester Evening News had been running stories for years about how awful it was'.[15] Not only was the Factory based there but so were many of the bands, along with fanzines like *City Fun* and recording studios. One of the most famous images of Joy Division was taken from one of the bridges over the motorway that bisected the new Hulme. The photographer Kevin Cummins later recalled how 'the heavy bombing (of World War Two) along with an ill-conceived 1960s regeneration programme conspired to make Manchester redolent of an eastern European city. Revisiting my photographs, I see the bleakness of a city slowly dying. A single image taken from a bridge in Hulme of Princess Parkway, the major road into Manchester, features no cars.'[16] Yet this image of a depopulated, Brutalist Manchester as a sort of English Eastern Europe resonated in a less clichéd manner with those who chose to live in Hulme—it was welcomed. Naylor remembers that the entire scene was obsessed with Berlin—'we weren't sure whether east or west Berlin'—a fixation that also dictated what they listened to: 'Iggy Pop's *The Idiot* and Bowie's "*Heroes*", was *the* music'.[17] This extended to the films they saw at the Aaben, the estate's arthouse cinema, where Fassbinder or *Nosferatu* would be eagerly consumed by the area's overcoated youth.

There was an attendant style to go with the Germanophilia. In her far from boosterist history of the area *Various Times*, Naylor writes that 'during the early 1980s there was a "Hulme look" when the whole male population of Hulme seemed to be wearing the clothes of dead men and everyone looked as if they had stepped out of the 1930s with baggy suits and tie-less shirts'.[18] The early 1980s scene in Hulme, which included Factory bands like A Certain Ratio or 'SWP types' like Big Flame and Tools You Can Trust, was perhaps a romanticization of these surroundings, of the stark, 'eastern European' aesthetic, the sense of a modernist utopia decaying, gone crumbled and decadent. Naylor remembers it being very comfortable in this period, 'not scary', an arty scene rather than the macho Mancunia that has dominated since the late 1980s. Although post-punk Hulme could be seen as a sort of slumming, with the families long since decamping to more hospitable areas, Naylor argues that rather than being just a form of urban tourism, this Hulme 'became almost an independent city, another town within a town with a shifting stream of young, single people with their own dress codes'.[19]

Especially intriguing is that this scene constituted itself *here*, in this bastardized approximation of New Babylon, this space of walkways, streets in the sky and vertiginous pedestrian bridges, rather than amidst old terraces or in-between serried tower blocks. Partly this is happenstance: the City Council was essentially giving away the empty flats left by the families who escaped. But it is also surely to do with the possibilities of the structure itself. All the things bemoaned in a 1978 *World in Action* documentary as deleterious to family life—the labyrinthine complexity of the blocks, the noise and sense of height and dynamism, the lack of a feeling of 'ownership' in the communal areas—were perfect for the purposes of a self-creating urbanism. In the minimal, atmospheric productions of Martin Hannett you can hear the ambiguous spaces created by the blocks' enclosures; in tracks like A Certain Ratio's 'Flight' or Section 25's 'Flying', you can hear the light-headedness of attempting to live in crumbling edifices somewhere in the air. Section 25 exploited the space and the walkways' sense of drama and movement in the video for 1984's proto-techno 'Looking from a Hilltop', where they feel less like dystopia and more like Constant's ludic, self-creating landscape.

A sense of *space* is one of the most salient things about Manchester's post-punk, a dreaminess necessitated by low land values, where the very fact that the spaces were unused or even unusable led to a sense of possibility absent from the sown-up, high-rent city of today. Naylor stresses that rent is the great unspoken factor behind culture, and in Hulme, she points out, 'hardly anyone was even paying any rent, including the rent boys'.[20] The very emptiness retrospectively claimed as the blight from which regeneration saved the city was instead the source from which it drew its power. 'The centre of Manchester', she says now, 'was like a ghost town. From 1979 to '81 I'd walk around it, and no-one was there. Now, if you go to the centre of Manchester at 10 am there'll be a line of people from Liverpool queuing for Primark.'[21] Although she warns me that her views might now be coloured by nostalgia, Naylor raises the possibility that Hulme 'became functional for people in a way that hadn't been anticipated by the planners',[22] or rather, in a way that was anticipated by the people the planners had drawn their ideas from, like Constant or the Smithsons, but which they had long since forgotten.

Naylor remembers the overriding feeling of Hulme's sense of itself as an enclave, embattled but cohesive: 'there's no future, but if we stay here we'll be all right'.[23] Nonetheless, from the mid-1980s, the drugs had shifted from speed to heroin, crime had become more common, Tory election landslides led to despair, 'people started being mugged for their Giro', and many of those associated with the post-punk scene moved on.[24] Yet the New Brutalist Hulme went on to become a (fairly crusty, by many accounts) centre for the rave scene in Manchester, with the Kitchen, a club made by knocking through three council flats, being the Hacienda's hidden reverse. In the mid-1990s, on the eve of the Crescents' demolition as a ritual sacrifice to New Emerging Manchester, there was another television documentary made about the place, this time for *The Late Show*. Only just over a decade later, and we are miles from the hand-wringing of the *World in Action* documentary, with no condemnations of the idiocies of planners from the inhabitants. Instead, the Crescents' occupants fiercely defend the estates' light, air, and openness—the possibilities of the streets in the sky and the richly creative community that had established itself there, even in a context where crime and deprivation was still rife. One comments that a friend's daughter 'only found out she lived in a slum when she heard it on the news'. Meanwhile, if the streets in the sky had come full circle, back to New Babylon, then this is entirely supported by the documentary, which features images of travellers' caravans in the open space between the blocks, reminding that the hypermodernist, Situationist urbanism of New Babylon was originally inspired by gypsy camps.

Conclusion

In *The Road to Wigan Pier* George Orwell claimed, convincingly, that the failure of an idea so self-evidently sensible as Socialism to make real inroads into British society—to put it in terms he would not have used, to become counter-hegemonic— was at root a failure of propaganda and aesthetics. Socialism was associated with the following two tendencies, which sound rather mutually exclusive. First, the back-to-nature 'prig's paradise' of the garden cities, 'sandal wearers', faddists and ruralists; and second, an H. G. Wells-like science fiction machine utopianism, which often tied in with the techno-romanticism of the 'cult of Russia', all those Constructivist photos of glittering tractors and the Dnieper dam. Arguably, twentieth-century architectural modernism was something that tried to tie these two together, and Orwell insists that they are equally alien to the British worker and the part of the middle classes disaffected enough to be won to the cause. The ordinary British proletarian, for Orwell, is essentially conservative, wanting little more out of life than a comfy chair, the kids playing in the corner, the dog lying by the coal fire, the wife sewing and the paper with the racing finals: a 'perfect symmetry … on winter evenings after tea, when the fire glows in the open range', etc. Yet modernism was, supposedly, bent on wiping all this out. 'Hardly one of the things I have written about will still be there … it is hardly likely that Father will be a rough man with enlarged hands … there won't be a coal fire in the grate, only some kind of invisible heater. The furniture will be made of rubber, glass and steel … And there won't be so many children, either, if the birth-controllers have their way.'[25]

Over seventy years later, if we look at the art forms thrown up by sections of the class Orwell idealized, what are they actually like? Watch, for instance, any footage of New Order in the early 1980s. These three men and one woman, all from working-class backgrounds in postindustrial, council-estate Manchester—the grandchildren of those sturdy Wigan men reading the racing pages—were playing music which would have astonished and mortified Orwell, with its blocks of overwhelming electronic sound, unnatural bass rumbles and technocratic shimmers. These extremely modern sounds were then experienced in the modern spaces of nightclubs in concrete housing estates, former warehouses in London and Manchester, or disused steelworks in Sheffield. Evidently, many of the descendants of these placid proletarians ended up embracing some kind of modernist environment.

It could be retorted that all this is just a reflection of the environment and that in a better world, the East End electronic musicians of Grime, to name a recent example, would not be making sharp, angular, brutal noises via pirated computer programmes but sitting around the fire after a roast dinner. If ordinary people are so hostile to new forms, new noises and new shapes, then how did the last forty years of all kinds of jarring, avant-garde street music manage to happen? How have the Teds, the mods (modernists, as they were originally known), glam rockers, punks, junglists, even the kids in provincial towns getting wrecked on Saturday nights to the ludicrously simple and artificial hard house or happy hardcore managed to be written out of the story of the encounter of working-class people and modernism? Perhaps pop was actually in many ways the grass roots equivalent to, not the repudiation of, the modern movement?

Notes

1 Quoted frequently, but see most recently Richard Weight, *Mod—A Very British Style* (London: Bodley Head, 2013), 4.

2 'The Syd Barrett Story by Syd and Those Who Knew Him', http://www.pink-floyd.org/barrett/quotes.html, accessed 19 August 2013.

3 Mark Owens, 'New Brutalists/New Romantics' in Zak Kyes and Mark Owens, eds. *Forms of Inquiry—The Architecture of Critical Graphic Design* (London: Architectural Association, 2007), 146.

4   Royston Landau, *New Directions in British Architecture* (New York: George Braziller, 1968), 30.

5   J.L. Womersley et al., *Ten Years of Housing in Sheffield* (Sheffield: Corporation of Sheffield, 1962), 47.

6   Kelvin was, even more inexplicably, restored shortly before it was demolished in 1995 and is interestingly described in Peter Jones' *Streets in the Sky—Life in Sheffield's High-Rise* (self-published, Sheffield 2008). A musician and former tenant of all three deck access blocks in the 1980s and 1990s, Jones claims Kelvin Flats, the least famous and least publicly lamented of the three, had the warmest sense of community, while the re-clad, heavily surveilled Hyde Park was the least enjoyable place to live.

7   Nick Johnson, *Park Hill. Made in Sheffield, England* (Manchester: Urban Splash, 2006), 75.

8   Gina Morris, 'Pulp's Guide to Sheffield', *New Musical Express*, 3 April 1993, cited on Acrylic Afternoons, http://www.acrylicafternoons.com/nmesound.html, accessed 11 September 2013.

9   John Mulvey, 'Ten Years in a Jumbo-Collared Shirt', *New Musical Express*, June 1992, cited on Acrylic Afternoons, http://www.acrylicafternoons.com/nme92.html, accessed 11 September 2013.

10   Ian Nairn, *Nairn's London* (Harmondsworth: Penguin, 1988), 178

11   Jon Savage, *Time Travel* (London: Vintage, 1997), 361.

12   'Formulary for a New Urbanism' was most recently reprinted in Tom McDonough, ed. *The Situationists and the City* (London: Verso, 2009), 32–41.

13   'Another City for Another Life' from *Internationale Situationniste* 3 (December 1959), translated by Paul Hammond. See, Situationist International Online, http://www.cddc.vt.edu/sionline/si/another.html, accessed 12 December 2013.

14   Ibid.

15   Interview with the author in June 2009.

16   Kevin Cummins, 'Closer to the Birth of a Music Legend', *The Observer*, 12 August 2007, http://www.theguardian.com/music/2007/aug/12/popandrock.joydivision, accessed 11 September 2013.

17   Liz Naylor, *Various Times* (unpublished manuscript).

18   Ibid.

19   Ibid.

20   Interview with the author in June 2009.

21   Ibid.

22   Ibid.

23   Ibid.

24   Ibid.

25   George Orwell, *The Road to Wigan Pier* (Harmondsworth: Penguin, 1988), 104–5.

12

Edinburgh on the Couch

Richard J. Williams

Edinburgh's problem

Scotland's capital is a city of just less than half a million, built on the remnants of a 325-million-year-old volcano. An architectural as well as a geological spectacle, it has one of the world's best assemblages of neoclassical buildings, recognized by UNESCO, which awarded it World Heritage status in 1995. It hosts what is generally regarded as the world's largest arts festival and it is, after London, by some way, the most visited city in the UK. Since 1999 it has been the home of the devolved Scottish Parliament, and despite the post-2008 slump in financial services to which it was highly exposed, it remains the motor of the Scottish economy.[1] An essential part of the UK's urban imagination, it represents for many an urban ideal.

However, Edinburgh has peculiar problems when it comes to contemporary urban design and, for that matter, contemporary urban development of any kind. This has long been the case, as the campaigner and critic Colin McWilliam explained in 1974: the city is 'inclined to conservatism, and to conservation'; changes to the built environment have been the result of a 'laborious' process of public consultation and 'the expression of strong interests tempered by rules on the one hand, (and) open criticism on the other'.[2] There is no obvious direction of travel. All of its large-scale urban projects since 1999 have been accompanied by controversy. The Scottish Parliament, designed by Enric Miralles, cost £431 million, ten times its original budget when it opened in 2004.[3] A later project to bring light rail to Edinburgh ran three times over budget for a scheme a third the size of the one originally planned.[4] The development of the waterfront has delivered so little of what was promised that a big shopping mall at its core may yet close.[5] Edinburgh became known for prevarication and political infighting, in marked contrast to England's big cities, which seem to have reached a growth-oriented consensus with a legible impact on design, at the same time.[6] In respect of its attitude to the future, Edinburgh closely resembles Venice, which I described in 2013 as a 'once-great city state, now in frank decline'.[7] Edinburgh is not yet a city in decline, but it is one that one way or another certainly cultivates the *look* of decline. In any case, Edinburgh's distinctive sensibility bears exploration, because—eccentric or not—it is widely held to represent some sort of utopia.

Recovering that sensibility is another matter. A 'sensibility' is something highly ephemeral. It is an attitude, a tone of voice, a carefully directed look, a raised eyebrow, or just gossip.[8] It certainly exists, however. You find it in its unmediated form in private conversations, in the pub, over dinner, or in the back of taxis on the way home. Those things condition a lot of what follows. In terms of print sources, the nearest thing to data is perhaps the debate in the digital media, which although moderated, is often highly intemperate in tone. Then there are the sources produced by campaign groups, of which Edinburgh has a lot. Again, here the discourse has a visceral quality, which is important. I refer to official documents too, to assorted plans and public statements, but these are of relatively less interest because they represent the post-hoc rationalization of feeling, and (in Edinburgh's case, without a doubt) they moderate the intensity of feeling to a high degree. Edinburgh's official urban discourse can be extremely dry.[9] In private, it is anything but. It should also be said that in Edinburgh's case, the usual narratives of agency also do not convince. The city council is often assumed to have power where it does not, for example, and developers seem more reluctant than elsewhere to build, despite having planning permission.[10] What I am trying to recover is therefore something like a city's unconscious, to use that much-abused but still suggestive psychoanalytical term. And to continue that theme, exploring its unconscious involves digging around in the past.

Cockburn's letter

Edinburgh is an antiquarian's city, so as good a place as any to start is a letter by a famous local antiquarian, Henry Thomas, then Lord Cockburn, to the Lord Provost of Edinburgh [Fig. 12.1].[11] Written in 1849, it outlines 'The Best Ways of Spoiling the Beauties of Edinburgh'.[12] Cockburn was (in the words of his present-day followers) a 'controversialist', a 'passionate defender of Edinburgh', and 'a serious pain in the neck'. A liberal as regards the law, in matters of architecture he was a fundamentalist. The publication formed the basis of the Cockburn Association, founded in 1875, probably the modern world's first society directed towards architectural conservation.[13] The society continues to the present day and holds much influence. Its publications include Cockburn's letter, which you can buy in an annotated and illustrated version from 1998; my reading of it relies on this version as it makes repeated connection between Cockburn's city and the city of Edinburgh now. Despite its age (164 years at the time of writing), it defines more succinctly than anything else the city's peculiar sensibility. And in Edinburgh, as the visitor soon realizes, 164 years is nothing. The New Town (finished 1830) really is, for many residents, still new.

Melancholy pervades the letter: it is predicated on loss, specifically that of historic buildings and views. Cockburn's fears are deeply held and powerfully expressed: he speaks of 'alarm' at proposed developments; of the 'sorrow' a future Edinburgher might feel at the loss of the beauty that once was; and of the 'shudder' he experienced

FIGURE 12.1 *Portrait relief of Henry Thomas (Lord Cockburn) at No. 1 Cockburn St, Edinburgh.*
© Richard Williams.

on seeing a recent addition to the castle.[14] It is visceral stuff. So much has been lost, Cockburn writes (remember, this is 1849). The city, 'the scene of so much history' has been eviscerated. It used to be 'so full of historical remains' but 'many of them are gone, and many are going. The antiquarian sighs over their disappearance....'[15]

Curiously, though, Cockburn's melancholy arises from the fear of what *might* happen in the future rather than what has happened in the past. His fiercest remarks are saved for ongoing proposals to remodel Princes Street, then, as now, the city's main artery and the dividing line between Old and New Towns. Cockburn objects in particular to the street's proposed completion with buildings on the un-built south side. Again, the loss is not actual but feared. The scheme is 'infernal', writes Cockburn; it only failed through luck; 'those who remember the battle have scarcely drawn their breath freely since'.[16]

A proposal to move a church stone-by-stone meets Cockburn's disapproval, again on grounds of loss: it is not preservation or the 'extenuation of what has been done'. He quotes Ruskin in full Old Testament Prophet mode from the recently published *Seven Lamps*: 'The glory of a building is not in its stones, nor in its gold. Its glory is in its age and in that deep sense of voicefulness, of stern watching, of mysterious sympathy, even of approval or condemnation, which we feel in the walls that have been long washed by the passing waves of humanity.'[17] The fear expressed here is provoked by the mere thought of loss. There is little that is rational or realistic about this melancholy. Specifically, it is *picturesque*: an eighteenth-century aesthetic beloved by the English aristocracy and which cultivated an air of romantic gloom. Visually, it could be produced by the Claude Glass, a darkened mirror designed to turn any view into an approximation of a painted landscape cracking under layers of varnish.[18]

Romantics care for atmospheres, not function. So Cockburn is extremely exercised about the proposal to build on the south side of Princes Street, as we have seen, for the sole reason that it will spoil the view ('… the absolutely insane project of *building houses*…' (Cockburn's emphasis)).[19] He is, if anything, more bothered by the abortive works to fill in the valley now occupied by Princes Street Gardens, a scheme designed to produce valuable—and rare—flat land for building. The entire point of this part of Edinburgh, Cockburn argues, is the formal contrast between Old and New Towns; to build is to destroy the 'composition'. 'For effect', he continues, 'the deeper this valley be kept, the better'.[20] (This attitude strongly persists: in Edinburgh, 'looks are everything', as the architect Neil Gillespie has written. Utility counts for nothing.)[21] Finally, Cockburn argues that there should be 'Cities of Refuge', meaning bulwarks against modernization, and, frankly, work. (Visitors often discover Edinburgh to be a lazy city. It is, and here is one of the founding texts of its indolence.) There are 'apparently those who long for steam engines, and docks, and factories', writes Cockburn. 'But I do not believe this', he writes. 'It is incredible.'[22] Cockburn's distaste for work extends even to washing clothes, as he inveighs against the 'pollution' of a 'public washing green' on Calton Hill.[23] Cockburn's horror of laundry is matched by his fear of markets, and very likely, considering the traditional Scottish diet, vegetables. A proposal for Princes Street Gardens would be dreadful: 'booths and stalls; rotten cabbage and bruised onions; cripple carriers with nasty baskets, old female hucksters and wrangling'.[24]

The list goes on. Every part of the letter eulogizes a city that is a work of art, and a refuge from the world of men, but one that through the messy intrusion of humanity is as good as lost. Really the only permissible inhabitant appears Cockburn himself, free (ideally) from other men to contemplate the city as a work of art. His disdain for any form of modernization is, even now, striking.

Cockburn in the afterlife

Cockburn is a nineteenth-century figure, but unlike Manchester's Engels or London's Dickens, he is still alive. At a certain level of Edinburgh public life, every committee has at least one Cockburn. Cockburns stalk Parliament House, the home of Scotland's Supreme Court. Most of all, we know Cockburn is alive because the Cockburn Association says he is. Their republication of the letter in 1998 comes with annotations and illustrations, not to say a modern cover in san-serif type, indicating that the letter is as relevant now as it was in 1849. So the annotations cover such un-Victorian issues as the 1949 Abercrombie Plan, the 1963 St James's Centre, the 1980s Waverley Shopping Centre, and the privatization of British Rail. If there is any further doubt, a preface in large type proclaims 'the views he expressed so scathingly in 1849 as relevant now as they were in his own time. Would that there were more like him now.'[25]

Without a doubt, Cockburn was colourful. Unfortunately his latter-day followers are not. Whereas the 1849 letter is Swiftian in character, using hyperbole to get attention, the pronouncements of the Cockburn Association are merely stubborn. They have (using Freud's memorable terminology) a distinctly *anal* character, which is to say they are 'orderly, parsimonious and obstinate'.[26] Freud, as always, says these characteristics are essential to the furthering of civilization but that they can be overdeveloped and productive of neurosis. In terms of architecture and urbanism, the anal sensibility might be associated with preservation over-development. It is necessary for the construction of a balanced city but can be overdone.[27]

The trauma of George Square

We could invoke another of Freud's terms in relation to the Cockburn Association, 'mourning'. There is a distinctly melancholy tone to a lot of what Cockburn says (and what his followers elaborate) but it is not the melancholy of the depressive: it has too active a character and too clear an object. If the association is melancholy, it is melancholy *about* something. Things outside their narrow range of interests—like Dundee—just do not excite their passions at all.

No, Cockburn's worldview is much more like mourning, which Freud memorably described in 1916. It is 'the reaction to the loss of a beloved person or an abstraction taking the place of a person, such as fatherland, freedom, an ideal and so on'.[28] It has certain characteristics in common with melancholy, namely the loss of interest in the outside world and a fixation on the lost object of affection. It too can be neurotic when the mourner turns away from reality and 'holds on to the object through a hallucinatory wish-psychosis'—in other words, that state of mourning in which the mourner neurotically holds on to the lost object even though it has gone, bringing it to life through hallucination. Also neurotic can be the more recent idea of *anticipatory mourning* which can be found in use in contemporary clinical psychology, a condition in which the object of mourning is still alive but understood—correctly or otherwise—to be approaching death. Now this is a modern concept, but there is certainly something like this in Cockburn's letter and in the work of his latter-day followers. They have so much invested in their imagination of Edinburgh's demise that they sometimes behave as if it were, in fact, already dead.[29] Edinburgh's traumas are often anticipatory in nature.

Edinburgh did, however, suffer one genuine trauma in the twentieth century, the rebuilding of George Square, the University of Edinburgh's main central city site. (Here the word 'trauma' is used advisedly. Edinburgh has not suffered any of the things that have threatened every other large British city: no aerial bombardment, no terrorism, no riots, no fires, no large-scale deindustrialization, and bar the occasional flooding of the Water of Leith, not even particularly severe weather.) But what happened at George Square from 1949 to 1980 was widely, perhaps mostly, seen as trauma—and the trauma persisted for decades after the original events, as any visitors to the university can attest. Although entirely legal, sanctioned by the university, the city council and the Secretary of State for Scotland, after the first demolitions, it was widely decried: it was a 'rape', 'a terrible mistake', 'a shambles', even 'a holocaust'.[30] Its author was principally the university, acting through two professors of architecture, Percy Johnson Marshall and Robert Matthew, who contributed plan and architecture respectively. The university was widely criticized. It had demonstrated the 'arrogant indifference of Edinburgh University to the opinion of its own graduates and of the citizens of Edinburgh' and was 'the cuckoo in the nest'.[31]

George Square lies on the south side of the city, slightly less than a mile from Princes Street. Laid out in 1766 by James Brown, it was one of the first large-scale developments outside of the Old Town. It consisted of a large green surrounded by houses of no more than four storeys, small by comparison with later developments. There is a notably rusticated quality to the stonework and particularly the pointing ('cherrycock'), although the treatment of the doorways is more delicate.[32] The trauma began in 1949 with the publication of what has come to be known as the Abercrombie Plan, or more accurately *A Civic Survey and Plan for the City and Royal Burgh of Edinburgh* by Patrick Abercrombie and Derek Plumstead.[33] By the time Abercrombie turned his attention to the Scottish capital, he was probably the English-speaking world's most eminent planner. He was no *tabula rasa* modernist, as the historically respectful opening pages of the plan make clear. But he did not think much of George Square.

A caption to a photograph of the (still extant) numbers 55 and 56 asks simply: 'Why allow them to stand in the way of a great project?' The façades—plain, small windowed, and lacking the brick-bonded stonework at ground level—are compared unfavourably with buildings on Queen Street. The square, writes Abercrombie, 'has a domestic character of some considerable charm', but because of detrimental alterations to the north side in the nineteenth century, the square, as a whole, should not be regarded as highly as Moray Place or Anne [*sic*] Street where 'no such incursions have occurred'.[34] Cognizant of the pressures of student numbers—the university wished to double its intake—and the difficulty of finding another location for expansion, Abecrombie recommended sensitive redevelopment, involving just the north side in the first instance and the retention of existing rights of way and the remaining three sides of the square.

The Plan allowed the principle of redevelopment to be considered for the first time; Frederick Appleton, the university's Principal appointed in 1949, concurred and by 1951 the rebuilding of the square was approved by the University Court, based on the now public rationale of growth. The chief architect appointed by Appleton, Basil Spence, publicly agreed with Abercrombie: after 'mature reflection', he wrote,

> I am convinced that the charm of George Square is due to its atmosphere created by the height of its buildings and its trees. I am certain that Edinburgh must be given something from this generation to preserve in the future [...] as Robert Adam did when he destroyed Kirk o' the Field to create the Old Quad.[35]

Spence produced some highly rhetorical sketches from the south side of the Meadows, a public park adjoining the university. These elegant pen-and-wash drawings draw on a picturesque rather than modern aesthetic. Redolent of John Constable's early nineteenth-century sketches of Salisbury Cathedral from that city's own Meadows, they depict the new buildings as benign horizontal and vertical accents, emerging naturally from the foliage. They do not in any way represent the modern as disruption, or even especially new; the modern is natural, timeless, but rooted.

Spence's sense of visual rhetoric may have been enough to assuage any doubt inside the university, but it was not enough to forestall the development of opposition. The plans led to the constitution, in 1956, of the Georgian Group of Edinburgh, later (1959) the Scottish Georgian Society, the key figure being Colin McWilliam. The Society was chaired by George Baillie-Hamilton, the 12th Earl of Haddington, and their activities had the strong support of the Cockburn Association. Under pressure from both societies, and a well-orchestrated anti-development campaign, the university partially relented.[36] The David Hume Tower and Library were built, along with an addition to the Medical School and two pavilions by Robert Matthew, Percy Johnson-Marshall and Partners (completed 1967), and their Lecture Theatre (also 1967) [Fig. 12.2]. The Department of Pharmacology completes the redevelopment, leaving the original west side entirely intact, as well as half of the east. The nineteenth-century fragment of George Watson's Ladies College, now (2013) occupied by the School of Philosophy, Psychology, and Language Sciences, also remains.

At issue in George Square are two competing theologies. Both are agreed on the importance of the past, but one is essentially liberal, the other fundamentalist. As Miles Glendinning has argued, this is entirely consistent with the origins of the conservation movement. Worldwide, an interest in architectural conservation develops hand-in-hand with modernization: often (as here), the advocates of modernization also wish to preserve the past—just different bits of it.[37]

FIGURE 12.2 *Basil Spence, University of Edinburgh Library, George Square, 1965–7.*
© Richard Williams.

Abercrombie was a founder member of the Council for the Protection of Rural England (CPRE). In Abercrombie's mind, there was no essential conflict between conservation and development. The same can be said of Robert Matthew, who simultaneously designed major buildings for George Square and campaigned to preserve the New Town. By the standards of the day, the past was carefully contextualized.[38]

The Abercrombie Plan is a strongly visual document, heavily reliant on black and white photography. The Plan opens with a full-page image of Calton Road, looking north underneath Waterloo Place, photographed in bright early morning sun, the cobbles glistening; looking up at the grand open portico on Waterloo Place, the image represents a city of immense grandeur and self-confidence which commands respect and amplification.[39]

The fundamentalist interpretation of George Square emerged after 1958. According to Miles Glendinning, the principles of the 1949 plan as regards George Square had long been accepted: 'the fundamental reality of the scheme was that outline planning permission for zoning change had already been granted in 1954', he wrote, and in 1958, the Secretary of State for Scotland refused the Cockburn Association's demand for a public enquiry.[40] The following year, 1959, the then Edinburgh Corporation granted outline permission to the scheme, confirming basic issues such as the demolition required, scale, massing and density. Only at that point did the fundamentalist position properly emerge, via 'a wide coalition in the time-honoured Edinburgh tradition of cultural-environmental outrage campaigns'.[41] The University of Edinburgh developed a (largely unfair) reputation for callousness.

Nevertheless, it came to pass, albeit in a truncated form. What survives, curiously, is the wound: it is a square of abrupt contrasts. The highly saleable picturesque vision of the square is still present in the views of the library, and in the right conditions, the David Hume Tower; but at the north-eastern corner, the contrast between the Georgian houses and Reiach and Hall's neo-Corbusian Appleton Tower is abrupt, while the hard landscaping and the downdrafts from the tower make for an uncomfortable experience at ground level [Fig. 12.3]. To the north, the square reads as a series of fragments, perversely keeping the sense of disruption alive. Developments since the 1960s have served to reinforce the wound—so on the eastern side of the square, the big 2008 development on the former Crichton Street car park by Bennetts Associates with Reiach and Hall, the Informatics Forum, takes up the restrained modernist language of the Matthew complex. On the western side of the square at the same time, numbers 17–19 have been extensively renovated, restoring the very striking cherrycock mortar on the building façade.

The Scottish Parliament

The ironies of the George Square redevelopment are considerable. Its author (Robert Matthew) was also a key figure in the conservation movement, and its new buildings have all been listed by the same organizations that fought to stop them being built. There are many other contradictions. Nonetheless, the redeveloped George Square is almost universally perceived as a wound, and

FIGURE 12.3 *Reiach and Hall, Appleton Tower, University of Edinburgh, George Square, 1963–6. Terraces on eastern side of the square in foreground built 1774–9.*
© Richard Williams.

privately, the university's attitude towards critics is conciliatory, often apologetic, while it continues (as in the refurbishment and extension of the William Robertson building during 2012–14) to entrench the stylistic disjunction brought into being in the 1960s. This contrast is not in itself a problem and has been in many other cities embraced as an ethic and an aesthetic. In Edinburgh, it continues to represent a wound.[42]

That sense of modern architecture as trauma was not unique to Edinburgh, but the events of George Square meant that it persisted there longer than anywhere else (get into a conversation with almost anyone about architecture in the city, and in under a minute, typically, you are onto the evils of modernism and the rape of George Square). George Square was followed by the growth of the heritage industry; in 1974 the *Architect's Journal* published a special issue devoted to the city and its conservation. In 1996, the city was awarded UNESCO World Heritage Status, which preserved the unique conjunction of Old and New Towns. Against this background the new Scottish Parliament building appeared, designed by the Catalan architect Enric Miralles and opened in 2004 [Fig. 12.4]. Much celebrated by critics from outside of Edinburgh at the time of its completion, it well represents the contradictions of the George Square project. To build *anything* in this context was to risk public vilification: added to an already toxic mix was the uncertainty about the Parliament itself. A legal entity since 1999, the Parliament was nevertheless insecure about its identity and purpose in these early days and lacked

FIGURE 12.4 *Enric Miralles/RMJM, Scottish Parliament Building, detail of entrance, 2000–4.*
© Richard Williams.

any existing model in the UK. That existential confusion is arguably represented in a commissioning process that very publicly lost control of its brief early on. A commission for a debating chamber costing some £40 million became a project for, in effect, a political campus with accommodation for Members of the Scottish Parliament (MSPs), facilities for the public, and significant areas of public space. The final bill was £431 million, an increase by a factor of ten. The epic quality of the overspend has inevitably overshadowed all perceptions of the building.[43] I would make two comments about that: first, as the critic Charles Jencks observed in early 2005, regardless of the starting point, £431 million is the order of magnitude one would expect for a public building of this scale and complexity. Second, the liquid character of the building in its design stages is *entirely* consistent with the circumstances that produced it, namely a city with a longstanding suspicion of anything modern and a Parliament with, at that time ,only a vague sense of its identity. In retrospect, it is only surprising it did not cost more.

The Parliament is best described as anxious: it is extremely eager to please its constituents and also keen to avoid offending its host city.[44] The result is an extremely odd building, one whose eccentricities speak of the need to satisfy multiple and conflicting demands. It is tempting to say that only Edinburgh could have produced a building quite like it—and that nothing like it is likely to appear anywhere else again. Its oddness is clear enough in its resistance to description. It is, as several critics noted, a sort of anti-monument around which it is possible to walk without realizing that it is a Parliament at all. Its northern flank, along the lower part of the Royal Mile, incorporates the eighteenth-century Queensberry House as well as the smaller and less distinguished Canongate Building. There is a concrete wall encrusted with decoration, but in general the impression this side of the Parliament gives is less of a single building than the boundary of some kind of campus. Turning the corner to the south front, and it is Holyrood Palace and the Queen's Gallery that draw attention: the Parliament's public entrance (for this is where it is found) is low key, and undemonstrative, either in its original iteration (2004) or its more recent one (2010). Both comprise small doorways into a largely horizontal, single-storey structure in concrete that emerges from the grassy terraces swooping down to Holyrood Park. From the southern side of the Parliament, you have the clearest sense of the complex as a whole. At ground level it is defined by a series of high concrete walls guarding the Parliament's service entrance. Above this rises the highest part of the complex, the debating chamber, containing (still) the germ of the original idea: a handful of scattered leaves (or boats, or shells) rendered in glass. Then to the left, looking northwards, is the mysterious slab containing the MSPs' offices: each is defined by a projecting window, in which one can sit; a tiny contemplative space, drawing on monastic imagery but also (it was said) abstracting the silhouette of Henry Raeburn's skater, the subject of his iconic 'Reverend Robert Walker Skating on Duddingston Loch' (c. 1790) [Fig. 12.5]. A left turn beyond this block brings the visitor back to the Royal Mile and the Queensberry House entrance.

The critical reception of the Parliament in 2004 was overwhelmingly positive but also showed some exasperation, as if the building simply exceeded the language available to describe it or (commonly) the Parliament was simply too much to take in. No Presbyterian restraint here: it was a place of Romantic excess ('a heady, hedonistic brew [...] A Celtic-Catalan cocktail to blow both minds and budgets').[45]

FIGURE 12.5 *Enric Miralles/RMJM, Scottish Parliament Building, 2000–4. Detail of MSP office wing, Salisbury Crags in the background.*
© Richard Williams.

A decade on, that excess is still legible, but perhaps more clearly now in terms of its excess of signification; it is not the excess of luxury such as you might find at the Trump Tower or the Burj Khalifa, but the (to my eyes) anxious desire to please everyone, through which there is a nod to almost every conceivable Scottish visual cliché, while the building itself recedes as a totality. That desire for inclusiveness is so exaggerated here that it reads now as anxiety; it speaks of a fundamental lack of confidence, an issue that has in fact been widely discussed in contemporary Scottish life.[46] It stands for everything and nothing at the same time.

But perhaps the most curious quality of the Parliament, and the most pertinent here, is its anti-urban quality. This was present in Miralles' original design brief which spoke of a building located in 'the Scottish Land' (his emphasis) and one that 'should originate from the sloping base of Arthur's seat and arrive into the city almost out of the rock'.[47] It conspicuously does not address its urban context; in fact, it seems if anything to shrink from it. Its formal reference points are the slopes of the extinct volcano of Arthur's Seat and the sea at Portobello. So the terracing of the public entrance on the eastern side of the building emerges from the landscape of the park, while the imagery of the debating chamber ('upturned boats' said Miralles) invokes fishing in the North Sea. Then there is the repeated imagery of vegetation: oak poles, arranged in an open lattice form shade the western-facing windows of the MSP complex, while the same materials are found on the entrance canopy; echoes of the lattice form can be found as concrete reliefs and a bamboo garden for MSPs. It is no monument in any conventional sense; it shrinks from the landscape, if anything. It adds nothing—literally nothing—to the existing skyline. You have to be taken to it to know it is there at all. For the most part, these qualities were praised by early critics, but interestingly the category used to describe them was the extremely difficult one of primitivism. So, it is 'National Romanticism [....] tapping deep into primeval folk consciousness' (*Architectural Review*);[48] it 'conjectures a mythical origin for the newly devolved nation' [...] and 'a £432 million primitive hut' (*Building Design*);[49] it is an 'organic, non-hierarchical building'; its rooflights resemble 'prised-open clams' (*RIBA Journal*);[50] it is a 'knitting together of nature and culture [...] a rocky outcrop [....]', and then 'Scottish identity is closely associated with the rugged landscape and the urban experience in which it has grown' (Charles Jencks in *Architecture Today*).[51] These responses (and there are many more like them) take their cue from Miralles himself, who stated clearly that in his view Scotland was a 'Land', not 'a series of cities'.[52]

All these words prepare the visitor for an experience of a building that is rooted in the landscape; they draw our attention away from the city, and towards the land; they remind us that the views from the debating chamber are indeed directed at the cone of Arthur's Seat, and to the sea beyond; they affirm that the materials (the granite, for example) come from the land. All this produces a *gesamtkunstwerk* directed at a blood-and-soil narrative of Scotland. Now there are several points to make about this. First is that it was, and is, popular. The Parliament received 250,000 visitors in the first six months of opening and now takes around 400,000 visits annually, a large number for a building never conceived as a tourist attraction.[53] While 'popular' does not equate to 'good', the large numbers suggest an empathy with the Parliament's concept. Second is the positive crucial reception by the architectural profession, culminating in the Stirling Prize in 2005, the highest award of the Royal Institute of British Architects ('a statement of sparkling excellence [...] the building embodied the transition between the city and the drama of the Scottish countryside surrounding it. Extremely successful landscaping made this transition even more striking.').[54] But the third point to make is, simply, that the Parliament reiterates Edinburgh's peculiar architectural sensibility. In 1849, Lord Cockburn imagined a city that was, in effect, finished, a city of such beauty that no further additions were possible. Its only future was genteel decline, overseen by Cockburn himself, and perhaps a few followers. Cockburn's decadent urbanism was reiterated in the furore around the George Square redevelopment ('a holocaust'), the subsequent rise of the conservation lobby, capped with the award in 1995 of UNESCO World Heritage Status, which congratulated the city on that most delicate of urban phenomena, its 'townscape'.[55] In such a context—an aestheticized, conservation-minded, growth-wary, risk-averse, decadent city—the only possibly Parliament, you might say, was this one. It makes no claim on the city's skyline, in effect burying itself, at the lowest point of the Old Town, and looking anywhere but the city. The brief was for a Parliament for Scotland, not (in Miralles' phrase) for a 'set of cities'. That said, Scotland's population is overwhelmingly urban, and that urban identity, strangely, has no representation here.

Conclusions

Assuming any of the above is true, what does it matter? Edinburgh, as its city council never tires of reminding us, is uniquely blessed: visitors flock to it; its citizens are ever wealthier and happier by comparison with their counterparts elsewhere. And, it should be said, in those areas of work we have learned to call creative industries, people seem content enough to re-inhabit the monuments of the past: Summerhall, the former Royal (Dick) School of Veterinary Studies is a case in point, successfully reinvented as a centre for entrepreneurship in digital media. My own anxiety, I suppose, concerns the future. Edinburgh's design tradition is one that has cultivated what Cockburn termed 'refuge', taking pride in an awkward, eccentric, and highly resistant approach to the modern world. The touristic appeal of this is undisputable, likewise its appeal to aesthetes. Its charms are less clear to (say) families on average incomes who struggle to find affordable housing within the city boundaries. The appeal to aesthetics (as has been so evident in central London) makes the city ever more a site of speculation, with housing a 'global reserve currency' as Michael Goldfarb of the *New York Times* memorably put it.[56] By Edinburgh City Council's own statistics, the city is strikingly rich, single, and grey: it comprises, in other words, precisely those people who can afford to cultivate the city as an aesthetic phenomenon.[57] Everyone else has been pushed to the margins. Arguably more than anywhere else in the UK, Edinburgh's design sensibility is an aristocratic one. Bizarrely for a city that likes to profess a taste for Scandinavian-style social democracy, its aesthetics are those of the eighteenth-century English aristocrat. The city, insofar as it allows such an impolite thing can exist at all, is an object of spectacular pleasure, a work of (historical) art to be consumed by the dilettante. I exaggerate, but not by much. While that sensibility dominates urban conversations, the much-touted Scots dream of a social democracy will remain just that.

Notes

1　Measured in terms of GVA per capita, it outperforms the general Scottish economy by a factor of 1.6 (2011 figures). See http://www.edinburgh-inspiringcapital.com/invest/economic_data/economy/gross_value_added_gva.aspx, accessed 15 November 2013.

2　C. McWilliam, 'Edinburgh Conserved', *Architect's Journal* (16 January 1974): 109.

3　S. Bain, *Holyrood: The Inside Story* (Edinburgh: Edinburgh University Press, 2005).

4　'Edinburgh Trams: Timeline of Twists and Turns', *Scotsman*, 12 April 2002, http://www.scotsman.com/news/scotland/top-stories/edinburgh-trams-timeline-of-twists-and-turns-1-2229133, accessed 15 November 2013.

5　J. McClellan, 'Holding Back the Fort Won't Save Leith', *Scotsman*, 25 October 2013, http://www.edinburghnews.scotsman.com/news/opinion/john-mclellan-holding-back-fort-won-t-save-leith-1-3157545, accessed 15 November 2013.

6　London and Manchester in particular. Both have had strong municipal leadership with an interest in design, and tall buildings, in particular.

7   See R.J. Williams, 'Scotch this Plan', *Foreign Policy*, 13 February 2013, http://www.
     foreignpolicy.com/articles/2013/02/13/scotch_this_plan_edinburgh_scotland_
     independence, accessed 15 November 2013.

8   Gavin Butt's work on gossip in the New York art scene is of tangential interest here—
     he wrestles with the same problem of recovering what can only be described as a
     feeling. G. Butt, *Between You and Me: Queer Disclosures in the New York Art World
     1948–1963* (Asheville, N. Carolina: Duke University Press, 2005).

9   See, for example, Edinburgh City Council's Local Plan, http://www.edinburgh.gov.
     uk/info/178/local_and_strategic_development_plans/1005/edinburgh_city_local_plan,
     accessed 15 November 2013.

10   Conversation with Euan Leitch of Built Environment Forum Scotland, November 2013.
     Most development sites in the city have planning permission: the widely perceived lack
     of development cannot (all) be attributed to the city council. See, http://www.befs.org.uk/

11   Lord Henry Thomas Cockburn, *A Letter to the Lord Provost on the Best Ways of
     Spoiling the Beauties of Edinburgh* (Edinburgh: Cockburn Association, 2006).

12   Ibid.

13   For more on the Cockburn Association, see http://www.cockburnassociation.org.uk/

14   Cockburn, *Letter*, 5, 11.

15   Ibid., 13.

16   Ibid., 11.

17   Ibid., 14.

18   For more on the picturesque as an urban sensibility, see R.J. Williams, *The Anxious City*
     (London: Routledge, 2004), 25–53.

19   Cockburn, *Letter*, 9.

20   Ibid., 9.

21   N. Gillespie, 'Flower of Scotland', originally in *Architect's Journal*, 17 January 2003.
     Reproduced at http://www.reiachandhall.co.uk/Library/Interview/flower_of_scotland.
     html, accessed 15 November 2013.

22   Cockburn, *Letter*, 6.

23   Ibid., 15.

24   Ibid., 10.

25   Ibid., 1.

26   S. Freud, 'Character and Anal Eroticism', in *The Penguin Freud Library Vol. 7: On
     Sexuality* (London: Penguin Books, 1991), 205–16.

27   Edinburgh's decision-making culture has long been tortuous, as if designed to produce
     negative rather than positive outcomes. See McWilliam, 'Edinburgh Conserved', 109.

28   S. Freud, *Murder, Mourning and Melancholy* (London: Penguin Books, 2005), 201–18.

29   For a discussion of anticipatory grief as a cultural phenomenon, see R. Fulton,
     'Anticipatory Mourning: A Critique of the Concept', *Mortality*, 8/4 (2003): 342–52.

30   McWilliam, 'Edinburgh Conserved'.

31   M. Glendinning. *The Conservation Movement: A History of Architectural Preservation,
     Antiquity to Modernity* (Abingdon: Routledge, 2013), 158.

32   J. Gifford, C. McWilliam, D. Walker and C. Wilson, *The Buildings of Scotland:
     Edinburgh* (London: Penguin Books, 1991), 251–2.

33 P. Abercrombie and D. Plumstead, *A Civic Survey and Plan for the City and Royal Burgh of Edinburgh* (Edinburgh and London: Oliver and Boyd, 1949).

34 Abercrombie, *Civic Survey and Plan*.

35 Spence, quoted in C. Fenton, *Appleton's Architects: Building the University of Edinburgh 1949–65*, PhD Thesis, University of Edinburgh (2002), 70.

36 Fenton, *Appleton's Architects*.

37 Glendinning, *Conservation Movement*. See also R.J. Williams, *Brazil: Modern Architectures in History* (London: Reaktion, 2009). Lucio Costa headed up SPHAN, the Brazilian conservation body at the same time as planning Brasília.

38 Later accounts of the city's modernization depict an apocalyptic rupture with the past. See for example D. O'Leary, 'Conservation Body Discovers Book of Radical Plans for Edinburgh circa 1949', *Scotsman*, 19 January 2013, http://www.scotsman.com/news/scotland/top-stories/conservation-body-discovers-book-of-radical-plans-for-edinburgh-circa-1949-1-2747564, accessed 18 November 2013.

39 Abercrombie and Plumstead, *Civic Survey and Plan*.

40 Glendinning, *Conservation Movement*, 158.

41 Ibid., 158.

42 The university's apologetic attitude is best represented by an anecdote. When I was inducted as a new member of academic staff in October 2000, I was addressed—as part of a cosmopolitan group of fifty or so, all new to Edinburgh—by the then principal. The *very first* thing he did was to apologize for the ugliness of the Appleton Tower, which up until that point none of us had even noticed.

43 For more on the financial management, see the public enquiry chaired by Lord Fraser of Carmyllie ('The Fraser Enquiry') which reported in 2004. Available online at http://www.holyroodinquiry.org.

44 I use the term 'anxious' in the same way as it is used in my book *The Anxious City*, in other words, an object subject to too many competing and contradictory demands.

45 C. Slessor, 'Scottish Parliament, Edinburgh, Scotland', *Architectural Review*, 116 (November 2004): 48.

46 See C. Craig, *The Scots' Crisis of Confidence* (Glendaruel: Argyll Publishing, 2011). Also see the Scottish Government's Curriculum for Excellence (2004 to date). A quarter of school education is now directed towards building 'confidence'. See Scottish Government, 'Curriculum for Excellence' (1 November 2004), http://www.scotland.gov.uk/Publications/2004/11/20178/45862, accessed 18 November 2013.

47 Miralles quoted in The Scottish Parliament, 'About the Parliament: Landscaping', http://www.scottish.parliament.uk/visitandlearn/15914.aspx, accessed 18 November 2013.

48 Slessor, 'Scottish Parliament', 62.

49 E. Woodman, 'Out of the Shadow', *Building Design* (15 October 2004): 13.

50 C. Wright, 'Study: Scottish Parliament, Edinburgh', *RIBA Journal* (October 2004): 38.

51 C. Jencks, 'Charles Jencks on the Architectural Territories of the EMBT/RMJM Parliament Building', *Architecture Today*, 154 (January 2005): 32.

52 Very widely quoted. See for example J. Knox, 'Holyrood; The Inside Story', *BBC News Website*, 4 September 2004, http://news.bbc.co.uk/1/hi/scotland/3627152.stm, accessed 19 November 2013.

53   The Scottish Parliament, 'Holyrood Visitor Figures Hit the Heights', 4 January 2010, http://www.scottish.parliament.uk/newsandmediacentre/17720.aspx, accessed 18 November 2013. For comparison, 1.9 million visited the National Museums of Scotland in 2012, but that is a multi-site operation whose business, so to speak, is visitor numbers.

54   RIBA Stirling Prize website, http://ribastirlingprize.architecture.com/the-scottish-parliament-edinburgh-2005, accessed 19 November 2013.

55   UNESCO, 'Old and New Towns of Edinburgh', http://whc.unesco.org/en/list/728, accessed 19 November 2013.

56   M. Goldfarb, 'London's Great Exodus', *New York Times*, 12 October 2013, http://www.nytimes.com/2013/10/13/opinion/sunday/londons-great-exodus.html?_r=0, accessed 19 November 2013.

57   City of Edinburgh Council, *Edinburgh By Numbers 2013–14*, http://www.edinburgh-inspiringcapital.com/invest/economic_data/publications/edinburgh_by_numbers.aspx, accessed 19 November 2013. The number of single-person households is approximately twice the UK average; the number of 'traditional' families (two parents, one or more children) in single figures, half the UK average.

13

Heatherwick Studio: A New Bus for London

Abraham Thomas

In an interview conducted by Abraham Thomas, Director of Sir John Soane's Museum, London, and former Curator of Design at the Victoria and Albert Museum, Thomas Heatherwick discusses the iconic London Routemaster bus and Heatherwick Studio's design for a new bus for London.

Thomas, what was your key interest in taking the commission for the new London bus?

I was once asked to appear on The Culture Show, and they'd asked different people to pick their British design icon of the last century. One person jumped in and argued for Concorde, and I did the same for the London Routemaster bus. I found myself sitting there explaining what was so special about it. The thing that was very striking about that bus was that it was thought through as a truly cohesive and integrated design project. Now that does sound special when you acknowledge that for the past twenty or thirty years the environments within buses have failed to convey any sense that there is some sort of design force holding the elements together. It just feels like buses recently have resulted from a conglomeration of health and safety concerns, public pressure initiatives … the design has just been layered and layered.

The design vision has been diluted?

Yes, in fact, that's on top of the fact that these buses weren't particularly appealing to start off with. Some of the 1980s bus types were just taking regulations literally. If there was a regulation about how long a bus needed to be, or how high it could be, the result would be simply to make a box to those dimensions. The only constraint that seemed to exist for London's Transport Authority in terms of the design was that it should be *red*. It seemed that there was this job to transport people around

London—somebody buys a ticket and they walk through that door, and that's it. From there onwards there was no true recognition of human spirit, of the human experience that we share, and how that affects the way we feel about the world around us.

I'm sure a crucial factor there is—and I know this is something that you and I have talked about before—the role of London Transport as a bold commissioning body— the perception of a 'golden age' state-sponsored design programme, incorporating vehicle design, textiles, graphic design, and so on.

I guess it depends on what your objective is. If your objective is just to take money off people and take them somewhere, then that's one thing—and some people might argue that even that isn't always successfully achieved. But there is also a civic role—a cultural societal role that public transport infrastructure provides as a backdrop to our lives. Many, many hours of your life are spent within the transport system—and that can be neutral; it can be negative; or it can actually enrich your life. Back in the 1930s and 1940s, there was a level of confidence in the provision of transport infrastructure in London. There was leadership when it came to the procurement of the stations, the buses, the rolling stock and other elements, and people understood that there was this civic role present at the same time. But if you don't value that aspect, if you don't truly contribute something, then you are quite possibly doing cultural damage to society. I think human beings are very sensitive and attuned to these things, but I think that many people treat human beings as if they are very basic. It's as if some of those values only matter if you've studied design or art. I think those values mean something to everybody, regardless of whether you've been trained in that or not. You still feel that you're affected. I think it's been very under-valued in recent years. That's most clearly, and shockingly, apparent when you realize that the last time a bus was designed specifically for London was more than fifty years ago. The old London Transport authority commissioned a design team to think about all of these factors together, but in the intervening years society has changed. London has changed. With the level of traffic we have, the reliability of the buses is not just about the traffic; it's also how quickly you can load and unload the passengers. When you have only one door, there is a real difference between three people getting on and getting off, and a queue of passengers waiting whilst seventy people get off and then seventy get on. Having three doors means that you're more likely to load and unload within a more consistent time frame, which means the bus is more likely to keep to its timetable. There was a great romance to the old buses, but it took more than fifty years for the true functionality of buses to be addressed again. How you feel is part of the function. Getting you there is the function. How much it costs and how much energy it uses. They're all, I believe, vital functions for a sustainable transport system. If you feel okay—if you feel that you're being informed well, looked after, and you're not in discomfort—then you don't mind so much if the bus is four minutes late.

That definitely seemed to be a real concern for Frank Pick when he was the design commissioner for London Transport during the 1920s and 1930s. He had a real ambition to improve commuters' lives, to think about all the tiny details—every single little thing that might have some sort of impact on that commuter's experience, whether it was the design of a poster or the moquette fabric on a tram seat or the way in which signage worked to get you from one part of the station to another.

In some sense, what you're describing chimes with the London 2012 Olympics cycling success. The success in the Velodrome was this thing that everyone has been talking about: the marginal gains. By looking at *everything* about that cyclist's life, and everything about the way they behave and live, and eat and sleep, and what they do in the hour between the heats and the finals … it all adds to that success. I've always felt that in our work, you need to think about everything. In effect, how you described Frank Pick thinking about the tickets and the lighting and the signage and the flooring, it all really adds up to something. Recently, it feels as though there has been this very crude view, which was just 'none of that nonsense'; it's been about saving money and so on—but it's so clearly a false economy. If you stop caring and don't value these things, if the world around you has little care in it, then in turn you will care little about *it* … and things escalate from there. In all our projects we deliberately focus on every possible thing we could possibly care about. The new London buses will be around for many, many years and we want to be able to sleep at night, knowing that we did everything we possibly could.

With the bus, it was just about trying to strike that balance, between all of those factors, believing that you can aggregate all of those 'marginal gains'. Why not aspire to every single bit of your experience being the best it can be? One striking element within the brief was the requirement that it mustn't be possible to kill the driver with a *sword*. Things like that. You just shuddered inside, creeped out by this factor. The drivers' unions needed the driver to be encased. We felt it was really important, therefore, to make the driver's enclosure not look like the driver thinks you're going to kill him with a sword. We didn't want this 'embattled citadel' that the driver is in reinforcing any sense of mistrust in the relationship between driver and passenger. We should *celebrate* the drivers. We're grateful and thankful that they're there making London work and taking us to our destination. They're our chauffeur. We felt that our role was to *elevate* the driver.

For me, I'm so proud of public transport. I feel very lucky to have been born and brought up in the city that pioneered the world's public transport ideas. London had the first underground system, and it's famous for its red double-decker buses. It's just amazing that if you ask someone on the other side of the world about their image of London, they're likely to say Tower Bridge, Big Ben, Red Bus. If you were to Google 'London view', you'd probably end up with the Houses of Parliament and a red double-decker bus. Given that, it's extraordinary how we have failed to cherish the red double-decker bus; failed to buff, polish and nurture that as a key part of our distinctiveness in the world. When people say, 'I'm looking forward to coming to London, and I'm going to go on a red double-decker bus', you're quietly thinking to yourself, 'No, really, don't'—because they're no longer special.

Yes, they don't really match that picture-perfect postcard view of London, do they?

They no longer match up, unless you're lucky enough to catch one of the heritage buses. It's very striking that, when we talk about London Transport and people go a bit misty-eyed, and you think of the examples, there is nothing from the last forty years that is particularly cherished. It's always further back beyond that. I think we should get properly embarrassed about that and use that force of being embarrassed to take inspiration from the confidence of the commissioning that was carried out in the early twentieth century.

Throughout the world many countries have a national day. Of the approximately 250 countries, 247 have a national day where they celebrate being a country together. The United Kingdom is one of the very few countries not to have a national day. We don't actually have anything where we come together, unless you are particularly focused on royal occasions. I think royalty does that, but that isn't always shared by everybody. We are less religious than ever. There are various forces at play. That's why the Olympics were so extraordinary. They brought us together and then we looked at each other and thought, 'Actually, we're all here together and, yes, other countries are special but we're special too. This is a special country'. In a way, to me, our public transport, it's like the BBC. What the BBC was, and what I hope it still represents—it's what brings us together.

Yes, the Olympics surprised us all. I think people were very cynical about the Olympics beforehand, assuming it wasn't going to be celebratory, but it absolutely was. People talked about it in such glowing terms—almost unanimously, and perhaps because we've gone for so long without that reason to celebrate and come together. Similarly, with public transport, people have forgotten the positive impact that transport can potentially have on everyone's lives.

It affirms the collective quality in all of us. There are so many things in life that break us down to be by ourselves and to become individuals. The Olympics had a moment where it was 'we'. It certainly had a moment of, 'Here we are, all together'. Maybe I'm sounding really soppy and sounding too romantic about it, but I love those moments when you're just standing on a tube train and there are strangers all around you. Actually, your safety exists because there are strangers, and we're all looking out for each other. There's that sense of being able to be by yourself because you're there with others; you can just be there with the population around you. For me, I suppose I'm speaking in celebration of cities. I do love that, that sense of togetherness, trying to make things happen. I believe in the chemistry of people together. Our transport system, for me, is very important. It's the way we see each other and keep our feet on the ground.

Let's explore that idea of the impact on the wider city. You said part of the appeal of the London bus project was that it had an impact on so many different lives. As an object within the city it has an amazing presence. What was the design thinking behind this bus presenting itself as an architectural elevation? How does it fit in to the rest of the urban fabric?

I did my undergraduate degree in Manchester; this was back in the very end of the 1980s, beginning of the 1990s. There they had these double-decker buses, moving the people of Manchester around the city. But they were all operated by different bus companies, and each operator changed the colour of their buses—so there were blue buses, green buses, grey buses, white buses. They had different logos and branding. The streets felt like a mess.

Nothing was coming together.

Nothing. You'd be waiting, and different people had passes for different bus operators, so you'd be waiting at a bus stop and a bus would come that could take you to where you want, but because it's not the right bus company for your pass, you'd wait until one of the blue ones comes, rather than the green one. Then inside the buses themselves—some of them had purple fabric with yellow spots, some had yellow fabric with birds on it, and others just had plastic seats. Just utterly fragmented. You'd look back at London, and Manchester really felt like it was the Wild West of public transport systems. When you're getting a bus, you don't care who the operator is. You don't want to know. I don't want to have to remember bus operator company names. You just want to be moved to where you want to go to. Manchester seemed an extreme example of something, of turning a city into a mishmash. Then coming back to London, where I was born and brought up, it seemed clear that there was this way of thinking about the buildings in the city, and the control systems that apply. You could propose a single two-storey building in North London that might be very controversial; it might meet huge resistance from landowners or the local authority planning department. There might be an independent design review panel, and English Heritage could have a view, or the Mayor's office might even call in if they think that the design isn't suitable. You get all these different people who are commenting on one building, and that could be a simple two-storey building. Are the materials in the local vernacular and is it in keeping with the existing palette of materials? Has it got the correct lead flashing? Is it real slate; was it quite the right quarry of stone that was used? And so on and so on—and that is one two-storey building. London has 7,000 two-storey buildings on wheels. There has been no control other than the transport authority saying: '*Is it red*?' But these are two-storey buildings that move around in front of you, every day in the city. You're more likely to see the elevations of those buses than any single building. You see a bus more than the tallest building in London, because that's all the way over there, and there aren't 7,000 of them.

Crucially, as a pedestrian you're on the street, and you're surrounded by these mobile objects.

You're on the street. A starting motivation for us was to draw no differentiation between objects in London. Whether an object is static or mobile, it's still an object in London. It seemed funny that there might be all these restrictions and interest groups relating to the construction of a new community centre, yet absolutely no oversight of the 7,000 two-storey buildings on wheels. We call one thing architecture, and we call that other thing infrastructure. There's nothing to say that in 300 years' time we'll still be using those terms—but they are all objects. They'll still be objects in 1,000 years. These are still surfaces, people remain the same size, and these objects will still create barriers to your view and impact how you feel. There seemed to be a great opportunity to see infrastructure through the same eyes and with the same care. We're not saying it's wrong to care about a two-storey building that's not moving; we're just saying, why don't we have an equivalent care? It represented to us a blind spot, like in someone's car mirror. As if, 'No, I can't see those 7,000 two-storey glazed, heated environments with seventy-five people in them.' Most two-storey buildings don't have seventy-five people in them.

That was inspiring for us. The studio isn't motivated by a starting impulse to express ourselves; instead our interest is: where can you make a difference? Where can you be useful? If things are already fantastic, there's no urge—the motivation plummets—to be involved. With the London bus, it really felt like there was this vast opportunity to make a positive improvement, as objectively as possible, rather than producing something deeply subjective.

With the bus, it seemed that you were taking an inside-out approach, looking at the experience of the passenger first. There's quite a details-focused approach to the design, whether that's the hand poles or the texture of the floor surface. But it's also about the passenger's view out into the city beyond.

In very simple terms, during the intervening period since the last time a team had been commissioned specifically to produce a bus for London, there hadn't been a design team thinking about the experience of the passenger—and a lot can go awry during those years. Instead, the focus has been on an incremental accommodation of different health and safety regulations and budgetary and engineering issues—but it's not necessarily been focused on the human passenger experience. That felt very basic to us, to see the bus through the lens of the human experience. So our approach ranged from trying to get more wool back into the fabric of the seats, rather than nylon, to the quality of light hitting your skin. Of course, yes, you need to meet a certain lux level because there's a regulatory requirement; that's fine—but there have been over-reactions to each health and safety regulation. A regulation might come in specifying how much light was required to hit the floor for passengers, but then because it's a little bit challenging, someone just takes a blanket approach and puts fluorescent tubes absolutely everywhere, and you end up with far too much harsh light flooding the space [Fig. 13.1].

And I guess that's because you have all these individual teams working on different elements, one team working on the lighting, one team working on the seats, and so on—and none of them are communicating with each other effectively.

Well, they're just solving a narrow thing, in their own compartment. They're not being pulled back, all at the same time, a bit like a zoom camera. I've often felt that our role on all our projects is a bit like that noise you hear when you're standing next to somebody taking a photograph. You can hear their autofocus zoom, you can hear it going, 'zzz zz zzz', backwards and forwards. With those zoom lenses, you can zoom right into a detail, but equally you can pull back and see the whole thing. Our role, I felt, was to pull right back and see everything, but then to be able to zoom into something in greater detail, keeping both in balance, so one isn't at the detriment of the other. Otherwise it just feels like someone has either stepped back and not looked at detail; or they've looked at one single detail and they haven't

FIGURE 13.1 *New Bus for London.*
© Heatherwick Studio.

asked themselves about the impact, the knock-on effect, of that single solution on other aspects of the functionality. It has to be accepted that how you *feel* is one of the functions of a piece of infrastructure. Human beings have feelings and responses and that is, we would argue, part of essential functionality.

The other day, I was speaking at the annual Google Zeitgeist conference, and I said something which suddenly led to spontaneous applause from the whole audience. I was discussing the bus project, and I was describing the fact if someone is really rich and they have a Ferrari, they drive around London in their Ferrari and that's fine—but the thing that I love about double-decker buses is that, however rich you are, you cannot beat being at the front at the top of a double-decker bus. It's the best view of London. The whole room just broke out into this huge applause!

I agree, it's definitely the best view. I always try to get that seat.

It's romantic. It's something that you lose if you see it as just a bus. I met someone once who is very wealthy, and we were talking about aeroplane travel. This person has had their own aeroplane for more than thirty years, and so for the last thirty years they've never got on a commercial passenger flight; they've never gone on a train, and they've certainly never been on a bus. Culturally, just imagine what they've missed out on…

Yes, no communal travel experience whatsoever.

No sharing. Society has this amazing power when it's good, it's wonderful. Those moments of shared humour when suddenly, with a bunch of strangers, you're all sitting on a train and the announcement comes through, where the personality of the driver comes through as he's announcing something.

And he tells a bad joke or something like that.

Makes a funny joke about some issue as to why you're delayed for a minute or something.

Everybody smiles, everybody laughs.

Everybody smiles, and you share. Some of those things can be magical in a way. There is something collective. It's offering you something that you can't get in other ways.

One of the most enjoyable aspects of the new London bus is the dialogue you have with the city around you and that's because of the way you've thought about the amount of glazing. The windows seem to coincide with moments of transition, like the two staircases.

Well, there was this very practical thing that we were working on together with the manufacturers, Wrightbus and Transport for London—and that was to make a bus that would use 40 percent less fuel than the existing diesel buses on the streets. That meant that the bus needed to be lightweight, which in turn meant that we were going to need to use composites in the manufacture. Saying 'composites' is just an exotic way to say fibreglass, and when you say fibreglass—especially in this country— something plummets inside of you. But fibreglass is actually an amazing material. You can use this material for the structure of the bus, but also for the finish. With the right coating it can become the fire-protective surface of the bus. All wrapped up in one element, so there isn't a separate structure underneath [Fig. 13.2]. What you're standing on is what's holding the whole back of the bus together, so it's very efficient. There was this sense that some of the buses of recent times have used fibreglass very pragmatically, but it's been really in your face. There's something a bit creepy about having fibreglass in your face, and having to touch it. There are some bizarre alcoves underneath staircases which are just a giant bit of fibreglass with one weird seat, where they've obviously been trying to cram another seat in. But it's just an ugly form, and experientially really abysmal. As a first impression, you enter the bus environment and there's this fibreglass material right in your face. If you're squeezed in on a packed bus, it's literally a few inches away from your face. There's very little you can do to make that special. One of the worst bits is often the staircase. You go up the staircase and it's just a tube of plastic. We felt that, experientially, we needed to make sure that passengers weren't walking up through a tube of plastic. The staircases are a moment where you're there, rising upwards, doing something you could never do in a car or a taxi—looking out over London—and that's something to celebrate. With the staircase for the new bus we tried to make that experience

FIGURE 13.2 *New Bus for London (upper deck).*
© Heatherwick Studio.

something grand. Staircases are often the grandest bits of buildings—for example the stereotype of a stately home where someone sweeps down the grand staircase in their ball gown or something.

It's about performance and spectacle.

It's a spectacle, exactly. We were also aware that security was an issue, that you can feel vulnerable in that staircase 'moment' when you're actually quite hidden from the world around you. It seemed that if you could let the windows follow you up the stairs, you'd see the city outside. It's an exciting, dramatic moment where you look out on to the city—and the city can see you. At no point in the bus are you hidden from other motorists, other people in buildings or on pavements. Actually, it's lovely watching people move around and within buildings. You see staircases as a moment when you can watch people moving through buildings—and it seemed, well, why can't we treat this big object on wheels similarly to how we treat a big object without the wheels?

The staircase that you designed for the Longchamp store in New York offers a moment of performance and spectacle similar to the theatricality of the staircase on the new London bus.

I think a staircase has theatre whether you like it or not, and it's just a question of whether it's bad theatre or good theatre. We could either make this bus staircase feel like the pokiest staircase ever or make the staircase feel expansive by sharing the surrounding city with the passenger. We wanted to really add something to the experience. It wasn't just us thinking 'well wouldn't it be nice to have diagonal lines on the outside of the bus'—that wasn't the motivation.

It's about creating a sense of difference, a special experience.

As you can tell, we're interested in cities as a collective experience, and I think we live in an interesting time because the older cities of the world evolved oblivious of each other, largely. Most people in those cities didn't travel to lots of other places, and initially not at all. So they developed through the materials that were available nearby, what the climate was like, what the landscape was like. There was this pragmatic sense of a city relating to itself. Now, with global communication and transportation, cities become acutely aware of every other city. So, in the past cities developed their own character and idiosyncrasy because they were not aware of how other cities were evolving—but now we're all so aware of everyone else. So if you think, ooh that's good, that city's doing a bike system, then you go, ooh, let's have our own bike system—and you suddenly find there's a trend of cities getting their own bike systems. People saw what happened in Barcelona for the 1992 Olympics, looked at the way they commissioned artistic buildings and thought, well why don't we do that? City officials and mayors go on an away weekend to explore a place and bring back various ideas. Or they go to Bilbao and think, oh that's good; I'd like an amazing art museum here. So, I find myself going to new cities and wishing that I'd gone to them twenty or thirty years earlier, because they're all becoming more and more similar to each other.

There are isolated pieces of difference, but increasingly you'll find that, for example, the bus system is really similar to, if not employing, the exact same buses as your own city. Or the metro system is really similar, if not the same, because it's been procured from Siemens or whoever is doing the global procurement. With office buildings, you see the emergence of a global generic office. Whether it's arctic or equatorial climates, you still see the same blue-coloured glass and extruded aluminium. So you become aware that with the global experience of our planet, it's more and more down to *details*. You'll find yourself in another city being delighted at a bus ticket, simply the fact that the ticket is different—'oh look, they've got tickets which have a hole, look at the way they do tickets'. To me, it's a little bit pathetic that it's the ticket that we're cherishing. I'm pleased at difference, but you pick your friends, not because they're versions of other people, but for their particularity and their unique qualities. I'm fascinated with how, rather than looking for a single solution, we allow countries, cities and regions to have their own idiosyncrasy. I think there was a certain romance in the past for the unique qualities of a place—what's the phrase I mean?

Genius loci?

Yes, that's it. We respond to the genius loci, the spirit of place. That really did apply when you made your buildings from materials that were there and when it was humans lifting and carrying, and the presence of a hill meant that you would respond to it. I feel that we've now overpowered all that. A piece of local topography has to be very strong to be able to match global procurement. Otherwise it's wiped away very, very quickly. It's romantic to talk about, but there's not much pushback from genius loci, no sense of it really stamping its ground against lorry sizes and economics. Our motivating factor in the Studio is how we allow places to have their own spirit and character. I think it's a big challenge to us now; how we can use procurement and good practice and global examples of success stories without imitating them, without imitating *ourselves*, and endeavouring to help a place to find its own character. The infrastructure is the armature within which you fill. The road systems, public transport systems, postal systems, bridges, rivers and canals—these all provide an armature within which there is a requirement for a joined-up thought process. And that, probably more than anything else, is where you can express the character of the city.

So the experience of working on a bus and working with a commissioning body like Transport for London—has that fed an appetite for doing further projects that will have a city-wide impact? As you say, enforcing a character on the city in some way.

I think the positive response to the bus project has actually given us a platform, and we've tried to maximize what was possible within that parameter. Together with the other national-level projects that we've been involved in—the Shanghai Expo UK Pavilion and the Olympic Cauldron—these are all projects that needed to achieve some sort of strategic national objective. They are all very different from each other, but they have allowed us to not be immediately written off as freaks, because they've had a degree of success, and they've proven that we don't have to resign ourselves to bland, characterless failure if government is involved. We've forgotten that national projects can really contribute something to a country's society. We tend to look back romantically and roll our eyes, and say, well in the past they did that but now the way things happen government ruins everything. I think even government quietly believes that it ruins everything, and doesn't want to admit it. I feel that with those three projects, what I was most proud of was actually government in a sense. There were different governmental regimes that we worked with, but they all employed certain people who believed that projects mattered just as much as policies. Projects can really manifest something if they're done confidently and are not driven by fear. So our hope is to use the platform of confidence that has built up through those three projects, and create some momentum for this idea that government can create projects that are experientially special for society.

I feel determined to encourage the same confidence of commissioning that allowed us to do those three projects. That means there's an onus on designers to inspire confidence and creativity in the commissioners and the patrons. I think that's been underplayed in the past. There's been a huge emphasis on creative talent and the assumption that it's an inert role to commission someone, but it's truly a process, and you develop a project together; you're not in isolation. If a project is a success it's because of both of you, and if a project is a failure it's because of both of you.

I don't know how to put this best, but there is an enormous opportunity in Britain to take infrastructure and to apply a cohesive piece of thinking. To try and avoid a collection of disparate initiatives of different levels of success that quietly complicate, and fail to assert a sense of clarity. When you get on an underground train you don't need to feel that every station is different; you actually want reassurance and confidence that this is a joined-up system that will work, and that once you walk through that door into the underground station you're now within something that holds you, looks after you, gets you to where you need to be.

It's not about creating a transformative moment, simply giving people a certain quality of experience.

We worked with an extraordinary priest, on a different project, who had written a book about happiness. What I found very interesting was that, although we think of happiness as being a big smile on your face, his definition of happiness was just an *absence of unhappiness*.

So, in terms of specific ambitions in the wake of those three national projects, are there other areas of public infrastructure that really interest you?

I think every aspect of how you stitch together the armature of infrastructure is extremely interesting for us. Whether we can make a living out of it, I don't know. It's also very hard to do. In the popular media, design has been portrayed via this 'Changing Rooms' notion, that your artistic person does a sketch, there's the idea, and magic and elves in the night, and *pa-ding*, there it is. I think that the historic bits of London's transport infrastructure that we appreciate were not done in a Changing Rooms, overnight, magic elves, kind of way. They were developed over a number of decades, with two or three key people who just continued working, focusing, over a prolonged period of time with an intensity and a vision. It seems to me that this isn't a sprint; it's a marathon. This is a long piece of work if you're going to really make an impact, rather than contribute yet another layer to the problem. So something like this I see as a long-term engagement and relationship which as a Studio, we would love to work on. If you're going to give many, many years of your life to something, you must really believe in it. Something like that would be extremely motivating if we could get that chance.

So the key thing would be to use these three projects to build on existing relationships with institutions like Transport for London or the Greater London Authority and to develop long-term strategic partnerships?

Yes, to try and reassert the human experience and the completeness of transportation and not to just see it as way-finding or architecture or whatever. It's an experience made up of many, many elements.

Is that why city-scale design interests you, because it's an opportunity to break out of individual design disciplines and to instead look at everything as a single cohesive system?

It's harder than ever to actually get that clarity back because London is more complex, much more complex, than forty or fifty years ago. That means that only the most determined people will be able to make true quality happen. I know that we're very determined. I know that it will need determination, long-term gruelling determination, to really make a difference.

We also are working on an idea for a piece of infrastructure in London which is for a new garden. I do see London's parks and gardens as part of the infrastructure of the city, and London is the greenest city of its size on the planet. So we're exploring the notion of adding another garden to London, and you might think, well where? How can you add another garden, are you going to bulldoze something? But this is a garden right in the centre of London, and it's an idea that was originally developed by the actor Joanna Lumley, who had this idea a number of years ago and we've been working with her to try and see whether it's possible to make this happen. The unique thing about this garden is that it isn't just plonked somewhere; it can also do another job which is to connect South and North London together. It will act as a bridge across the River Thames. So it's extremely ambitious, but in a way it's not that ambitious because in the intervening years since we first started talking to Joanna about her idea, in New York there has been a project to put a garden on a disused rail line, The High Line. That surpassed everyone's expectations of success. I was just recently in New York meeting the landscape designers for the project, and some of the planners who made it happen. None of them knew that it would capture the imagination in such a way. The High Line isn't in the centre of New York, and it doesn't even function as a way of connecting people between two different sites. The garden that we've been developing for London is right in the centre. It's positioned between Waterloo and Blackfriars, in a location that appears really perfect, where it would really contribute something important. The bridge would not only create a garden but also help stitch together two very different parts of London that are relatively close geographically. We've got our cultural arts area on the South Bank and we've got our cultural West End, with Covent Garden and Leicester Square, but when you actually look at how you can get between those two—when you walk across Waterloo Bridge—you are actually walking across a road bridge. The pedestrian is secondary. Unlike in Paris where the Seine is, on average, around 100 metres wide, London's river is a quarter of a kilometre wide, so it's over 250 metres wide. We're looking at whether we could create the slowest possible route across the Thames.

An experience purely for pedestrians.

It's a place where you could spend an hour if you wanted; or all the commuters coming into Waterloo could use it as a way to get across into the West End, and instead of jumping onto the tube, they could walk. I feel like my job is to be a humble design slave to try and see if we can take forward this idea that Joanna originally developed and that has captured our imagination.

SELECT BIBLIOGRAPHY

Abercrombie, P. and D. Plumstead. *A Civic Survey and Plan for the City and Royal Burgh of Edinburgh*. Edinburgh and London: Oliver and Boyd, 1949.

Ackroyd, P. *Albion: The Origins of the English Imagination*. London: Chatto & Windus, 2002.

Addison, P. *No Turning Back: The Peacetime Revolutions of Post-War Britain*. Oxford: Oxford University Press, 2010.

Anderson, B. *Imagined Communities: Reflections on the Origin and Spread of Nationalism*. London: Verso, 1983.

Antram, N. and N. Pevsner. *The Buildings of England: Sussex East with Brighton and Hove*. New Haven and London: Yale University Press, 2013.

Augé, M. *Non-Places: An Introduction to Super-Modernity*. London and New York: Verso, 1995.

Bain, S. *Holyrood: The Inside Story*. Edinburgh: Edinburgh University Press, 2005.

Barber, J. *South Africa in the Twentieth Century: A Political History, in Search of a Nation State*. Oxford: Blackwell, 1999.

Beaton, C. *Fashion: An Anthology by Cecil Beaton* [Catalogue of an exhibition held at the Victoria and Albert Museum, October 1971–January 1972]. London: Victoria and Albert Museum, 1971.

Berghahn, M. *Continental Britons: German-Jewish Refugees from Nazi Germany*. 2nd ed. Oxford: Berg, 1988.

Berridge, G. R. *Economic Power in Anglo-South African Diplomacy: Simonstown, Sharpeville and After*. London: Macmillan, 1981.

Berridge, G. R. *The Politics of the South Africa Run: European Shipping and Pretoria*. Oxford: Clarendon Press, 1987.

Black, G. *Living up West: Jewish Life in London's West End*. London: The London Museum of Jewish Life, 1994.

Bracewell, M. *England Is Mine: Pop Life in Albion from Wilde to Goldie*. London: Flamingo, 1998.

Bracewell, M. *The Nineties: When Surface Was Depth*. London: Flamingo, 2002.

Breward, C., B. Conekin and C. Cox, eds. *The Englishness of English Dress*. Oxford: Berg, 2002.

Breward, C., E. Erhman and C. Evans, eds. *The London Look*. New Haven and London: Yale University Press in association with the Museum of London, 2004.

Breward, C. and G. Wood, eds. *British Design from 1948: Innovation in the Modern Age*. London: V&A Publishing, 2012.

Brown, N., A. Forsyth and D. F. Gray, eds. *Lyons Israel Ellis Gray: Buildings and Projects 1932–1983*. London: Architectural Association, 2004.

Brubaker, C. W., R. Bordwell and G. Christopher. *Planning and Designing Schools*. New York: McGraw-Hill, 1998.

Bryson, B. *Notes from a Small Island*. London: Black Swan, 1995.

Buckley, C. *Designing Modern Britain*. London: Reaktion, 2007.

Burke, C. *A Life in Education and Architecture. Mary Beaumont Medd 1907–2005*. London: Ashgate, 2013.

Burke, C. et al. *Principles of Primary School Design*. Cambridge: ACE Foundation and
    Feilden, Clegg and Bradley Studios, 2010.
Bush, B. *Imperialism and Postcolonialism*. Harlow and New York: Pearson Longman, 2006.
Butt, G. *Between You and Me: Queer Disclosures in the New York Art World 1948–1963*.
    Asheville, NC: Duke University Press, 2005.
Butt, J. and K. Ponting. *Scottish Textile History*. Aberdeen: Aberdeen University Press, 1987.
Campbell, L. *Coventry Cathedral: Art and Architecture in Post-War Britain*. Oxford:
    Clarendon Press, 1996.
Campbell, L., M. Glendinning and J. Thomas, eds. *Basil Spence: Buildings and Projects*.
    London: RIBA Publications, 2012.
Caudill, W. W. *Toward Better School Design*. New York: F. W. Dodge Corp., 1954.
Cherry, B. and N. Pevsner. *The Buildings of England: Devon*. 2nd ed. Harmondsworth:
    Penguin, 1989.
Clarke, N. L. and W. H. Worger. *South Africa: The Rise and Fall of Apartheid*. Harlow and
    New York: Pearson Longman, 2004.
Cockburn, Lord Henry Thomas. *A Letter to the Lord Provost on the Best Ways of Spoiling
    the Beauties of Edinburgh*. Edinburgh: Cockburn Association, 2006.
Cohn, N. *Today There Are No Gentleman*. London: Weidenfeld & Nicolson, 1970.
Colley, L. *Britons: Forging the Nation 1707–1837*. London: Yale University Press, 1992.
Conekin, B. *The Autobiography of a Nation*. Manchester: Manchester University Press, 2003.
Conekin, B., F. Mort and C. Walters, eds. *Moments of Modernity: Reconstructing Britain*.
    London: Rivers Oram Press, 1999.
Cook, P. *Fashioning the Nation: Costume and Identity in British Cinema*. London: BFI
    Publishing, 1996.
Cornforth, J. *The Inspiration of the Past: Country House Taste in the Twentieth Century*.
    London: Viking, 1985.
Cox, A. *ACP/Architects Co-Partnership, First Fifty Years 1939–1989*. Potters Bar, Herts: The
    Firm, 1989.
Craig, C. *The Scots' Crisis of Confidence*. Glendaruel: Argyll Publishing, 2011.
Cullen, G. *The Concise Townscape*. London: The Architectural Press, 1961.
Damant, H. *Golden Run: A Nostalgic Memoir of the Halcyon Days of the Great Liners to
    South and East Africa*. Cape Town: Print Matters, 2006.
Daniels, S. *Fields of Vision: Landscape Imagery and National Identity in England and the
    United States*. Cambridge: Cambridge University Press, 1993.
Darling, E. *Re-Forming Britain: Narratives of Modernity before Reconstruction*. Abingdon:
    Routledge, 2007.
Daunton, M. and B. Rieger, *Meanings of Modernity: Britain from the Late-Victorian Era to
    World War II*. Oxford and New York: Berg, 2001.
Davey, K. *English Imaginaries: Six Studies in Anglo-British Modernity*. London: Lawrence &
    Wishart, 1999.
De la Haye, A., ed. *The Cutting Edge*. London: V&A, 1996.
Donnelly, M. *Sixties Britain*. London: Pearson, 2005.
Dormer, P. ed. *The Culture of Craft*. Manchester: Manchester University Press, 1997.
Dunleavy, P. *The Politics of Mass Housing in Britain, 1945–1975*. Oxford: Oxford
    University Press, 1981.
The Editors of Fortune, eds. *The Exploding Metropolis*. Garden City: Doubleday Anchor
    Books, 1958.
First, R., J. Steele and C. Gurney. *The South African Connection: Western Investment in
    Apartheid*. Harmondsworth: Penguin, 1972.
Fowler, J. and J. Cornforth. *English Decoration in the 18th Century*. London: Barrie &
    Jenkins, 1974.

Fox, C. *Watching the English*. London: Hodder & Stoughton, 2004.

Glendinning, M. *The Conservation Movement: A History of Architectural Preservation, Antiquity to Modernity*. Abingdon: Routledge, 2013.

Goldie, M. *Corbusier Comes to Cambridge*. Cambridge, Churchill College, 2007.

Goodrum, A. *The National Fabric: Fashion, Britishness, Globalization*. Oxford: Berg, 2005.

Gorman, P. *Mr Freedom—Tommy Roberts: British Design Hero*. London: Adelita, 2012.

Graves, J., *Waterline: Images from the Golden Age of Cruising*. London: National Maritime Museum, 2004.

Greenhalgh, P. *Modernism in Design*. London: Reaktion Books, 1997.

Greg, A., ed., *Primavera: Pioneering Craft and Design, 1945–1995*. Gateshead: Tyne and Wear Museums, 1995.

Hall, S. and T. Jefferson. *Resistance through Rituals: Youth Subcultures in Post-War Britain*. London: Hutchinson, 1975.

Harris, C. J. and B. Ingpen. *Mail Ships of the Union-Castle Line*. South Africa: Fernwood Press, 1994.

Harris, J. *The Last Party: Britpop, Blair & the Demise of English Rock*. London: Fourth Estate, 2004.

Harrison, B. *Seeking A Role: The United Kingdom 1951–1970*. Oxford: Oxford University Press, 2008.

Harrison, B. *Finding A Role? The United Kingdom 1970–1990*. Oxford: Oxford University Press, 2010.

Harrod, T. *The Crafts in Britain in the 20th Century*. London: Yale University Press, 1999.

Harwood, E. *England: A Guide to Post-War Listed Buildings*. London: B.T. Batsford, 2003.

Harwood, E. and A. Powers, eds. *The Sixties—Life: Style: Architecture*. London: The Twentieth Century Society, 2002.

Hatherley, O. *A Guide to the New Ruins of Great Britain*. London: Verso, 2010.

Hebdige, D. *Subculture: The Meaning of Style*. London: Methuen, 1979.

Hilton, M. *Consumerism in 20th Century Britain*. Cambridge: Cambridge University Press, 2003.

Hobsbawm, E. and T. Ranger, *The Invention of Tradition*. Cambridge: Cambridge University Press, 1983.

Hoggart, R. *The Uses of Literacy*. Harmondsworth: Penguin, 1958.

Honey, W. B., *The Art of the Potter. A Book for the Collector and Connoisseur*. London: Faber and Faber, 1946.

Hornsey, R. *The Spiv and the Architect: Unruly Life in Postwar London*. Minneapolis: University of Minnesota Press, 2010.

Hoskins, L. *Living Rooms 20th-Century Interiors at the Geffrye Museum*. London: Geffrye Museum, 1998.

Hunt, L. *British Low Culture: From Safari Suits to Sexploitation*. London: Routledge, 1998.

Huygens, F. *British Design: Image & Identity*. London: Thames & Hudson, 1989.

Hyam, R. and P. Henshaw. *The Lion and the Springbok, Britain and South Africa since the Boer War*. Cambridge: Cambridge University Press, 2003.

Jack, I. *The Country Formerly Known as Great Britain*. London: Jonathan Cape, 2009.

Jackson, L. *Contemporary: Architecture and Interiors of the 1950s*. London: Phaidon Press Limited, 1994.

James, A. S. *Sketches from a Life*. London: Michael Joseph, 1993.

Jeremiah, D. *Architecture and Design for the Family*. Manchester: Manchester University Press, 2000.

Johnson, N. *Park Hill. Made in Sheffield, England*. Manchester: Urban Splash, 2006.

Jones, P. *Streets in the Sky—Life in Sheffield's High-Rise*. Sheffield, http://www.freewebs.com/lifeonkelvinflats/KELVIN%20PDF.pdf, 2008.

Klein, B. *Eye for Colour*. London: Bernat Klein, 1965.

Klein, B. *DESIGN Matters*. London: Martin Secker & Warburg, 1976.

Klein, B. and L. Jackson. *Bernat Klein: Textile Designer, Artist, Colourist*. Selkirk: Bernat Klein Trust, 2005.

Kyes, Z. and M. Owens, eds. *Forms of Inquiry—The Architecture of Critical Graphic Design*. London: Architectural Association, 2007.

Kynaston, D. *A World to Build: Austerity Britain 1945–48*. London: Bloomsbury, 2007.

Kynaston, D. *Smoke in the Valley: Austerity Britain 1948–51*. London: Bloomsbury, 2007.

Kynaston, D. *Family Britain 1951–57*. London: Bloomsbury, 2009.

Landau, R. *New Directions in British Architecture*. New York: George Braziller, 1968.

Lawrence, A.W. *Greek Architecture*. Revised 5th edition by R. A. Tomlinson. New Haven: Yale University Press, Pelican History of Art Series, 1996.

Lawrence, D. *Underground Architecture*. Harrow Weald: Capital Transport, 1994.

Leavis, F.R. *Two Cultures? The Significance of C.P. Snow*. London: Chatto & Windus, 1962.

Lees-Milne, J. *Through Wood and Dale: Diaries 1975–1978*. London: John Murray, 2003.

Light, A. *Forever England: Femininity, Literature and Conservatism between the Wars*. London: Routledge, 1991.

London, L. *Whitehall and the Jews, 1933–1948, British Immigration Policy, Jewish Refugees and the Holocaust*. Cambridge: Cambridge University Press, 2000.

Long, P. and J. Thomas, eds. *Basil Spence: Architect*. Edinburgh: National Galleries of Scotland in association with the Royal Commission on the Ancient and Historical Monuments of Scotland, 2007.

Louw, E. *The Rise, Fall, and Legacy of Apartheid*. Westport, CT and London: Praeger, 2004.

Louw-Potgieter, J. *Afrikaner Dissidents: A Social Psychological Study of Identity and Dissent*. Clevedon and Philadelphia: Multilingual Matters, 1988.

Lubbock, J. *University of Essex: Vision & Reality*. Colchester, University of Essex, 2014.

MacCarthy, F. *British Design Since 1880: A Visual History*. London: Lund Humphries, 1982.

MacDonald, S. and J. Porter. *Putting on the Style: Setting up Home in the Fifties*. London: Geffrye Museum, 1990.

MacLure, S., *Educational Development and School Building: Aspects of Public Policy, 1945–73*. London: Longman, 1984.

Marr, A. *A History of Modern Britain*. London: Macmillan, 2007.

Martin, J. L., B. Nicholson and N. Gabo, eds. *Circle: International Survey of Constructive Art*. London: Faber and Faber, 1937.

Martin, L. *Whitehall: A Plan for the National and Government Centre*. London: HMSO, 1965.

Martin, L. and L. March, eds. *Urban Space and Structures*. London: Cambridge University Press, 1972.

Matless, D. *Landscape and Englishness*. London: Reaktion, 1998.

McCay, G. *DIY Culture: Party & Protest in Nineties Britain*. London: Verso, 1998.

McDermott, C. *Street Style: British Design in the 80s*. London: Design Council, 1987.

McDermott, C. *Made in Britain: Tradition and Style in Contemporary British Fashion*. London: Mitchell Beazley, 2002.

McDermott, C. *Design: The Key Concepts*. London: Routledge 2007.

McDonough, T., ed., *The Situationists and the City*. London: Verso, 2009.

McKellar, S. and P. Sparke, eds. *Interior Design and Identity*. Manchester: Manchester University Press, 2004.

Meecham, P. and J. Sheldon. *Modern Art a Critical Introduction*. Oxford: Routledge, 2005.

Mitchell, W. H. and L. A. Sawyer. *The Cape Run*. Lavenham: Terence Dalton, 1984.

Monro, J. *11 Montpellier Street: Memoirs of an Interior Decorator*. London: Weidenfeld and Nicholson, 1988.

Murray, M. *Union-Castle Chronicle: 1853–1953*. Harlow: Longman, Green, 1953.

Muthesius, S. *The Post War University: Utopian Campus and College*. New Haven and London: Yale University Press: 2000.

Nairn, I. *Nairn's London*. Harmondsworth: Penguin, 1988.

Nairn, I. and N. Pevsner. *The Buildings of England: Sussex*. Harmondsworth: Penguin, 1965.

Newell, P. *Union-Castle Line: A Fleet History*. London: Carmania Press, 1999.

Orwell, G. *The Road to Wigan Pier*. Harmondsworth: Penguin, 1988.

Paxman, J. *The English*. Harmondsworth: Penguin, 1998.

Perry, V. *Built for a Better Future: The Brynmawr Rubber Factory*. Dorchester: White Cockade Publishing, 1994.

Pevsner, N. *The Englishness of English Art*. Harmondsworth: Pelican, 1956.

Pool, M. J. *Twentieth Century Decorating, Architecture and Gardens: Eighty Years of Ideas and Pleasure from House and Garden*. London: Weidenfeld & Nicholson, 1980.

Powers, A. *In the Line of Development, Yorke Rosenberg Mardall*. London: Heinz Gallery, 1992.

Powers, A. *Britain: Modern Architectures in History*. London: Reaktion, 2008.

Reynolds, S. *Rip It up And Start Again: Post Punk 1978–1984*. London: Faber & Faber, 2006.

Saint, A. *Towards a Social Architecture: The Role of School Buildings in Post-War England*. London and New Haven: Yale University Press, 1987.

Samuel, R. *Patriotism: The Making and Unmaking of British National Identity*. London: Routledge, 1989.

Sandbrook, D. *Never Had It So Good: A History of Britain from Suez to the Beatles*. London: Little Brown, 2006.

Sandbrook, D. *White Heat: A History of Britain in the Swinging Sixties*. London: Little Brown, 2007.

Savage, J. *England's Dreaming*. London: Faber & Faber, 1991.

Savage, J. *Time Travel*. London: Vintage, 1997.

Sinclair, I. *Lights Out for the Territory*. Harmondsworth: Penguin, 1997.

Smith, S. B. *In All His Glory: The Life of William S. Paley*. New York: Simon and Schuster, 1990.

Snow, C. P. *The Two Cultures and the Scientific Revolution*. Cambridge: Cambridge University Press, 1959.

Spence, B. *Phoenix at Coventry: The Building of a Cathedral*. London: Geoffrey Bles, 1962.

Sparke, P., ed. *Did Britain Make It?: British Design in Context, 1946–86*. London: Design Council, 1986.

Sparke, P. *An Introduction to Design and Culture in the Twentieth Century*. London: Routledge, 2000.

Sparke, P. *Elsie de Wolfe: The Birth of Modern Interior Decoration*. New York: Acanthus, 2005.

Sparke, P. *The Modern Interior*. London: Reaktion, 2008.

Stone, J. *Colonist or Uitlander: A Study of the British Immigrant in South Africa*. Oxford: Clarendon Press, 1973.

Street, S. *British National Cinema*. London: Routledge, 1997.

Sudjic, D. *Design in Britain: Big Ideas (Small Island)*. London: Conran Octopus, 2009.

Thompson, E. P. *The Making of the English Working Class*. Harmondsworth: Penguin, 1963.

Tuan, Yi-Fu. *Space and Place: The Perspective of Experience*. Minneapolis: University of Minnesota Press, 1977.

Turner, G. *British Cultural Studies*. London: Routledge, 1990.

Tyack, G. *Modern Architecture in an Oxford College: St John's College 1945–2005*. Oxford: Oxford University Press, 2005.

Urban, W. J. *More Than Science and Sputnik: The National Defense Education Act of 1958*. Tuscaloosa: University of Alabama Press, 2010.

Van Heyningen, E., et al. *Cape Town: The Making of a City: An Illustrated Social History*. Claremont: David Philip, 1998.

Votolato, G. *Transport Design: A Travel History*. London: Reaktion, 2007.

Walker, J. A. *Left Shift: Radical Art in 1970s Britain*. London: Macmillan, 2002.

Ward, S., ed. *British Culture and the End of Empire*. Manchester: Manchester University Press, 2001.

Wealleans, A. *Designing Liners: A History of Interior Design Afloat*. London: Routledge, 2006.

Weight, R. *Mod —A Very British Style*. London: Bodley Head, 2013.

White, R. J. *The Conservative Tradition*. London: Nicholas Kaye, 1950.

Whiteley, N. *Pop Design: Modernism to Mod*. London: The Design Council, 1987.

Wiener, M. *English Culture & the Decline of the Industrial Spirit 1850–1980*. Harmondsworth: Penguin, 2004.

Williams, R. J. *The Anxious City: English Urbanism in the Late Twentieth Century*. London: Routledge, 2004.

Williams, R. J. *Brazil: Modern Architectures in History*. London: Reaktion, 2009.

Womersley, J.L., et al. *Ten Years of Housing in Sheffield*. Sheffield: Corporation of Sheffield, 1962.

Wood, M. *Nancy Lancaster: English Country House Style*. London: Frances Lincoln, 2005.

Wood, M. *John Fowler: Prince of Decorators*. London: Frances Lincoln 2007.

Wright, P. *On Living in an Old Country*. London: Verso, 1985.

Zucker, P. *Town and Square from the Agora to the Village Green*. New York: Columbia University Press, 1959.

INDEX

Note: Locators followed by the letter 'n' refer to notes.

427501